ADI 19.85/13.37

Loving This Planet

ALSO BY HELEN CALDICOTT
FROM THE NEW PRESS

Nuclear Power Is Not the Answer

The New Nuclear Danger: George W. Bush's Military-Industrial Complex

War in Heaven: The Arms Race in Outer Space (with Craig Eisendrath)

LOVING THIS PLANET

Leading Thinkers Talk About How to Make a Better World

Helen Caldicott

I dedicate this book to my two radio producers: Scott Powell, whose persistence, perseverance, and dedication over the years assured the creation of my radio show, and to Jasmin Williams, my loyal and clever friend whose technological knowledge allows us to record and produce the show in a tiny Australian fishing village made famous by the fisherman and author Zane Grey.

Requests for permission to reproduce selections from this book should be mailed to:
Permissions Department, The New Press, 38 Greene Street, New York, NY 10013.

Published in the United States by The New Press, New York, 2012
Distributed by Perseus Distribution

LIBRARY OF CONGRESS CATALOGING-IN-PUBLICATION DATA

Caldicott, Helen.
  Loving this planet : leading thinkers talk about how to make a better
world / Helen Caldicott.
    p. cm.
  ISBN 978-1-59558-806-7 (pb : alk. paper)
1. Environmentalism--Philosophy. 2. Environmental responsibility. 3.
Environmental protection. I. Title.
  GE195.C35 2012
  304.2--dc23
                    2012004565

Now in its twentieth year, The New Press publishes books that promote and enrich public discussion and understanding of the issues vital to our democracy and to a more equitable world. These books are made possible by the enthusiasm of our readers; the support of a committed group of donors, large and small; the collaboration of our many partners in the independent media and the not-for-profit sector; booksellers, who often hand-sell New Press books; librarians; and above all by our authors.

www.thenewpress.com

Composition by Bookbright Media
This book was set in Garamond Premiere Pro

Printed in the United States of America

10 9 8 7 6 5 4 3 2 1

CONTENTS

INTRODUCTION

Delivering the Message to
Love This Planet

From an early age I discovered the tremendous importance of disseminating knowledge and information. As a young girl in Australia, with the Good Samaritan as a guide, I decided that I wanted to be a doctor so that I could help people. At the age of seventeen, a cloud developed on my horizon. Just as I was about to enter medical school, I read a novel by Nevil Shute called *On The Beach*, which described a nuclear war that killed everyone in the northern hemisphere. Eventually the radioactive cloud engulfed Melbourne, where I lived, signaling the end of human existence. That image branded my soul and remained with me throughout medical school, indeed throughout my life. While learning basic genetics during my first year in 1956, the United States and Russia were irradiating millions of people by testing nuclear weapons in the atmosphere. And it became obvious to me that many people would develop deleterious genetic mutations, and that they would pass inherited diseases on to their offspring.

I moved to Boston in the late 1960s, which were years of intense political turmoil. The civil rights and anti–Vietnam War movements were flourishing; Martin Luther King Jr. and Bobby Kennedy were assassinated; and Richard Nixon was elected president. Aside from caring for three small children, I had a part-time job at Harvard Medical School, and while not having much time to participate in any political activities, I observed a potent democracy in action.

Upon my return to Australia I discovered that the French were contaminating our land with radioactive fallout from their atmospheric tests. I decided to write a letter to the local paper describing how children could develop leukemia and cancer from these tests. Suddenly, as an informed voice, I was given access to nightly television news programs to explain to Australians how radioactive fallout could induce mutation, cancer, and genetic diseases. Within nine months of my writing that letter, 75 percent of the Australian populace rose up in indignation, prompting our prime minister, Gough Whitlam, to take France to the International Court of Justice, which forced France to move its testing underground. I had a revelation as I saw firsthand the extraordinary power of viable media to educate the public and promote democracy.

Soon after this victory I discovered that the same prime minister wanted to export uranium to be used in nuclear power plants around the world (Australia owns 40 percent of the global supply). I traveled throughout Australia, teaching the union movement about basic genetics related to the dangers of uranium mining. The mining and export of uranium was banned for five years, marking another victory achieved by education through the media.

In 1976 I joined the faculty of Harvard Medical School as a pediatrics instructor in the Cystic Fibrosis Center at the Children's Hospital in Boston. But at the same time that I cared for children in the clinic, my deep concern about all things nuclear persisted. The policy victories back home led me to revive a moribund Physicians for Social Responsibility in 1978, and over a period of five years, we recruited 23,000 members and created 153 chapters throughout the country. I encouraged the members to make full use of the media by writing op-ed pieces, appearing on radio shows and television programs, and conducting public meetings about the medical consequences of nuclear power and nuclear war. A nation that had been tightly in the grip of Cold War logic had been transformed. By 1983, 80 percent of the population opposed the concept of nuclear war, because they understood that it would create the final epidemic of the human race.

Deeply encouraged, I began initiating similar physicians' movements in many other countries throughout the world, including Canada, Australia, New Zealand, Japan, Belgium, Germany, England, Scotland, Ireland, Sweden, Norway, and Denmark. A massive global physicians' movement developed, helping to fuel a changing dynamic between Reagan and Gorbachev that eventually led to the end of the Cold War. We were granted the Nobel Peace Prize in 1985 for our work.

That was then, and this is now. The problem today is that science has been applied in industry, medicine, agriculture, and in many other aspects of daily life to do terrible things to society and the planet. For instance: we live in a cocktail of over eighty thousand chemicals in common use; agricultural corporations have introduced genetically modified food that is reaping disastrous consequences in the third world; nuclear power plants spill radioactive elements over nearby populations continuously, and they sometimes erupt with atomic vengeance to irradiate millions of unsuspecting people; coal plants emit carbon dioxide at a rate that is destroying the ecosphere by global warming; and thousands of nuclear weapons stand ready to be launched with a press of a button by either Putin or Obama to create nuclear winter, inducing the end of all planetary life.

The sophistication and misapplication of science has thus left the average citizen far behind. People are vaguely aware that things are not going well despite the fact that they are constantly being reassured by corporate shills and skillfully orchestrated advertising campaigns—by institutions such as Monsanto, General Electric, BP, Shell, Lockheed Martin, and Boeing—that the interests of the common man and woman are being protected.

In our world today the question then becomes, How does one educate the body politic in a time of precarious planetary ills? How do we relay life- and planet-saving information when so many people are addicted to media outlets like Fox, or similar radio and television entities, that trumpet climate change skeptics and give unfettered access to scientifically illiterate politicians? Many people, in particular the youth, turn to Facebook, Twitter, and other superficial media outlets, where it can be difficult to verify the accuracy of the information being shared. While not decrying the utility of the Internet and the remarkably efficient way that it can be used to spread ideas and obtain information, being well-informed is key to utilizing it productively.

I often reference Thomas Jefferson's poignant observation that an informed democracy will behave in a responsible fashion. My experience over the last forty years has taught me that the best way to educate the democracies in the developed world efficiently is through the media. Independent media is therefore imperative in this day and age, and there is simply too little of it. Even public television now takes advertisements, euphemistically called "underwritings," from the Nuclear Energy Institute and other such iniquitous institutions, thus severely damaging its so-called independent status.

My belief in the power of independent media is what inspired me to create a weekly radio show. With the generous help of the Pacifica network, I interview the world's leading scientists and global thinkers on many of the issues that are threatening our very survival. The eye-opening knowledge and brilliant intellect that has been shared on the program served as the impetus for developing this book—a collection of some of the most informed and intriguing voices of our time.

In this book I have selected twenty-five interviews with the world's leading thinkers and scientists, in which we discuss many of the most pressing challenges facing humanity today. The conversations cover an extraordinary amount of ground, including everything from the U.S. military-industrial complex, global warming, sea-level rise, and the destruction of the world's forests to the role of the media in politics, the WikiLeaks controversy, and how popular entertainers can influence important issues in our society. The book includes an astonishing interview demonstrating the absurdity of storing radioactive waste for one hundred thousand years, information on the persistent march toward nuclear annihilation, and a moving discussion of the cancer epidemic arising from over one thousand American nuclear tests in Nevada. I talk to an expert on brain cancers related to cell phone use and reflect on the Chernobyl catastrophe, the coming global water deprivation, and the fragility of global agriculture.

While the discussions herein have been edited down for the book, the essence of each has been carefully maintained and is enriched through philosophical musings and social analyses on the subjects included. As I read the transcripts of these interviews, I had indeed forgotten much of what had been discussed. Not only did I find the interviews fascinating all over again, but I was stimulated by a renewed energy to continue spreading this important knowledge. My hope is that this book will inspire readers to genuinely love this planet and become actively engaged in protecting the health of our world and all its inhabitants.

—⦿⦿⦿—

I would like to thank the New Press for instigating this book and for recognizing the value of these radio interviews, which were conducted over a period of two years.

MAUDE BARLOW

Maude Barlow is national chairperson of the Council of Canadians and former senior adviser on water to the president of the United Nations General Assembly. She chairs the board of the Washington-based Food & Water Watch and is a counselor to the Hamburg-based World Future Council. Maude is a recipient of eleven honorary doctorates, the 2005 Bright Light Award, and the 2008 Canadian Environment Award. She is the author of *Blue Covenant: The Global Water Crisis and the Coming Battle for Water*.

—∿∿∿—

HELEN CALDICOTT: You're in Australia at the moment, and you're Canadian, so you've come to help us with our water, right?

MAUDE BARLOW: I'm not here to say how wonderful Canada is at handling our water. If I'm critical about what Australia is doing, I'm critical about my own country as well. The only difference is that we have more water to be cavalier about.

HC: Let's look at the world water situation in terms of global warming, sea-level rise, people in Bangladesh and their wells becoming salty, and the like.

MB: The big story is that the world's running out of freshwater. In about grade six we all learned that there's a finite, fixed amount of water, and it goes around and around in the hydrological cycle and can't go anywhere. But that's not true, it turns out. A combination of polluting surface water and overmining groundwater and extracting our rivers to death takes water from where it's needed, not only for a healthy ecosystem and for the actual hydrological cycle to function, but also, for instance, in cities; when we're finished with it we dump it into the ocean, but we don't return it to the land. As a result, we are creating what scientists call hot stains. These are parts of the world that are actually physically drying up. These are not cyclical droughts but rather growing deserts.

One is northern China. China uses its water to produce many of the toys and running shoes for the world, so it is removing water from its watersheds for industry. China is creating an area of desert the size of Rhode Island every year. India has 23 million bore wells going 24/7 just pumping water out of the ground. Chile, big parts of southern Europe, around the Mediterranean and other points, all are in trouble. Mexico City is sinking on itself. They've taken all the water from under the ground. There are twenty-two countries in Africa in crisis, and every one of their 677 lakes is in crisis. The Southwest of the United States is in crisis, as is the Colorado River, which is declining. I would argue that Australia is one of these places that has built an economic miracle on the notion that there were unlimited resources. It's not true. Close to a billion people live in water-stressed regions of the world. Close to 3 billion have no running water within a kilometer [about a half mile] of their homes. And every eight seconds, somewhere in our world a child is dying of a waterborne disease, because the number-one cause of mortality, more than HIV/AIDS, accidents, and war put together, is dirty water. So I feel that the global water crisis is the number-one ecological and human crisis of our time. Our governments continue to deny the problem and have these great hopes that somehow big technology will save us.

HC: What about overpopulation? What role does that play in water shortage?

MB: Well, it's huge. But it's not population by itself; it is population plus a certain kind of development—Western, urbanized, consumer-based. As our populations increased threefold, since the 1950s, our water use has increased sevenfold. And I've been in communities in, say, rural India, where there are very dense populations per square kilometer [about a third of a square mile], but they live the way their great-great-grandparents lived, and they take care of the water. They don't pollute and they don't waste it. In countries like India and China, we physically are using more water than we have. The statistics are so stunning; looking ahead at 2025, 2035, 2050, no one knows where the water that we will need is going to come from, and there's no way yet to manufacture new sources of water.

HC: Politicians in Australia are talking about desalination plants. We're either called to produce more energy, which aggravates global warming, or build nuclear power plants to desalinate water.

MB: There's a true belief here that these private markets and the "three Ds"—dams, desalination, and diversion—are an economic miracle. It's a myth. As you say, desalination is very energy intensive, and it gives off CO_2 pollution. There are exorbitant expenses. It's important that we stop and remember that we're handing off to some parts of the environment what we don't want to continue to create in another part. Biofuel cuts down on fossil fuel for our cars, but we use land and water to grow food to feed those cars. We're creating problems with water to solve fossil fuel issues. With desalination you are abusing the ocean to provide water. Desal plants release a very intense brine back into the ocean. So there's the combination of the intense salt that gets stuck behind, the chemical that's used for the reverse osmosis process, and then this aquatic brine that is sucked in and sucked back out. I've been hearing from technicians who say, "We're just going to build a pipeline and send it farther out into the ocean."

HC: They always say that.

MB: And then it will kill the ocean a little farther out. The notion that the oceans are here for us to abuse is really a dangerous one. There are a number of new books, one by a terrific Canadian author, Alana Mitchell, called *Sea Sick*. What we're doing to the ocean is criminal, with the used plastic and the overfishing that's going on.

HC: What used plastic? Gyres?

MB: Yes, the great big whirlpools of plastic in the ocean that won't stop growing.

HC: There's a collection of plastic in the North Pacific. How large is it?

MB: The size of Mexico. The plastic breaks down, and then it gets into all the animals, the aquatic life. We really have to stop thinking of the ocean as the place where we can dump the problems that we haven't learned to live with on Earth. For me, desalination is what you do when you have run out of every single other answer. There's actually a place now, Salisbury, a suburb of Adelaide, where they're collecting the storm water and the human waste and recycling it through natural systems. They show that the city of Adelaide could provide water for its needs using this method at far less cost than their desalination plant. But they refuse to go to the natural model. We humans somehow think building these new technologies will take care of things. It's a very expensive mistake.

HC: I used to live in Adelaide, and we all used to have water tanks to collect the rainwater from the roof. I now live in a small fishing village, and I rely upon rainwater. And it should be imperative in a time of crisis that every single household on earth has a rainwater tank, and when it rains you collect the water from your roof.

MB: I absolutely agree with you. But we have come so far from that. Where does water come from? It comes from the tap or it comes from a bottle at Walmart. We don't have a relationship with water that says, This water must be returned to the land. It must be returned to the rivers and the aquifers. We've got to build our solutions on agreed-upon principles. And if we don't get those principles right, we're going to get the answers wrong.

HC: What principles would you follow?

MB: There are five I would suggest for Australia. The first is that the national government might declare Australia's water to be a public trust. Now I understand under the constitution in Australia water does belong to the people in the states; but this principle has been compromised under the 1994 law that allowed the opening of water trading between private brokers and the sellers. That's the privatization of the Murray-Darling river system, the irrigators who got the water for free using public money, to grow food; now they own that water from this 1994 legislation, and now they are saying to the government, "Well, maybe we'll sell it back to you, maybe we won't."

HC: I've never heard anything so ridiculous.

MB: The government needs to say, That water does not belong to you, it never belonged to you, and it's only for you to grow food. That doesn't mean that there isn't a commercial use for water, but we need to regulate it. The first thing to do is the reappropriation of public water. The federal government has to say, Water belongs to all Australians, the ecosystem, and the future. Period. Stop. The next principle is watershed protection and restoration. If we don't let enough water back into these water systems like the Murray-Darling system, we won't have enough water. We'll be refugees here.

HC: The Murray-Darling river system goes from the north of Australia and Queensland through New South Wales, through Victoria, to South Australia. It's the only river system we have in Australia, and Australia is the size of the United States, so you can imagine how precious that is.

MB: The Murray-Darling is where most of the agriculture in Australia takes place and where much of the food is grown.

The third principle would be conservation. Conservation is the soft path, as opposed to the hard path of technology. It's a different form of food production, more local, more sustainable. You pass a law so that you have a very strict code of conservation—collecting the storm water, the gray water, new building codes, all of that. The next principle is fair allocation. We have got to create a world built on the notion of water justice. And that means no one should be denied water because they cannot afford it. We have to say that water for living comes first, and local sustainable food production comes before commercial use. I tell people about the state of Vermont, where they have a lot of good groundwater, and water companies were coming in and pumping it up and sending it to cities in California. They passed a law saying that water belongs to the people in Vermont; it's their aquifer system and their future. If you use more than a certain amount a day, you have to have it licensed. And we have the right to revoke that if we feel your use is unsustainable. So the control is always back to the people, through their government.

The last principle is one we're working very hard on at the United Nations, and that is that water is a human right. I just came from Istanbul, and the World Water Forum says it's a need, which means that the private sector can deliver it on a for-profit basis. If somebody has been helping himself or herself to water for profit, then there's somebody else being denied that water. We need to establish once and for all that water is not running shoes, water is not Coca-Cola, water is what you need for life. And no one should be denied water from an inability to pay for it. We're hoping the nation-state constitutions will be amended to reflect this. We want a full covenant or treaty at the UN saying once and for all that water is a human right.

HC: I'm always shocked when I hear that corporations are moving into countries and saying, "We own the water, and you've got to buy it from us."

MB: In the global South the World Bank and the Regional Development Bank have promoted water privatization very strongly. For about fifteen years now the World Bank has extended money for water services in the global South contingent upon accepting private companies. Usually it's one of the two biggest companies, Suez and Veolia, who've run the water systems in France for many years, and who are about to lose their contracts for the first time in the city of Paris, which is about to go public. Everybody's very excited.

Suez and Veolia are all over the global South and in parts of the global North, delivering water on a for-profit basis, to people who can afford it. They have to take the same amount of public money that the public sector uses, but they have to profit from it, for their shareholders. Generally they lay off workers, and in some cases they triple the rate charged for water. There is a ferocious fight taking place all around the world, from La Paz, Bolivia, to Argentina, both of which kicked Suez out, to Atlanta, Georgia, which two years into a twenty-year contract said, Get out, don't come back. We can't believe what you did to our water system. But governments bought into the notion that the private sector can always do it better, especially in municipalities that are cash strapped. There's a fierce battle in the global South around this issue of the right to water.

HC: This is obscene, Maude, that the World Bank, which was set up to help developing countries and those of the third world, actually supports private companies who totally exploit the natural resources in the third world.

MB: It's a disaster. Even the UN under Kofi Annan supported privatization projects.

HC: Did he really? Why?

MB: I think that he really felt that playing with the big boys meant playing with the World Bank and the IMF. It was under Kofi Annan that the UN created the Global Compact, which is a voluntary agreement between the United Nations and a bunch of big corporations, some of whom are environmental and human rights abusers. Many of these companies have wrapped themselves in the UN flag. There's one for just the water companies, called the CEO Water Mandate, and it's all the big bottled water companies, all the utility companies. As somebody who's advising the president of the UN General Assembly, I criticize this corporate involvement in the one international institution left that has not been taken over by corporate interests. It's a very serious problem.

HC: They're being bought off. What happens to the poor people in these countries? How can they afford water?

MB: They can't. In Johannesburg, South Africa, Suez came in, and they bring water into the townships, but they installed prepaid water meters. And I remember standing in one of the townships with burning tires and garbage and what you call "flying toilets" where they defecate into plastic bags and just throw them. You can imagine this place when it rains. Then they suddenly have water coming into these communities, one of these pipes per block. But between the pipe and the tap is a water meter. You charge up your electronic key and then you touch this water meter that counts every drop. When you're talking 85 percent unemployment in a community like that, people laugh. Well, laugh and cry. And then they take their buckets, and they walk five kilometers [three miles] to a river that has cholera-warning signs on it, and they carry it back for drinking water. Or they buy water from private vendors at many more times the amount than they would have had to pay had they been able to hook up to the system. But they can't.

HC: Why don't they break the meters?

MB: They do. And what I love is that, in South Africa, some of the municipal South African water workers install the meters during the day and come back at night and show the people how to do that. It's one of my favorite stories.

HC: All this privatization of water. Soon we'll be walking around with oxygen bottles on our back, and they'll privatize the air.

MB: You know, in a way, carbon-emission trading is exactly privatizing the air. The whole notion of being able to buy your way out of polluting is a form of privatization of the air. I've just written a report called "Our Water Commons" about how to take back this notion of the commons, which was very much a part of thinking in many communities around the world. The modern enclosure of the commons has been privatization of these areas that we thought were sacred. I would include health care.

HC: Certainly in America.

MB: And education certainly needs to be seen as part of the commons. But there's nothing you can point to that more urgently needs to be designated as part of the commons than water. Bottled water is really one of the ways that we start the privatization process. Because if we've decided we're not going to trust that tap water, and you're only going to go to bottled water, then you're not going to care what comes out of that tap, and therefore you're maybe not going to want to pay taxes to make sure that that tap water's clean or that the infrastructure was upgraded or that the source was protected, because you've lost faith in it.

HC: You don't know where the bottled water's coming from.

MB: There are so many studies that tell us that bottled water is probably not as safe as tap water in many places. We had a big scandal in Canada, when it was admitted by the food protection agency that they haven't inspected the bottled-water plants in over six years. It's completely left up to the industry to regulate.

HC: Think of Coors beer, next to the Rocky Flats plutonium production plant where there was a huge fire. People have no idea where this water comes from.

MB: I know. In Canada we've now had twenty-seven municipalities, most of them are cities, ban commercial sales of bottled water. This has been a real campaign. We've had dozens of school boards across the country ban bottled water, and the Federation of Canadian Municipalities at their annual meeting passed a motion for a full ban across the country. They will not buy or sell a single plastic bottle or container on their premises. And it makes sense. If you are putting all this money into cleaning water and testing it, regulating it and protecting the source, why would you then compete with that by providing bottled water sales? A lot of restaurants are moving to their own filtering and so on.

HC: You don't need to filter tap water in the developed countries.

MB: It's perfectly safe and foolish to worry about it. But a lot of people have bought into that mythology. I walk down the streets here in Australia, and with all of the water crises, people are guzzling bottled water. When plastic is left in the sun, even in a car, the sun's rays heat the plastic up, and then you put the bottle into the fridge to cool it down. You shouldn't be drinking that water.

HC: No, that's right. And production of plastic produces nasty carcinogens, which are thrown into the air.

MB: And CO_2 emissions.

HC: Plastic turns into dioxins, and then stays in the rubbish heaps for thousands of years. People in swimming pools are guzzling bottled water—everyone has to have a bottle, and if it's not milk, it's water.

MB: In my province in Canada, Ontario, there was this kid who came up to the mic, braces and all, he must have been about fourteen. He said, "I can't imagine being without my bottled water," and he was really serious. And I said, "Well you're not going to believe this, but there was a time when people ventured out without their hydration vehicle."

HC: And people also think—this is a medical myth—that the more water they drink the healthier they are.

MB: That came from the bottled water companies.

HC: Did it?

MB: Absolutely. If you do drink eight glasses a day, and this is in London, Ontario, every day for a year, it will cost you $1.88. If you go to a vending machine, it's going to cost you $2,190. When I tell people that, I say, "You want to save money? There's a good spot to start."

HC: Let alone the strain on the poor old kidneys that have to filter out all that extra water.

There are two other things I'd like to cover. One is industrialization. In China they are using huge quantities of water to make sneakers. It is industrialization that's (a) using the water, and (b) polluting it, right? We've really gotten out of control, and isn't that reflected in what Wall Street did through the excessive use of capitalism, and where it's led us all?

MB: Yes, absolutely. And I keep saying, If we don't trust these people with our money, why would we trust them with our water? We have really allowed unbridled pollution. Actually, I'm working here with a group called SOS that is calling for a one kilometer [about a half mile] buffer zone around all waterways where mining is taking place. Industry has been given a free rein in all too many parts of the world.

HC: In the middle of our desert in southern Australia there's a huge uranium copper mine called Olympic Dam, and they're using

33 million liters per day out of the Great Artesian Basin, which is ancient archaeological water that feeds cattle stations and aboriginal people who use mound springs. That water then becomes polluted with radiation. It either is evaporated in ponds, the birds drink it, and they die, or it goes back into the underground water system, and we don't know how long that water's been in the Great Artesian Basin. And they're about to enlarge Olympic Dam by five times to make nuclear power plants and nuclear weapons.

MB: That's appalling. I go back to my principles. If we say that water is a public trust, and a human right, and has to be preserved in the ecosystem, we would place a priority on it that would be based on the soft path of conservation and source protection. You wouldn't be allowed to do that. We need politicians who will see beyond the four years that they're in office.

We're in the same situation in northern Alberta, with the massive destruction of our water table to provide energy for the United States. We have uranium mining in northern Saskatchewan, and now in southern Ontario and Quebec. One of my favorite quotes is from Martin Luther King Jr., who said, "Legislation may not change the heart, but it will restrain the heartless." We have to have laws, and they must be based on a set of principles that put water in the center, and nature in the center, and they must say that everything we have and are has come from nature, and if we destroy it we destroy our future as well. If we truly understood that, what you describe about the uranium mining would not be allowed to continue.

HC: In the southeast of Australia we're getting hardly any rain; it really is drought stricken. I know you're against us taking water out of the Murray Darling river, but it's terribly frightening.

MB: My point is that we mustn't underestimate that we're all contributing to this global warming by our abuse of these water systems. If we were to return water to watersheds, and really retain water, and restore the ecosystems, the rain would return. The water becomes a moderating influence in climate change.

HC: And trees and forests play a large role.

MB: We cut down trees. Trees drink the water, and they shoot it back out into the hydrological cycle. If you take over water-retentive landscapes, the rain will leave. And you create deserts. Understanding the water cycle is part of understanding the larger issue, and it's also part of the solution. Your former prime minister, Howard, would say, "There's nothing we've done; it's global warming." It's kind of like, Global warming made me do it.

HC: He was a scientifically illiterate man, as are most politicians.

MB: I think that your current government is trying really hard. I do feel a difference in the acknowledgment of climate change, but they're still allowing privatization of the Murray-Darling. And I think in the end the issues are startling and need to be looked at in a very powerful new way.

HC: Our current government is still in the pocket of the coal companies, the natural gas industry, the uranium companies, and nuclear weapons, so from my perspective on global warming and nuclear weapons, they're very guilty.

MB: Well, we've got a powerful citizens' movement growing everywhere, and in so many ways, you've helped. ∿

BILL MCKIBBEN

B ill McKibben is an American environmentalist and writer who has published *Eaarth: Making a Life on a Tough New Planet*, *The End of Nature*, and *Deep Economy: The Wealth of Communities and the Durable Future*. He frequently writes about global warming, alternative energy, and advocating for more localized economies. He leads the organization 350.org, which in 2009 coordinated the largest ever global rally of any kind, with 5,200 simultaneous demonstrations in 181 countries.

———✦———

HELEN CALDICOTT: You've published a book called *Eaarth: Making a Life on a Tough New Planet*. I want you to tell us how you're feeling about things now. You understand what's happening to the earth in a very deep way.

BILL MCKIBBEN: I wrote my first book about climate change twenty-one years ago. The only thing we didn't know back then was how quickly all of this was going to happen. And the answer is, A lot more quickly than we feared. The last twenty years have seen a rapid development of big, systemic changes in most of the physical systems on the earth. Clearly we're moving out of what scientists called the Holocene—the ten-thousand-year period that governs the rise of human civilization. We're moving out of that into something else, and that something else is in great flux, and it's very dangerous, and we got an intense feeling of it in the northern hemisphere this summer [2010], by far the hottest most brutal summer that people can remember. Nineteen nations set new, all-time high temperature records. We were talking with our 350.org colleagues in Pakistan in May when one of them said, "Very hot here today." I was surprised, because it's often hot in Pakistan, and it had been the hottest day ever recorded anywhere in Asia. The temperature had reached 129 degrees Fahrenheit.

Those kind of numbers are in themselves horrific. We got a good sense of what they meant in practice when we saw things like the continued rapid melt of the Arctic this summer. The volume of ice has reached a new record low. In Russia, they had the worst heat wave ever recorded across the middle of Russia. Moscow had day after day of 100-degree heat and horrible fires. That was enough to convince the Kremlin to stop grain exports to the rest of the world— from the third-largest grain exporter on the planet—a move that instantly spiked the cost of corn and wheat around the world. We saw it most tragically in Pakistan. Warm air holds more water vapor than cold, and that sets us up for these tremendous downpours and floods. Across the headwaters of the Indus up in the Hindu Kush it produced the most devastating flood anyone can remember any- where. Twenty million people out of their homes, on the move, be- tween a third and a fifth of the country underwater. Just epic.

HC: Biblical?

BM: Yes. The thing that's scariest is that this comes with human beings having raised the average global temperature about 1 degree. Climatologists tell us they're confident that if we keep burning fos- sil fuel, that number will be 5 degrees before the century is out. If 1 degree melts the Arctic, we really do not want to find out what

5 degrees does. Your original question was the right one, about how one is personally feeling. That's why I wrote this book with the odd title, *Eaarth*. The climate still looks the same. It has the right number of continents, gravity is still functioning. But in very fundamental ways it's a different planet than the one you or I were born onto, and that shift has been profound. We need to start noticing, because it's that noticing that will drive us to the action that's necessary to prevent more destruction in the very near future.

HC: By the time politicians, and in particular corporations, wake up, it's going to be too late, right?

BM: Well, not too late. This is all relative, right? It's already warmed 1 degree. We've probably got another degree in the pipeline from carbon we've already emitted. But we have enormous latitude to keep it from getting worse. There's a world of difference between a 2-degree increase and a 5-degree increase in the global temperature. One will produce a difficult century, the other may produce an impossible one. And we still have it within our power to make that choice. You're right: we have to move pretty quickly. And at the moment, the politics of this is almost as discouraging as the science. The failure of the Copenhagen talks in December 2009 and the inaction of the American Congress earlier really seem to have doomed for the moment any chance of comprehensive legislation. I think what we have to do is build a powerful movement around the world, and especially in the United States to kick the offensive back. This is a hard task. We're up against the most profitable industry the world has ever seen. Fossil fuel makes more money for its patrons than any other industry. Since we're not going to match them dollar for dollar, we have to use our bodies and spirits and creativity to blunt their advantages.

HC: I think most young people have a very deep sense, intuitively, that their future looks really grim. Do you agree?

BM: We find an enormous willingness among young people the world over to take real action. They seem hopeful and optimistic. Maybe they're being more brave. We find it everywhere, from Australia to Latin America to Africa to Asia to North America. It's really profound to see. On 10/10/10 [October 10, 2010] there will be a truly enormous global work party on climate change.* We're expecting 7,000 events, a huge number of them across the Antipodes, and most of them organized by young people.

HC: What are they going to be doing?

BM: Well, you name it. Everything on that day will be aimed at having some practical effect on climate change. So people will be putting up solar panels, people will be digging community gardens, laying out bike paths. Across Auckland there are hundreds of bike mechanics who will be making sure that every bike in the city is working well so that people will be able to ride to work. In 2009 at our first attempt at a huge global political rally, we managed to organize 5,200 events in 181 countries. CNN called it the most widespread day of political action in the planet's history. It's going to be bigger this year. People may be discouraged by events in Copenhagen, but they haven't given up. The point of this day will be to show that there are things we can begin doing in our communities. We know they won't solve climate change by themselves—for that we need legislation that resets the price of carbon—but we want to send a credible message to our politicians. At the end of that day, people will put down their hammers and shovels, pick up their phones, and call their president, their prime minister, their politburo and deliver the same message all around the world: I'm getting to work, what about you? If I can climb up on the roof of the school and put in a new solar panel, you might be able to climb up to the

---

* This interview was conducted in early October 2010, prior to the events described in this passage.

floor of the Senate and hammer out a little legislation. That's the kind of change that we really need.

HC: It's really a revolution of a kind. I'm in the Antipodes, in Australia, and we are just one huge quarry. In fact, we're a third world country. One of the most lucrative raw materials that we export is coal. We're just full of coal. I can go out on the shore and see thirty huge cargo ships waiting to line up at Newcastle to load themselves with coal and go to China. When politicians talk, and journalists talk, they talk about jobs, they talk about money, and they don't talk about what's going to happen to the planet if we keep burning coal. And *the* most concentrated form of carbon is coal, and we really have to stop burning it, or we're doomed.

BM: The only thing that's going to change politicians' minds is a political movement that really pushes them. Australia's come closer than most countries on Earth, and that's because people rallied so well. You had an election that was fought on climate change. Mr. Rudd won and then backed away, and that cost him dearly. Those are good reminders that politicians need to hear. It's extraordinarily tough because of the concentration of money and power in those industries. Even if you're just thinking economically, we're making an extraordinarily shortsighted set of decisions. We're suckering the economies and industries of the past. We've known how to burn coal since the early eighteenth century. And yet it's pretty clear that the energies and industries of the future revolve around sun, wind, and renewables. Australia may buy itself ten to twenty years of coal-based prosperity, but it's going to be at the cost (a) of an uninhabitable planet, and (b) of sacrificing all of the next emerging economies to places like China, where they've begun to take seriously this revolution.

HC: You are right about Australia, because Prime Minister Rudd came in vowing to do something about global warming. He produced legislation that was almost worse than nothing, just to placate the corporations. And he got kicked out by his own party. The Australian people have spoken on global warming, and they're really annoyed. Still the politicians stand there listening to the corporations, all of which are foreign-owned, that are mining our coal. The profits go offshore, and not many jobs are created. The whole thing is crazy. We could be the leading global energy superpower by covering Australia with solar panels and windmills and geothermal energy. We're just waiting to use our natural resources.

BM: Yes, a coalition of people, Beyond Zero, put out a white paper in Australia explaining how the country could go carbon-free by 2020 with a real push to make use of all those things that you have in abundance. There's never been a place more favored with sun, with tide, with wind, and it's too bad that the fascination with black rocks is continuing.

HC: It's these blasted corporations and these very, very rich men who dominate the political scene. We come back to capitalism when you look at your Congress and our Parliament and how they're run by those who have the power, the money, and the access. A coal man can go to Parliament and meet with the secretary of energy for an hour, and yet someone from the Green Party—and, interestingly, the Green Party now holds the balance of power here—who cares about the future might get five minutes with an assistant to the secretary of energy.

BM: I predict that it won't change. We won't match BHP Billiton, Rio Tinto, and Exxon Mobil dollar for dollar. I think we better figure out a better currency to work in. And that's what we've been trying to do at 350.org. Australia's been one of the places that's best for our organizing. Our wonderful Australian coordinator, Blair Palese, and her crew have done an astonishing job. It's always going to be an extremely tough fight, simply because, beyond the financial power of the industry, we all benefit at some level from using fossil fuels every day. There's a certain kind of inertia that goes with it.

HC: We almost need to become Gandhis. There's always another way to approach it, and we're all searching for that particular asymmetrical approach to overturn the powers that be at the moment. I'd love to talk to you about what initiatives China is taking at the moment. I think everyone needs to know about that.

BM: China's a very interesting case. I was there doing a story for *National Geographic*. On the one hand, we've all seen the pictures of the enormous, smoky, coal-fired power stations, all the pollution that's plaguing China as it goes through rapid industrialization. All of that's very real and dangerous, although it must be noted that the average Chinese person uses about a quarter as much energy, and hence produces a quarter as much CO_2, than the average American or Australian.

The other part of the story is pretty exciting. The Chinese are quickly emerging as the biggest users of renewable energy around the world. I was in cities of seven hundred thousand or a million people where virtually every building has solar hot-water panels on the top. When about a quarter million Chinese take a shower, the hot water is coming from solar panels on the roof. They're by far the world's leader in installed solar capacity and installed wind capacity. They're making some remarkable strides. So the race between a green China and a black China is not yet decided. But I dare say they've done more than the United States as far as using renewables. And that's a pretty shocking thing to say. Last week in the United States we were caravaning around a couple of the solar panels that Jimmy Carter had put on the White House roof, and that Ronald Reagan had taken down. We were trying to convince the Obamas to put solar panels back up on the White House. We didn't have much luck, but we learned that one of those solar panels from the Carter White House is now in the private museum of the Chinese solar baron Huang Ming, whose company put about 60 million of these solar arrays on buildings throughout China.

HC: I read about your attempt to get the panels back on the White House roof. What happened?

BM: We talked to several high-ranking White House staff people. They wouldn't tell us why they didn't want them. Maybe they're afraid anything associated with Jimmy Carter would be seen in a bad political light. I think they're making a mistake. I think people love solar panels, even people who don't believe in global warming seem to like them. They'd get a lot of credit for putting them up on the White House, just like they got a lot of credit for putting a garden in the White House lawn. But they're not willing to do it right at the moment.

The good news is that on October 10, 2010, there will be other world leaders stepping up to the challenge. There is the wonderful president of the Maldives, Mohamed Nasheed, who is the leader of a country facing submersions in this century as the waters rise, and a country at this minute undergoing a hideous onslaught of bleaching of their vital coral reefs from warm water. Mohamed Nasheed will be up on his roof, of his official residence, installing solar panels on that day. It will remind other leaders that they could get to work, too.

HC: Germany is one of the leaders in renewable energy, is it not?

BM: Germany has put what's called a feed-in tariff that has allowed them to dramatically raise the amount of solar they've got online. If you are a German householder, and you put a photovoltaic panel on the roof, the electric utility pays a premium price to you for the power that's coming off of your roof into the grid. Germany is not a particularly sunny place; most of it is well north of the United States. But despite that they're probably the world leader in installed photovoltaic capacity.

HC: I want to move on to Exxon. I want you to tell us what they've been doing in terms of propaganda, injecting doubt into the debate, and the role they have played in inhibiting moves to prevent global warming.

BM: Exxon has provided a lot of the funding for disinformation groups in the United States, but also in much of the rest of the English-speaking world. They're not alone in doing this. Jane Mayer wrote a beautiful piece for the *New Yorker* about the billionaire Koch brothers, oil and gas and other resource barons in the United States, who have been devoting hundreds of millions of dollars to this task.

HC: And to the Tea Party, too?

BM: Exactly right, funding the Tea Party. We see now a powerful campaign by them, to get voters to overturn the landmark law in California that's the closest the United States has come to doing anything substantial about climate change, funded by these same forces.

HC: The climate skeptics funded by Exxon Mobil and these other corporations say the data's not really there. The Intergovernmental Panel on Climate Change, which is a huge international body of scientists looking at climate change, made one mistake. And if you make one mistake their whole database is ruled invalid. It's a very superstitious, ignorant way of thinking and approaching the problem.

BM: I think the right wing has done a commendable job of winning this fight. They have a fairly easy job, because they've got so much money. It's powerful. They're very good at this, and doubt is their product. All they need is doubt, because all they need is delay. The sad and ironic part of it is that everybody, including them, know that in sixty, seventy years from now the world will have moved on from fossil fuels. We'll have run out of many of them, and we'll be doing sun and wind. The problem is, if we wait sixty or seventy years we will have wrecked the planet for eons to come. If we do it in the next ten or twenty, it'll be more wrenching, but we'll stand some real chance of preventing the onrushing environmental destruction.

HC: They won't live to see the end results of what they've been doing. Do you have any spiritual beliefs that guide you, or are you coming from a scientific, rational perspective?

BM: I'm a Methodist. A large part of this for me is the incredible moral outrage of what's going on. The sheer fact that those people that cause the problem suffer from it less than those that don't cause the problem should be enough to spark a kind of moral outrage in all of us. Nobody in Pakistan is causing the climate to change. They're not burning enough fossil fuels to be more than a rounding error in the calculations. And yet they're underwater.

HC: Do you have training and education in science?

BM: I'm a journalist by background. My first job was at the *New Yorker*, where, in fact, *The End of Nature*, my first book on climate change, was serialized. My specialty is in talking to scientists and translating what they have to say so that people can understand it.

HC: Have you tried to get to the Obama administration?

BM: We did with the solar panel trip. The Obamas haven't taken a strong leadership role on climate issues. They decided to pursue health care reform instead in the first couple of years in office. The guy's got a tough job, he's in a tough pinch, and one hesitates to criticize too much. At the very least they could've been doing a lot more symbolic leadership on this issue than they have. The decision was made, I think, to not talk about climate change and instead to talk about things like green jobs. One result is that there's been very little push back to the right-wing forces that are trying to downplay talk of global warming. The poll numbers for skeptics increased over the last few years. We need to spend the next couple of years building a strong and committed movement that will be able to really take advantage of the next openings when they come. Be they political or be they the openings the natural world is going to continue to give us as conditions deteriorate.

HC: Yes, it's very scary. Do you want to say anything about the Tea Party?

BM: They've clearly seized on a kind of generalized American anger with the inefficiency and unproductivity of our government and its leadership. It's too bad that they've taken an exclusively right-wing direction. All forty candidates for the Senate from the Republican Party announced that they don't think climate change is real. That's a very scary and difficult place to be in. I think it's political calculation among people at the top. One of the things that's quite distressing is that it's become an article of true faith within the conservative movement that global warming isn't real. And it's a strange position for conservatives to be taking. One would think that if you are conservative, i.e., interested in stability, in keeping things as they've been in the past, then you would be at special pains to keep from trying to double the amount of carbon in the atmosphere and just seeing what happens. That's a pretty reckless, indeed radical, course of action to be pursuing.

HC: Let's get back to *Eaarth*. You talk about what's happening to the planet: warming, drying, acidifying, flooding, burning, but you also talk about solutions. I first want to ask you about your attitude to nuclear power, and then we'll move on to the other solutions.

BM: It isn't about solutions so much in the sense of, here's one technology, here's another; it's about rethinking the world. I think one of the things we have to come to grips with is that economic growth, the main driver of our politics around the world for the last couple of generations, is no longer an intelligent goal. We've probably grown as large as it's smart for us to grow, and somewhat larger. Therefore, one of the things that we really need to do over the next period is figure out how to scale down.

In recent years our financial system had gotten too big to fail, and yet it failed. It's important to realize that our energy and our agriculture systems are at least as overbuilt, vulnerable, brittle, prone to failure, and interlocked. If they start to go down they'll take a lot with them. The final solution to that is to decentralize some. When I think about nuclear power it's often in those ways. You're the expert on the health and safety risks, and I confess that those worry me less in certain ways than (a) the tremendous costs associated with trying to generate power in this way—you might as well burn $20 bills, and (b) the inherent centralization. We're at a moment when we have the real possibility of switching toward the sun and the wind, and with them a kind of democratic, dispersed, decentralized power. It would be a great shame to try to figure out yet another completely centralized, highly expensive form of energy to indulge in. At the very least we're running out of the money to do it with.

HC: Let's get on to other solutions. You've obviously thought about this in great depth. How can we as a people at all levels bring a halt to this catastrophe we're facing?

BM: The important legislative solution is to put a stiff price on carbon that reflects the damage that it does in the atmosphere, so that we'll use less of it. Once that starts to happen a lot of other good things will happen as a result, because the way the modern world works is a direct reflection of the constant availability of cheap fossil fuel. For instance, we can move quickly to a much more localized agriculture. At the moment we have an industrialized agribusiness approach that's heavily energy intensive. It uses immense amounts of fossil fuel. It's replaced human labor with fossil fuel, such that in the United States we went from 50 percent of us farming 150 years ago to less than 1 percent now. We're never going back to 50 percent, but last year, for the first time in 150 years, the United States Department of Agriculture reported that the number of farms in the United States was increasing instead of decreasing. That's because we have this rapidly spreading set of farmers' markets, the fastest growing part of our food system. Sales have been up 10 to 20 percent a year now, for more than a decade and a half. That's exciting. It would go much faster if we weren't directly and indirectly subsidizing agribusiness to the tune of billions of dollars a year. But even so, progress has been made. Much more will be made when oil costs what it should cost. At which time shipping a tomato five thousand miles will be seen for the crazy act that it is.

I think the same thing could happen in energy. The great vision for the future—what the engineers call distributed generation—is millions of people putting energy into the grid and taking it out. I have solar panels all over my roof; on a sunny day like today I'm a little power utility. It's a much nicer system in all possible ways, right up to and including the things that have been troubling the sleep of Americans for the last decade. A terrorist could theoretically take an interest in my solar panels, climb up on the roof, and smash them with a hammer, but if he did, deadly solar particles would not flow off into the atmosphere. I'd have a problem, but it wouldn't crash the grid. In a tough century we're going to need to work on making problems stay problems and not turn into disasters.

HC: Do you sell your solar power back to the grid?

BM: Yes. The stuff that we don't use directly, absolutely.

HC: That's wonderful. We have subsidies now in Australia to build solar hot water systems and solar panels. I've got a vegetable garden that I adore. I fertilize it with horse manure, since there are lots of horses around here. I don't have to buy artificial fertilizer made with fossil fuel, and it's such a lovely feeling to go out and pick my salad at night, or my spinach or kale. It's got no pesticides, it's clean as a whistle, and I grew it myself. It makes eating much more enjoyable, actually.

BM: Absolutely. I just made squash soup with the squash from our fall harvest this year. The apples have come in in Vermont. We're right at that magic moment in early autumn.

HC: When you think about centuries ago, people lived in New England and Vermont right through the winter without importing raspberries from South America and tomatoes from California, because they bottled their beans, they preserved. You can use the ice for refrigeration. Just have a little cupboard sticking out of your house, and you can store things the whole winter.

BM: There's lots of stuff we can do that would be wiser than the things we are doing. To me, the emblematic thing is that the clothesline would allow everyone to dry their clothes without having to think of the alternative. You can either hang your clothes on a clothesline and dry them for free, or you can go have somebody mine coal for you, ship it to where you need it to be, build a power plant, burn it, build a set of transmission lines, have somebody else build an expensive appliance, run the appliance from the lines into your house, and essentially use them to heat up your clothes and spin them around for a while. Both accomplish the same thing, but one is a marvel of complexity that degrades the planet that it lives on and the other is a marvel of simplicity that doesn't trouble anyone and might get you a few minutes outdoors every day to feel the sun on your back. Yet something like a third of Americans aren't even legally allowed to put up a clothesline, because they're in gated communities where they're not allowed to, because people might think they look bad.

HC: GE makes dishwashers, clothes dryers, washing machines, nuclear power plants, nuclear weapons, missiles, the whole thing. Social engineering has been very clever to brainwash people into thinking they need a dryer, where in the winter in Vermont you just hang your clothes on a clotheshorse next to the furnace and in the summer you hang them outside. We've always dried our clothes outside in Australia, and they smell so nice.

BM: You can hang them outside in the dead of winter, frankly, then shake the ice right off. They actually dry faster. They freeze-dry.

HC: America could survive without carbon energy production and nuclear power and fulfill its energy needs. By 2040 or 2050, with all the renewable technologies, America could be carbon-free and nuclear-free.

BM: Until we build a movement as strong as those other guys are, they're going to keep winning. There's no great mystery to it, and at some level, no use complaining about how the world works. It gives you some idea of what you have to do to make a change. We've managed to do that at some points in history. This is a uniquely difficult one, because everybody's implicated in the whole mess. We all use fossil fuel all the time, and we all like the things that it provides. But we've got to deal with it. It's not an ideological battle in the end; it's humans versus physics. I'm saying, You're not going to out-argue physics. It's declared its bottom line: 350 parts per million [ppm] CO_2 in the atmosphere if you want the planet to work the way it's supposed to work. And since we're at 390 right now, and rising, that's our problem.

HC: I think about how things have changed. When I was a kid— I'm seventy-two now and getting on—we had a little radio and electric lights, when I lived in Melbourne, Australia, but that's all. And now look at my house. I've got all this electronic equipment.

BM: I'm fairly sanguine about the ability of computers and computer networks to be an important part of things going forward. You can do about a thousand searches on Google for the amount of energy it takes to drive your car a kilometer [about a half mile]. So if we learn to travel in different ways, that will help. It's not a cure-all, but I know that we couldn't have done the kind of organizing we've done in the last few years without these kinds of technologies.

HC: We can also turn all of our appliances off at night. Stand-alone power uses about 6 percent of the electricity that we currently use.

BM: It's completely wasted, and the minute that we have a serious price on carbon, everyone will do it every night. I think the key is probably to put a stiff price on it and collect it from Exxon Mobil, and let them run the price up at the pump, and then rebate all the money back to people. You get a check every month for your share of the sky. And that'll allow us to get the price signal we need without being beggars in the process.

HC: You're doing fantastic work, but it's got to rise to the point where the politicians can't ignore us.

BM: Amen. That's what we're trying to do. Movements take a while to build, and it'll be a beautiful and powerful one. ∼

LESTER BROWN

L ester Brown is founder and president of the Earth
Policy Institute, a nonprofit environmental research
institution based in Washington, D.C. During a career
that started with tomato farming, Brown has been awarded twenty-four honorary degrees, and his books have
been translated into some forty languages. His most
recent book is titled *World on Edge: How to Prevent
Environmental and Economic Collapse.*

———∿∿∿———

HELEN CALDICOTT: I read the article in *Scientific American* called
"Could Food Shortages Bring Down Civilization?" The biggest
threat to global stability is the potential for food crises in poor
countries to cause government collapse. Now I know we talk about
global warming and deforestation and all sorts of things, but this
catastrophe is on the cutting edge: failed countries. Would you like
to define what a failed country is?

LESTER BROWN: The term "failed state" has just entered our working vocabulary within the last decade or so. But a failed state is one
where governments can no longer provide personal security. They
often lose control of part of their territory. Pakistan at the moment
is an example of that. And eventually, as governments weaken and

become less able to satisfy the needs of society, whether it's personal security or food or education or health care, they begin to lose their legitimacy. And there is now a very substantial list of failed and failing states, and they include countries like Somalia, the Democratic Republic of the Congo, Zimbabwe, Iraq, and Afghanistan. Pakistan, incidentally, is the first nuclear power to move into this category. A number of countries in Africa are in the failing states category, so this is a growing concern. And if I were to pick one political indicator that will tell us more about our future than any other, it would be the number of failing states in the world. If that list grows longer, it poses a difficult question, which is, How many states have to fail before we have a failing global civilization? We don't know the answer to that question, because we haven't been there before.

HC: Is there any historical reference to this present situation?

LB: I suppose the closest thing we have to it is the records of the early civilizations that failed. Like the Sumerians or the Mayans. There are many others, and we study their archaeological sites today. What we're seeing now, I don't think, has any modern equivalent. In the period since World War II we've seen the creation of a huge number of states, initially from decolonization, and then we had the breakup of the Soviet Union and Yugoslavia, for example. Now some of those states, particularly those that have had sustained rapid rates of population growth, are beginning to break down under the stress. And the stress includes everything from food shortages to the inability to build enough schools and the inability to provide security.

HC: I suppose if we looked at Zimbabwe, formerly—

LB: Northern Rhodesia.

HC: What's happened under Mugabe?

LB: What's so interesting about Zimbabwe is that, a decade or so ago, it was a model of how an ex-colonial country should work. And Mugabe was advised not to drive out all the European farmers in Zimbabwe, because they were such an important part of the economy, and to build around them, but in the end he ignored this advice. Zimbabwe was a model of development. And a similar thing happened in the Ivory Coast. Now both of them are high on the list of failing states.

HC: And there's Haiti. That's in a terrible mess, isn't it?

LB: It's a country where the deforestation came first, then the soil erosion and falling food production. Haiti imports 60 percent of its grain today. And it's really kept alive by the World Food Programme's food support system. Haiti, without this lifeline from the world food system, would probably go up in flames.*

HC: And who deforested Haiti? Was that foreign logging corporations or was it done domestically?

LB: I think in this case it was a matter of the population growing and the need for charcoal and more and more land to produce food. They kept clearing land, until today only 4 percent of the country is forested. And every time there's a heavy storm or a hurricane that passes near Haiti, it's a catastrophe. There's nothing to hold the water once it falls. It starts accumulating and doing enormous damage. Haiti shares the island with the Dominican Republic. And from the air you can see the territorial dividing line—the Dominican Republic is still 40 percent forested. The Dominican Republic is a reasonably stable country and doing all right economically, but Haiti has become an ecological, and therefore an economic, basket case.

HC: Like Easter Island, where they chopped down all their trees?

LB: Right, but even worse, because of the climate, the terrain, and

---

* This interview was conducted in June 2009, prior to the catastrophic earthquake that ravaged Haiti in January 2010.

the soil. And in Haiti, in addition to the World Food Programme lifeline, there's a UN security force that keeps armed gangs from taking over the country.

HC: Because they got rid of Jean-Bertrand Aristide?

LB: Right.

HC: We could go farther south, down to Brazil, Peru, Venezuela, and look at the Amazon, fast disappearing.

LB: We've seen, over the last century and a quarter, three sort of major land expansion efforts in the world. One came in the United States in the nineteenth and early twentieth centuries, and it culminated in the Dust Bowl of the 1930s. That's become a chapter in our history now. And it took a very strong, well-organized response to stabilize that situation.

HC: Was that because of deforestation?

LB: Not so much deforestation but overplowing of the grasslands in the Great Plains. As a result of the Dust Bowl, during the Roosevelt years—and this was also the Great Depression—there was an effort to take some of that marginal land out of production and put it back into grass, to plant trees and create shelterbelts, to change cropping patterns to alternate-year cropping and strip cropping. A whole series of conservation measures did stabilize the situation. In the late 1950s, the Russians, who wanted very much to overtake the United States in agriculture, decided they were going to plow up a lot of land, much of it in what's now Kazakhstan. In the early sixties, they plowed an area of grass equal to the wheatland of Australia and Canada combined. The agronomists were saying, Don't do it, but the planners in Moscow, the political types, were saying, We're gonna overtake the United States. And by the mid-sixties they had a huge dust bowl. And 40 percent of that land that they plowed has now gone back to grass.

And what we have in Brazil is the third great expansion of the last century. I have a feeling that it may end up in the same way. We're seeing both the clearing of the savannah-like region south of the Amazon and, at the same time, the clearing of the Amazon for agriculture. It begins by removing the trees, grazing the cattle, and then plowing the land and planting soybeans or other crops. But the inevitable result here, if the deforestation of the Amazon continues, is that the rain forest will begin to dry out and become vulnerable to natural fire, thunderstorms, lightning strikes. It may reach one of those key points when there's no return, so we could end up with the Amazon being, at best, some sort of savannah landscape and, at worst, a desert. How it's going to unfold is not clear. There is growing concern among ecologists that we're approaching the tipping point in the Amazon Basin. We could then have irreversible problems.

HC: And change the climate in North America, right?

LB: It will alter the climate systems in the world, because Brazil's a vast area, and one of the things that happens early on is that, as you deforest in the coastal regions, you reduce the capacity of the rain forest to transmit water inland. As moisture-laden air from the Atlantic moves westward across the Amazon toward the Andes, it carries moisture inland. As the air cools and this moisture is converted into rainfall, it waters the rain forest below. But if you begin clearing land then, when it rains, roughly three-fourths of the rainfall runs off and only one-fourth evaporates, leaving little to be carried inland. Whereas, in a healthy rain forest, when it rains only one-fourth runs off and three-fourths evaporates and is carried farther inland. So this mechanism is weakened by deforestation. The risk is that southern Brazil, northern Argentina, and Paraguay could begin to suffer from drought, and indeed, there are signs that that process has already begun.

HC: I've been to the Amazon and gone down to Venezuela into the Amazon River itself. Every afternoon there's a massive rainstorm.

I've heard that one tree transpires one hundred gallons of water a day from its leaves into the air.

LB: The reason tropical forests are called rain forests is that they do recycle water so efficiently. And if the air masses are moving inland, that carries the water inland. And as you know, it's very difficult to burn a healthy rain forest. You have to wait until the end of the rain season, and you have to cut some brush and dry it out. You have to really work to get a fire going. But as the rain forest dries out, as more and more plots are cleared, it becomes vulnerable to natural fire. That's the tipping point.

Brazilian cattle spend most of their life grazing, and then go directly to market off the range. In the United States, by contrast, the calves are born on the range, spend six or eight months there, until they reach about six hundred pounds, then they go to a feedlot, and they're fed until they weigh eleven hundred pounds. In the feedlot it takes about seven pounds of grain for each pound of live weight. In the case of Brazil, it's almost all grass-fed beef, and that's why they keep clearing more and more land, as the world demand for beef grows.

HC: Huge soybean crops are now being grown on cleared Amazon land. And now everyone thinks soybeans are good for us. Not just for human consumption, but I believe for animal consumption as well, particularly in Europe.

LB: And in China. Of the world's soybean crop, less than 10 percent will be consumed directly as food. For the great bulk of the world's soybean crop, the bean is crushed and the oil removed. That's 20 percent. The remaining 80 percent, the high-protein meal, is used everywhere in the world today for feed rations. For pigs, for chickens, for cows, on fish farms in China. China, which gave the world soybeans, is now far and away the largest importer. This year China will import some 55 million tons of soybeans. The big suppliers are the United States, Brazil, and Argentina. In the United States we now have more land in soybeans than we have in wheat because of the huge demand in China.

About 35 percent of the world grain harvest is now fed to cows, pigs, chickens, and fish. Fish farming is becoming huge, especially in China. What they're usually fed is a ration similar to what's fed to chickens: grains supplemented with soybean meal. It takes a lot of soybean meal to feed all the pigs and chickens, cattle and fish in countries like China, the United States, and places in Europe.

HC: How many more people could be fed if all that grain was fed to people and not animals?

LB: It's not quite as simple as it seems. If in the state of Iowa you had an acre of land, you could plant all the land in soybeans and consume the soybeans directly. You also could plant that acre in corn, and because the corn yield is three times as high as that of soybeans, you could feed that corn to chickens, and they require about two pounds of grain per pound of live weight. In a sense, it would be a more efficient use of land and other resources to consume poultry than to consume soybeans directly.

HC: Why is the world so hooked on soybean production if it isn't fully sufficient to feed both animals and humans?

LB: Because not much of the world's soybean harvest is consumed directly as food. What happens when you incorporate 20 percent soybean meal with 80 percent grain grasses is that, most important, soybean meal in the grain dramatically increases the efficiency by which livestock and poultry convert grain into meat or milk or eggs. That's where soybeans are playing an important role in the world food economy.

HC: Let's talk about feeding cars.

LB: In the last several years the price of gasoline has gone up in the United States, as it did right after Katrina hit at the end of August in 2005. The price of gasoline suddenly jumped to $3 a gallon. And at that time the price of corn was $2 a bushel. Since you could get gallons of ethanol from a bushel of corn to put in cars, it suddenly became highly profitable to convert corn into fuel for cars. We used to have a food economy and an energy economy. They were pretty much separate. But now, with the enormous investment in ethanol distilleries in the United States, we're converting roughly a third of the U.S. grain harvest into fuel for cars. What it means is that, given this capacity to convert grain into fuel for cars, the price of grain is now tied to the price of oil. Every time the price of oil goes up, it pulls the price of grain up behind it. If the food value of of grain is below the fuel value, the market for grain is in the energy sector.

So we have set up a competition between the owners of the world's one billion vehicles and the low-income people in the world. The interesting thing is that the average income of the people with cars is something like $30,000 a year. The average income of the 2 billion poorest people in the world is less than $3,000 a year. There's a real inequity. It's easy to see who's going to win in this competition. This is a major reason why the number of hungry people in the world has been increasing. In the last few years we have had a dramatic rise in the prices of wheat, rice, corn, and soybeans—they tripled between the beginning of 2007 and mid-2008, so the number of hungry people is now close to 1 billion. This is a social indicator, the increase in hunger, like the indicator we talked about earlier, the growing number of failing states in the world. Now we have an increasing number of hungry people in the world. This I think is a warning sign, because we could see more and more failing states as governments are no longer able to provide food security for their people.

The thing that's so interesting is that we have had, since the last half of the last century, price surges from time to time, but they were always event-driven. It was a poor harvest in the Soviet Union or a monsoon failure in India or an intense heat wave and drought in the U.S. corn belt. But this rise in prices is not event-driven. This current rise is driven by trends on both the demand and supply side. There are some 3 billion people who want to move up the food chain and this is creating an insane competition between automobiles and people for the food supply. We have new trends emerging that make it more difficult to increase the production. One is soil erosion—that goes back to the beginning of agriculture itself—taking more of the world's crop land than ever before. The second thing is falling water tables in countries that contain half the world's people. In some countries where the water supplies are running out, like Saudi Arabia, they're phasing out irrigated agriculture. They've been able to produce wheat by tapping an aquifer that's half a mile down. They've used oil-drilling technology, but that aquifer is essentially a fossil aquifer, which means it doesn't recharge. Now that the aquifer is largely depleted, they are facing an end of irrigated wheat production, and by 2016 they will be importing virtually all their grain. It's estimated that about 175 million people in India are now being fed with grain produced by overpumping, and about 130 billion people in China are in the same category. When wells go dry, as they're beginning to, and as they've already done in Saudi Arabia, the entire world will know.

HC: I want to go back to the grain in Iowa. I thought the drive to do this was that ethanol produces less CO_2 when burned than does oil.

LB: The ethanol fuel program in the United States was launched in 1978 after the Arab oil export embargo. What people said was, Well, we've got a lot of this land set aside under our farm programs. Why don't we just use it to grow corn for ethanol and burn the ethanol in our cars? It sounded like a pretty good idea. Because corn and soybeans share land, when corn production for ethanol distilleries expanded in the United States, it also meant the pressure on soybeans in Brazil intensified, because Brazil is the other big soybean producer. They have to clear more land to produce more soybeans. The net effect is, when you burn off forests and clear them, there are enormous carbon emissions. Not just from the aboveground vegetation, but from all the organic matter in the soils that comes from the heavy vegetation. So it turns out that most of the recent studies conclude that we have a net increase in carbon emissions when we grow corn to produce ethanol for our automotive fuel.

HC: Also, we have to put a lot of fertilizer in the ground to grow the corn, and oil is used to produce fertilizer. So the net decrease in CO_2 just doesn't occur. Ethanol produces, in the long run, through the whole cycle, more CO_2 than does oil, isn't that correct?

LB: That is correct, much to the surprise of many. A number of scientific studies have reached agreement on that point.

HC: You have some pragmatic suggestions about how to reduce CO_2 production by 80 percent by the year 2020. Have you had any contact with the Obama administration and Dr. Steven Chu, the secretary of energy?

LB: The person I know best is John Holdren, who's been the president's science adviser. They appointed some really first-rate people very much committed to taking the steps to stabilize the climate. The decision to raise automotive fuel efficiency to fifty-four miles per gallon in this country for new cars sold in 2025 represents a huge jump. Another interesting thing happening in the States now, which is more a result of the economic downturn, is that the rate of scrappage of old cars has exceeded new car sales. We're actually now seeing a shrinkage in the U.S. automobile fleet. Another interesting development, and this precedes the Obama administration, is the powerful grassroots movement opposing new coal-powered plants in the United States. We are very close to a de facto moratorium on new coal plants in the United States. Beyond this, 106 of the country's coal-fired power plants are now scheduled to close.

HC: James Hansen, who's the godfather of global warming science at NASA, says that we really have to stop burning coal, period.

Steven Chu comes from the Los Alamos nuclear weapons lab. Do you think they're really going to focus on stopping coal-burning electricity and getting into renewables in a very rapid way?

LB: From 2007 and 2011, carbon emissions from coal use in the United States dropped 10 percent. During the same period, emissions from oil use dropped 11 percent. Over the same time period, more than four hundred wind farms—with a total generating capacity of 27,000 megawatts—have come online, enough to supply 8 million homes with electricity.

HC: That's equivalent to thirty nuclear power stations. Do you think, then, that Dr. Chu would share your urgent need for the United States in particular, but the world in general, to get below 80 percent of CO_2 production by 2020?

LB: Steven Chu said, "If we don't get our act together, there won't be any agriculture in the state of California twenty or thirty years from now." So he's very much aware. Al Gore is calling for the phasing-out of all fossil fuel by 2020. If we don't do something like this, then we're going to be faced with so many climate-related issues—the melting of the glaciers in the Himalayas and in the Tibetan Plateau, for example.

It is the ice melt on these glaciers that sustains the major rivers in Asia during the dry season. This includes the Ganges in India and the Yellow and Yangtze rivers in China, and not only does the ice melting in the glaciers support these rivers during the dry season, they sustain the irrigation systems based on these rivers. If that flow is disrupted, as will happen if glaciers keep melting and eventually disappear, then we're looking at a dramatic effect on world food security. Most people don't know this, but China is the world's leading wheat producer. It's number one; India's number two. China and India together totally dominate the world rice harvest. So when you look at wheat and you look at rice, humanity's two food staples, what happens to those glaciers, those river flows, and the production of wheat and rice in China will affect every one of us. What we're looking at, from a U.S. point of view, is the prospect of 1.3 billion Chinese with rapidly rising incomes competing with us for our grain harvest, driving up our food prices. Historically, when faced with something like this, we would have restricted export, as we did in the 1970s. But China's now our banker. Each month the Treasury Department in Washington auctions off securities in order to cover our fiscal deficit, and many months the biggest buyer of these securities is China. So, like it or not, we're going to be sharing our grain harvest with China. ∼

JANETTE SHERMAN-NEVINGER

D r. Janette Sherman-Nevinger, a specialist in internal medicine and toxicology, is the author of the books *Life's Delicate Balance: Causes and Prevention of Breast Cancer* and *Chemical Exposure and Disease: Diagnostic and Investigative Techniques*. She is a contributing editor of the book *Chernobyl: Consequences of the Catastrophe for People and the Environment*. Janette Sherman has been an adviser to the National Cancer Institute on breast cancer and to the Environmental Protection Agency on the Toxic Substance Control Act and on pesticides. She was an adjunct professor at the Environmental Institute at Western Michigan University and a research associate and lecturer with the Radiation and Public Health Project. She is a resource person, adviser, and speaker for universities and health advocacy groups concerning cancer, birth defects, pesticides, toxic dump sites, and nuclear radiation.

HELEN CALDICOTT: I read the Chernobyl book. It's extremely important; over five thousand scientific and medical papers have been interpreted. Would you give us a history of the way the nuclear industry, the International Atomic Energy Agency, and the World

Health Organization have really not told the truth about data, nor explored what's happened to the people in Europe, Russia, Belarus, and Ukraine, etc., post-Chernobyl?

JANETTE SHERMAN-NEVINGER: The WHO and the IAEA covered only articles written in English when they came out with a report saying there really wasn't that serious a problem from Chernobyl. What has happened, however, was that Alexey Yablokov, who was an adviser to Gorbachev and Yeltsin and was instrumental in getting the nuclear testing stopped, and Vassily Nesterenko, who was head of the Ukrainian nuclear department, started collecting articles on Chernobyl. They collected something like thirty thousand. The five thousand they translated and abstracted are in the book that was recently published by the New York Academy of Sciences and Wiley-Blackwell, and these show an entirely different story than what the WHO and IAEA came out with. These articles were written by people on the ground who witnessed Chernobyl, largely the people from Belarus, Ukraine, and Russia, and also quite a few articles from Europe, Greece, and a few from the United States. They put together what they were seeing. These people were from various fields—social scientists, physicians, nurses, statisticians, epidemiologists—and when you look at the total picture from these many articles you've got a pattern of injury and environmental degradation.

HC: First of all, let's talk again about the relationship between the International Atomic Energy Agency and the World Health Organization, both of which are UN organizations. Why have they obscured the data and not looked at articles that were not written in English?

JSN: WHO and the IAEA have an agreement, which they signed in 1959, requiring each of them to get the approval of the other before they can release any information.

HC: Information about nuclear accidents?

JSN: Yes, nuclear accidents or the effects of nuclear accidents, nuclear radiation.

HC: Can you explain the philosophical morality, if you will, or amorality, of this agreement, and the fact that they have really never examined the profound medical consequences of the worst nuclear power accident in the world?

JSN: I don't think very many people have actually addressed it or looked at the agreement. Yablokov and his associates did. Rosalie Bertell has in the past, but very few people have evidently looked into it and questioned it.

HC: So it's imperative that we get this information out. As an epidemiologist, a toxicologist, and a specialist in radiation biology, first of all let's talk about the "liquidators." Tell us what liquidators were, what they did, what they are exposed to, and the medical consequences of that work that they did.

JSN: The liquidators were young men and women who were conscripted across the old Soviet Union and invited in by other countries. These young people worked directly on Chernobyl after the explosion to try and contain the radiation and the accident. Unfortunately, now, twenty-four years later, 80 percent of them are sick, and many have died. About 25 percent of the eight hundred thousand liquidators have died, and it's a tragedy.

HC: What have they died from?

JSN: All kinds of diseases: cancer, heart disease, pulmonary disease, brain damage. We've heard for years that radiation causes cancer and birth defects, but also the radioisotopes that were ingested by these young men and women, or inhaled, damaged the interior of their blood vessels, causing heart disease, and were transported to the brain, causing brain disease and, essentially, caused diseases throughout their bodies. The liquidators have had terrible health outcomes, as have their children.

HC: What are we seeing in their children?

JSN: We're seeing small birth weights, small head sizes, small chest sizes, mental retardation, and chronic ill health.

HC: Would that be a result of the ova and sperm being radiated and damaged before the babies were conceived?

JSN: Yes. There was lots of radiation in the bodies of these people. They left the site and went back to their hometowns, and they carried with them big doses of radiation.

HC: So many of those radioactive elements would have crossed the placenta into the developing fetus?

JSN: They certainly could have.

HC: Can you describe what the eight hundred thousand liquidators were asked to do? That's nearly a million people who were brought in, and there had to have been intensely radioactive material lying around the site.

JSN: They were doing cleanup work, welding, doing concrete work. They tried to cover the Chernobyl reactor with as much concrete and all the materials that they could, but twenty-four years later they're still talking about building a sarcophagus, a big metal dome over the top of Chernobyl. These workers were called in to work while the reactor was extremely radioactive.

HC: And extruding huge amounts of radiation as they were there. I believe that that reactor is still in trouble, because the remediation was so inexact and done so fast, with a sense of urgency. There is still a possibility that the Chernobyl reactor could have a meltdown again.

JSN: Let us hope not. Even if they get the reactor covered, we will have to be concerned about the bottom of the reactor, which they can't cover and which is leaking.

HC: Leaking? Into the water supplies? Leaking radiation?

JSN: Yes, of course.

HC: Then there are the helicopter pilots who dumped 6,720 tons of lead onto the reactor to try and stop the reaction from proceeding, the fission reaction. Were those helicopter pilots followed up with about health consequences in later years?

JSN: I'm not aware of any follow-up with the helicopter pilots. I do know that the lead that they dropped on the reactors landed on top of this extraordinarily hot radioactive mess and became vaporized along with the radioactive isotopes, so it was not only giving off radioactive materials, it was also giving off lead, which added to the poisoning of the whole area.

HC: In your Chernobyl book you write that lead can synergize or aggravate or potentiate the effects of radioactive materials in the body. Is that correct?

JSN: You're absolutely correct, yes.

HC: There is a thing called acute radiation illness, which we as physicians didn't know about until the bombs were dropped upon Hiroshima and Nagasaki. Would you describe the symptoms of acute radiation illness, what sort of radiation levels cause it, and therefore how many people died in Europe, Belarus, Ukraine, and Russia as a result of that acute initial dose of radiation?

JSN: I don't think we know the entire number of those who died very soon after. Certainly the control operators, there were several of them who died very quickly. The main thing that occurs is the complete depression of a person's bone marrow, so they get bleeding and infection. It's really quite a rapid death. But the thing I think is most important is the chronic low doses of radiation to which so many were exposed.

HC: People usually only talk about cesium 137, and about 40 percent of the European landmass is still contaminated with it, which lasts for about 300 to 600 years and is very carcinogenic. But so many other elements escaped and were measured, in fact, all around the northern hemisphere, including: silver 210, which has a half-life of 250 days; chlorine 36, with a half-life of 30,000 years; technetium 99, with a half-life of 23,000 years; and plutonium. A lot of plutonium got out, which has a half-life of 24,400 years. I could go right down the list, describing the radioactive iodine and all sorts of other terribly dangerous things. In other words, the whole inventory of radioactive materials escaped from Chernobyl, some short-lived and some very long-lived. Would you like to extrapolate on that?

JSN: The issue with this is the half-life. It takes about ten half-lives for an isotope to completely decay, so if you have a thirty-year half-life you multiply that by ten years, and we're talking about three centuries. Not only do we worry about the physical half-life of these isotopes, but one of the big issues is that they are brought down with rain and snow, go into the soil, the trees, and the plants, which absorb the isotopes, carry them back up the trees to the leaves, or in the plants to the leaves of the fruit and vegetables; the leaves fall again, they're highly radioactive, and then, of course, it rains and snows on them, and the isotopes go back into the soil, and then are picked up again by the plants. You have a biological recycling of these isotopes. Then, if there are forest fires, you have to worry about the transport of smoke, which is radioactivity that goes long distances.

HC: I hadn't thought of that. I know about the mushrooms and the reindeer in Scandinavia being extraordinarily radioactive, and the lambs in Cumbria and Wales still being radioactive. So people in Europe are obviously still eating radioactive food.

JSN: Yes, particularly people in Belarus and Ukraine.

HC: There is so little media about that. I've just been in Spain, and Spain got a big dose. In various selected areas where it rained, in hot spots, but there's absolutely no talk in the European media at all now about Chernobyl, is there?

JSN: I think there is very little talk anywhere. It was not covered in the major newspapers in the United States. The *Washington Post*, the *New York Times* did not carry anything about Chernobyl. The twenty-sixth of April [2010] was the twenty-fourth anniversary. There was nothing. The only information that I'm aware of is coming out on the Internet.

HC: It's a conspiracy by the nuclear industry and others to keep this quiet so the nuclear industry can get on with what it wants to do, which is build lots more nuclear reactors.

JSN: I fear you may be right.

HC: In the Chernobyl book there is a specific reference to children in Kiev, which is the capital of the Ukraine. It got a lot of radiation. Before the accident 90 percent of the children were healthy. But now only 20 percent of children in Kiev are, and in certain parts of the Ukraine, none of them are healthy. What are these children suffering from, twenty-four years after the accident occurred?

JSN: It's not just Ukraine; probably the most affected country is Belarus, which was just north of Chernobyl. The children are underweight, generally undersized. Many of the girls never start having their menstrual period.

HC: Never?

JSN: No. And they are immune-compromised, so they have lots of infections, asthma, and are just generally not well.

HC: Would you describe what you've seen in the film *Chernobyl Heart*?

JSN: It's an absolutely tragic film of children who are sick with birth defects, just not terribly bright, and that issue especially troubles me, because if you have a country where 80 percent of the children are not well, who are going to be the teachers, the musicians, the artists, the nurses, the transport workers? Who is going to carry on the country if you have 80 percent of the population not well?

HC: I too saw the film, and there are homes full of the most grossly deformed children I've ever seen. I'm a pediatrician, and my colleagues who are pediatricians in those homes say they've never seen anything like this before in their medical careers.

JSN: I don't know how a country can survive with that much of its population unwell, plus you have the enormous cost of caring for so many sick people.

HC: When the accident occurred, the old Soviet Union didn't have much money. They didn't even have machines to measure the platelets, the white blood cells, or get the complete blood pictures, let alone really care for these survivors of the catastrophe.

JSN: They did not, and I don't know if many of the areas still have adequate resources to care for sick people.

HC: It's beyond a major catastrophe, and it's covered up and hidden and so important for doctors to understand this. If there is a meltdown, for instance, thirty-five miles from New York at the Indian Point reactor, we're going to have to deal with these consequences in a Western population. It's imperative that all of us in the medical profession understand what's going on in Europe, Russia, Belarus, and the Ukraine so that we can prevent another catastrophe occurring.

JSN: I think it would completely wipe out New York City if there was a meltdown at Indian Point, which is very troublesome. Right now in the United States the news is on the big oil spill off the coast of New Orleans, off of Mexico, which is a major catastrophe. The only thing that could be worse would be if there were a nuclear meltdown in one of our 104 plants that exist in the United States.

HC: I was talking to a nuclear engineer recently, and I said to him, What are the chances of a meltdown in America? And just straight off he said, One in ten in the next ten years. Other nuclear engineers I know say it's not *if* but *when* that occurs. It seems to me to be imperative that we get this information out into our medical journals.

Let's talk about thyroid cancers. I actually have never seen a case of pediatric thyroid cancer. Can you tell us how many people have suffered and are suffering now from thyroid cancer related to the Chernobyl meltdown?

JSN: I can't tell you off the top of my head how many have had thyroid cancer, but it was the signature disease. The WHO predicted a few cases here and there. It turned out there have been thousands of cases of thyroid disease and many, many cases of thyroid cancer—thyroid cancers that were very aggressive and had a tendency to spread, which was a very serious problem. But you also may be interested to know that in the United States a colleague of mine by the name of Joe Mangano did a study of cancer in eastern Pennsylvania. The most elevated cancer rates for men, women, blacks, and whites are in places near nuclear reactors, such as eastern Pennsylvania, which is very significant, because it's downwind from the Three Mile Island, Peach Bottom, and Limerick nuclear power plants.

Back to Chernobyl. A good functioning thyroid, as you know as a pediatrician, is required for a healthy baby to be born, and if the baby is born with low thyroid function, the chances are that the child is going to have mental retardation. We not only have the disease of thyroid cancer, but we have thyroid disabilities that are affecting the general health of the population.

HC: So it's not just thyroid cancer; it's abnormalities of the babies. The data I've read from Russia is that over ten thousand people have had thyroid cancer. I often debate with members of the nuclear power industry, and they say, Oh, well, they haven't died. As you point out, it's a very aggressive sort of thyroid cancer, papillary carcinoma, which metastasizes fast. I can't get over the fact that these nuclear energy people—none of whom are physicians—lie. They just lie, and the public gets very confused, because they quote scientists, and the public doesn't really know whom to believe. Have you experienced that?

JSN: As far as education, it certainly is not all that great in the United States. You have to worry about people who are not really educated in science. When you ask somebody to take her hand and put it over her liver, not many people know where the liver is located.

HC: [*laughs*] I hadn't thought of doing that.

JSN: A lot of people really are not knowledgeable about disease, which I think is one of the ways that people get hooked into saying, Well, there is no such thing as evolution. You have a promotion of ignorance, which I think is very, very troubling. I don't know if this is occurring in Australia, but it's certainly a factor in the United States.

HC: That would be a good title for a book: *Promotion of Ignorance*. I've heard that five years after Chernobyl there was an epidemic of leukemia; is that accurate? Would you describewhat leukemia actually is?

JSN: Leukemia is a dysfunction of the bone marrow, and radiation exposure has been known for decades, since Hiroshima and Nagasaki, to result in leukemia. We certainly saw that in people who were downwind from the plant. It was predictable that there would be leukemia cases as a result of the radiation fallout. One of the isotopes that's given off from Chernobyl, and also from functioning nuclear power plants, is strontium 90. This all drifts off into the air, is precipitated by rain and snow, and goes into the grasses; the grasses get eaten by cows, and it goes into the milk supply. So pregnant women and nursing mothers and young children drink this milk and eat the dairy products that contain strontium 90. This radioactive element belongs to the same family as calcium and therefore goes to the bones and teeth of the unborn and young children. The bone marrow is where the blood cells are formed, and they are essentially radiated inside the child's body.

HC: So leukemia is really cancer of the white blood cells?

JSN: You can also have cancer of the red blood cells. Polycythemia vera is a red-cell leukemia.

HC: Is there any estimate of how many people developed leukemia after Chernobyl?

JSN: I would have to look up the exact number, but there will continue to be more.

HC: I've read estimates ranging from five thousand to fourteen thousand dead from leukemia already. And I've also read ten to forty thousand dead from thyroid cancer. It's estimated that nearly a quarter of a million people have died from general cancers. A quarter of a million people! It's been only twenty-four years post-Chernobyl, and people can be developing cancer for sixty to seventy years before they die, because the incubation time for cancer is extremely long.

JSN: Unless you're a child.

HC: That's right. Because they're very sensitive and get cancer much faster than adults. So we're really actually just seeing the tip of the iceberg.

JSN: I believe that's the case, and when you consider that there were people who were of reproductive age when Chernobyl happened, now we are in the third generation. If they were twenty at that time, add another twenty years for the second generation. Some of those people are now having children, which is passing on this contamination now to a third generation.

HC: Contamination from the radioactive food.

JSN: Right—the food and water that they ingested.

HC: And chromosomal defects, because radiation splits chromosomes, and the classic chromosomal defect is Down syndrome. But there are also genetic abnormalities, and there are over 24,000 genetic diseases now described. Over the generations, will they increase in frequency?

JSN: Unless some of the people who are born are just not able to have children. There is some limitation, because some of the girls never start having their menses and some of the boys have significant genital abnormalities and will not become fathers. So some of this will die out, but some will be passed on. Then of course there is the recycling of the isotopes through the food supply, affecting new generations. The ultimate result is very, very difficult to predict.

HC: Have they examined the sperm of the boys to see if there are chromosomal abnormalities? Are the sperm viable? Are they healthy?

JSN: I don't know if there has been any sperm testing. I do know that there were tremendous problems with reproduction in the liquidators.

HC: I'm sure. Let's talk about another element. You talked about heart disease and radiation inducing arteriosclerosis, heart disease, and strokes. The person who did the seminal work in this was Dr. John Gofman, who tied abnormalities of cardiovascular systems with radiation. We're seeing that now in the European population. What about accelerated aging related to radiation exposure?

JSN: That is absolutely fascinating, because we're seeing cataracts in children, almost unheard-of. The kinds of signs that you see in the elderly—loss of mentation, heart disease, arteriosclerosis, thickening of the arteries—this kind of thing is being seen in very young people, teenagers and young adults. We have accelerated aging. It's a catastrophe. But it's not just humans. When you go throughout the entire biosphere over there—not every system was studied, but every one that was studied, whether it was insects, mushrooms, bacteria, fish, or birds—no matter what was studied, everything was changed, and many of them were changed irreversibly.

HC: With genetic abnormalities and birth defects?

JSN: Yes, as well as other systemic abnormalities. They studied twenty-two generations of voles—these are little woodland creatures—and the genetic abnormality was constant throughout all twenty-two generations.

HC: That's a classic experiment done by Muller, when he irradiated fruit flies, which reproduce very fast, so he could watch the genetic abnormalities as they're passed on, generation to generation. He got the Nobel Prize for that. So we've actually known about this for a long time. I learned about it in medical school in 1956. Let's talk about how 57 percent of the radioactive elements fell outside the old Soviet Union. Which were the countries in Europe that were most exposed to the fallout?

JSN: It was originally picked up in northern Sweden, so it essentially has covered France, Germany, Sweden, Norway, Wales, Great Britain, Ireland, Turkey, and then far eastern Asia, and it essentially went around the entire northern hemisphere. There was some fallout in Canada and the United States but not nearly as much as in Europe and the Far East.

HC: It always amuses me that the French, who are so into nuclear power—80 percent of their electricity comes from nuclear power—said that the fallout from Chernobyl stopped right at the French border.

JSN: I know, isn't that marvelous? We should all know how to do that.

HC: [*laughs*] Now they're actually seeing an increase in incidents of thyroid cancer and other cancers related to the Chernobyl fallout in France, right?

JSN: It's very hard to get information from France. Very difficult. But we do know, for instance, that some of the latest studies show an increase in leukemia in Germany.

HC: And also in Sweden, the cancer has increased. I was interested to read in the Chernobyl book that fallout occurred more specifically in Alaska, Oregon, Idaho, New Jersey, New York, Florida, and Hawaii. In other words, the radiation is brought down from the troposphere and stratosphere by rain. If it's not raining, you probably miss out on the most acute radiation, and you don't get such hot spots. That's interesting too.

JSN: Yes, it's brought down by rain and snow, and the fallout from Chernobyl was not uniform around the planet. There are many hot spots.

HC: The other thing is that, initially, when there is a meltdown, a lot of elements get out that are short-lived, are intensely radioactive, and only live for hours or days before they decay away to zero radiation. Although they are short-lived, if you're immersed in a cloud of fallout from a nuclear accident, you are going to get one hell of a dose of radiation, right?

JSN: That's correct, but not many countries were taking measurements, so we don't really know how severe the fallout was, or the amount.

HC: Talk about people who live near nuclear reactors being given potassium iodide tablets. Why would they do that, and is it happening to people adjacent to reactors in the United States?

JSN: I like that question [*laughs*]. One has to take the potassium iodide within an hour so, or within twenty-four hours at the very most, of exposure to radioactive iodine. The potassium iodide is taken to block the uptake of the radioactive iodine in the person's thyroid. Right now there are no plans to hand out potassium iodide to people living around nuclear power plants in the United States. It's strictly voluntary. If there is a meltdown, how many people are going to go to a center of any kind and pick up the potassium iodide? After a meltdown it's not going to do any good if it's not taken within twenty-four hours of the accident, so it's not really going to help anybody. This is one of my pet peeves: the fact that the nuclear industry does not want to give out the tablets because it would make people worry, and maybe alert them that there might be a problem here. It's a very useful medication, but it blocks only the uptake of radioactive iodine. It doesn't do anything about any of the other isotopes . . .

HC: . . . that can cause cancer in many organs of the body.

JSN: Exactly. But even that is inexpensive, and it's relatively stable, so you can have a bottle of it on your shelf. It would be perfectly okay, but it's not being done.

HC: As a physician and an expert in this area, what would be your commentary on the nuclear industry in America at this time?

JSN: I think it's irresponsible that they want to build more nuclear power plants. I understand why they want to, because they are asking for enormous subsidies from us taxpayers, which would make lots of money for these companies. But we do not need nuclear power. It only produces between 15 percent and 20 percent of the power in the United States. We now are making great strides with solar and wind, and the one thing that we don't talk about is conservation. I think that if every person understood the hazards of nuclear power they would be willing to cut back their use of electricity by 20 percent, which is relatively simple. We could do away with these nuclear power plants. But in the United States we have one of the best Congresses money can buy.

HC: [*laughs*] That's a terrible thing to say.

JSN: It's true.

HC: What about the White House?

JSN: President Obama said that we would only look for safe, clean nuclear energy. That's an oxymoron—there is no such thing. Certainly the financial crisis in the world is against building any of these plants. Certainly the companies are not going to put their own money forward to do this. It's only with huge government subsidies paid by we the taxpayers that these plants will come about.

HC: So it's a socialized industry, like the weapons industry?

JSN: Exactly. Socialize the industry, and then we the taxpayers pay the price.

HC: Yes, well, you mustn't have socialized medicine, but it's all right to have socialized nuclear power and socialized nuclear weapons? What about you or I writing a letter to the editors of the *Journal of the American Medical Association*, the *New England Journal of Medicine*, and *Pediatrics* to say that this book has been published that summarizes some of the most important data? These publications do publish letters, and it could start sort of a campaign to get these facts known among colleagues in the medical profession.

JSN: I think that is a great idea. I would start with the pediatric literature, because this is the generation that's going to be most affected.

HC: This is very exciting, because this information is aching to be publicized. It's beyond imperative. Everybody in the world must know about what happened at Chernobyl, particularly the

American public, because they're being propagandized and brain-washed into thinking nuclear power is a good thing. What in fact we need to do is close down all the reactors in America, there are 104, and indeed throughout the world, so that this dreadful medical catastrophe never happens again. ∼

HUGH GUSTERSON

Hugh Gusterson's research focuses on the political culture of nuclear weapons scientists and antinuclear activists in the United States and the former Soviet Union. He is the author of *People of the Bomb: Portraits of America's Nuclear Complex*; *Nuclear Rites: A Weapons Laboratory at the End of the Cold War*; and is co-editor with Catherine Besteman of *Why America's Top Pundits Are Wrong: Anthropologists Talk Back*. After being a professor at MIT for fourteen years, Hugh Gusterson became a professor of sociology and anthropology at George Mason University, where he teaches classes on war and peace, ethics and science, drug politics and culture, and the sociology of science.

HELEN CALDICOTT: You lived and drank with the scientists at Los Alamos for up to a year, got to know them, their culture, and then you described how they see their bomb making.

HUGH GUSTERSON: Being an anthropologist, we tend to move in with the people we're studying: melt unobtrusively into the background; fit into the flow of daily life. I lived in three different houses at the weapons site for two years, with people who worked at the lab. I went to church every Sunday, different churches. I joined the lab's singles' group and its basketball and baseball teams. I tried to meet as many people who worked in the lab as I could. You get to know people in a really different way if you take the time to just become a part of the fabric of their lives. I want to put in a little plug for the anthropological method.

HC: As an Englishman, did you find it difficult joining the American cultural philosophy in the labs in Los Alamos and Livermore?

HG: I was accepted, and I was a little startled by this. I'd thought that as a foreign citizen trying to understand the culture of a top secret military facility I would have a very hard time, but it turned out not to be true. As you might know, in the United States the British tend to be treated with maybe too much reverence. There are two nuclear weapons labs: one is Los Alamos, which developed the bombs dropped on Hiroshima and Nagasaki, and the other is Lawrence Livermore in San Francisco, which was established in 1952. I have done extensive fieldwork at both labs.

I moved to Lawrence Livermore first, at the end of the Reagan years. I expected to find the people who worked on nuclear weapons to be Reagan Republicans, conservatives who thought that there was a real threat of communist domination. I was surprised to find that many of the weapons scientists I got to know were Democrats as well as Republicans; some had protested the Vietnam War when they were younger. They'd been active in the civil rights movement. There was an interesting mixture of conservatives and liberals. And I vividly remember one weapons scientist telling me that he could never work on conventional weapons, because it would be immoral. He felt much more comfortable working on nuclear weapons, because he was convinced that nuclear weapons would never be used. I was very struck that he felt morally cleaner working on weapons that could destroy a city than he would have felt working on napalm. The other thing I found was that about three fourths of the people I interviewed were some form of active Christian. Most of them belonged to fairly moderate, midline Christian denominations: Catholics, Methodists, Episcopalians, Lutherans. Relatively few belonged to the born-again Baptist sects. I did meet a few weapons designers who were evangelical. I found them the most troubling to get to know, because some of them believed that their work designing nuclear weapons was part of God's plan, described in Revelations, to dissolve the Earth in fire and bring about the day of judgment. But most of the weapons scientists didn't see much conflict between Christianity and designing weapons of mass destruction, and they were quite sure the weapons would never be used.

Critics of the arms race have focused on this strong belief held by weapons professionals, that nuclear weapons will never be used. Robert J. Lifton, the great antinuclear psychiatrist, has talked about it as a form of denial.

HC: Let's go deeper into what you discovered about these actual bomb designers.

HG: Since 1992 the United States hasn't conducted any nuclear tests, something that causes some pain to the nuclear weapons scientists who were practicing a form of science that's now a forbidden experiment. They can no longer test complete weapons, but they feel some bitterness about that. But back in the old days, up to 1992, life at the lab was structured around the design of new weapons and the testing of new weapons, so the lab produced nuclear tests. What they really lived for was to tweak the design of old weapons to figure out ways of making the weapons smaller and lighter, squeezing more explosive yield out of less plutonium, making them slightly different shapes. Weapons designers would compete with one another, proposing fiendish new design ideas that would be vetted by review committees within the Pentagon. If the designer was lucky enough to have one of the few ideas that made it onto the shot schedule, then they would work quite feverishly, often for months, as the tests neared completion. Particularly in the last weeks before a test, these designers could be working seventy-, even eighty-hour weeks. I would hear stories of people sleeping in cots in their offices in the lab. It culminated with a trip down to the nuclear test site in Nevada where nuclear weapons were tested. They would dig an enormous, great hole, and the device—it's never called a bomb—would be loaded onto a great canister with lots of very complicated, expensive diagnostic equipment. That diagnostic equipment would be completely destroyed in the nuclear tests. Its job was to measure the output of the nuclear device, in a fraction of a fraction of a fraction of a second, before it's vaporized by what it's measuring. These tests, by the late 1980s, were costing as much as $50 million apiece, and about eighteen a year were run. So you would watch the device being placed in this hole, with diagnostic equipment attached, and the hole gets backfilled, because it would have been a violation of international treaties for radiation to escape and cross international borders when the test happened. Then they would retreat to the control room, and from there they would watch a flickering of needles on the oscilloscopes, and that's all they would see. It wasn't like the old days, when nuclear weapons were tested aboveground and you would have to put on very thick glasses to protect your eyes from the flash, feel the heat and the shock wave and all that. It was more of a sterile experience by the 1980s, when nuclear testing had been forced underground. Then came the final stage of the process: within a few hours of the explosion usually an enormous crater would appear in the desert. The bomb would have vaporized enough of the earth that eventually a crater would collapse, and some of the designers to this day like to go down to the Nevada test site and look at their craters. These massive movements of earth.

HC: Which are radioactive.

HG: The idea is that the radioactivity is contained underground—

I'm not sure how 100 percent successful that was. I've done a tour of the Nevada test site. Officials have more confidence than they should have in the cleanliness of what they've been doing. There were parts of the test site they wouldn't take me into, because they were still radioactive, where they'd done a lot of aboveground tests. They claimed they sealed everything in. There was a test in Baneberry, Nevada, in 1970 that leaked a massive radioactive plume all the way to Canada, which put the United States in violation of its treaty obligations under the Limited Test Ban Treaty.

HC: Tell us about their psychological state as they built up to their very precious device.

HG: It's like any kind of creative process that's very intense. It's like someone working on a dissertation or a musician working on a recording. They become absorbed in the task. Unlike writing a book, this is a much more collective process, in which people have to interact with people in massive teams of chemists and engineers and machinists; people become quite tightly bonded. People would talk about feeling this psychological letdown when it's over. They'd been working so feverishly, and suddenly it was over—what do you do? It's a sort of vacuum that appears in their lives afterward. So the scientists are having this incredibly intense experience, bonding with their team. For their families this experience was a real loss. The scientists are often traveling, so they're not at home. Even if they're not traveling, they're working long hours in the lab and can't be home very much. They can't bring the work home, because it's secret, so wives of weapons scientists would talk about being science widows. Their husbands weren't dead, but they would be bereft of their husbands' presence. They became psychologically focused on something going on elsewhere that they weren't allowed to talk about, so their kids and wives would talk about this sense of having lost a family member in the process leading up to a test.

I'm talking about scientists' wives as if all of these people are men. The majority are men, but by no means all of them. In the 1980s in the United States only about 5 percent of physics PhDs went to women. Physics was a male-dominated discipline. Actually, at the weapons labs there was a slight overrepresentation of women weapons designers, more like 6 percent or 7 percent. One woman weapons designer at Los Alamos told me that she thought that the female mind was particularly well suited to nuclear weapons design, because when you change one variable everything else changes with it. She argued that women think more holistically, so they had a better aptitude for nuclear weapons design.

HC: In the past you've described some of the terminology the scientists use. One talked about giving birth to the bomb and the need to push. And then, after the explosion, they talked about postnatal depression.

HG: They also talk about missiles being connected to the outside world by umbilical cords. The very first bomb tested was referred to as Oppenheimer's baby. The one dropped on Hiroshima was Little Boy, so there is this language of metaphors of birth that surrounds this bomb enterprise. They talk about the results of radioactive decay processes as being daughter products. So there is this language of fertility and birth. There's a man called Brian Easlea who's a psychoanalytically inclined academic, and he's argued that this is all about men with birth envy. Because they can't give birth the way women can, they're trying to do something as awesome as birth. Testing a nuclear weapon is something as awesome as birth, so they're betraying their deeper unconscious motives by using all this language of birth. I've asked many weapons scientists why they use these birth metaphors, and they say, You use birth metaphors to describe any creative process, don't you? The language of death is banished from the world of nuclear weapons scientists; they don't talk about killing people; they talk about collateral damage. People are not incinerated; they're always carbonized—anaesthetizing language from which death is banished. But there's this very rich set of metaphors about birth. I've always wondered if that wasn't an attempt on their part to say, We're really about life, we're not about killing people. Which you can see as a form of denial.

HC: I see that it's giving birth to annihilation, which amazes me from a masculine perspective.

HG: I'm curious to know what you make of the women.

HC: They've probably got retinoblastomas on their ovaries, a tumor that secretes testosterone. I'm being facetious, but like Maggie Thatcher and Indira Gandhi, some voraciously join the male ethic to achieve.

HG: The weapons labs are very masculine environments. To be a woman scientist there is to be in a very small minority. Women often get forced into adopting male roles in places like that.

HC: Talk about the Replacement Reliable Warhead.

HG: In 1992, the administration of Bush the Elder agreed to end nuclear testing. When Bill Clinton came to power he decided to turn the moratorium on nuclear testing into a test-ban treaty, which his administration negotiated. The weapons labs were not very happy about this.

HC: They can still keep some in storage.

HG: They were worried that with this stockpile they could no longer work on improvements. Its design features were being frozen in place. They were worried about how to train a new generation of weapons designers without them being able to do any testing. Traditionally, the way you train designers is that you apprentice them until they get their own test. That whole system of apprenticeship can't work anymore. They were worried that these weapons they had designed were very temperamental, right on the edge of working properly. They were concerned that, as they aged, they might not work. They struck a bargain in which they agreed that if the Clinton administration gave them more money *not* to test nuclear weapons than they had given them *to* test nuclear weapons in the past, they would find a way of maintaining the stockpile and training new designers without nuclear testing.

They developed this enormous program of simulations called stockpile stewardship. It's a way of simulating aspects of nuclear tests; for example, the Lawrence Livermore lab is in the process of building the most powerful laser on earth. It's a $5 billion project. When it's finished it will create temperatures and pressures greater than those inside the sun.* It will do this about five hundred yards from a suburban housing development. When they push a button it will use the entire U.S. electricity supply for a fraction of an instant. So there's an astonishing machine that enables the scientist to figure out more about the processes within a nuclear explosion and offers a different way of training young scientists. Since the 1990s the weapons labs have been building this very lavish program of simulations, and they've been recruiting new young designers. These temperamental, high-end new weapons they designed—as the parts wear out you can't replace them with identical parts. They'd like to replace what is a stockpile of Porsches with a stockpile of Honda Civics. And the RRW, the Reliable Replacement Warhead, is a sort of funky bomb that will be superreliable. The point of designing it is also to give younger designers something to do so they can learn how to design a weapon. They had a design competition between Livermore and Los Alamos. Livermore won, and it looked as though they would be given $100 million to design a prototype RRW. Then Congress pulled the plug on the funding, and it's been completely canceled. The weapons labs were begging for $10 million just to keep hope alive, to do little computer studies on it, and

---

*The construction of the laser has since been completed.

Congress didn't even allow them to have that. So at the moment there's this standoff. The labs haven't given up on the RRW they're still pushing. But the current Congress has refused to give them any money.

It is notoriously difficult for the United States to kill a weapons program. President Jimmy Carter thought he'd canceled the B-1 bomber, but military contractors waited for a more sympathetic president and brought it back. Now it's flying around dropping bombs on Iraq.

HC: Isn't there a group of very eminent scientists, called the Jasons, who inspected all the bombs in the U.S. arsenal and said that almost all of them would be reliable for the next hundred years, and there's no need to replace them with the RRW?

HG: They reviewed scientific studies about the way plutonium behaves as it ages. The weapons designers are concerned that plutonium is a very temperamental substance that can behave unpredictably. As plutonium ages, the radiation it generates might produce chemical changes within the plutonium that would stop it from exploding properly. The Jasons concluded that they expected the plutonium to age "gracefully," as they put it; they think the plutonium cores of nuclear weapons will be quite reliable for eighty to hundred years, and they think that the arming detonation and fusing systems of weapons can be maintained so they'll be reliable. The Jasons are professors who do independent reviews of weapons programs for the Pentagon. The weapons scientists said, Who's the real expert here? We're weapons scientists. They're just Jasons. Certainly the study that the Jasons did is one of the reasons why Congress did not fund the RRW.

The other reason is that, at a time when the United States is putting pressure on North Korea to give up its nuclear weapons, putting pressure on Iran not to go down that path, and talking a lot about the importance of the nonproliferation of nuclear weapons, it makes the United States look like hypocrites if they design a new nuclear warhead, mass-producing it while they're lecturing the rest of the world on the importance of not making nuclear weapons. I went down to Congress. A number of congressmen were very concerned with how it would look to the rest of the world.

HC: It's totally hypocritical for the United States, even if they're not replacing their warheads, to lecture other countries about not developing their own warheads, when America still has in stockpile, ready to go, about ten thousand hydrogen bombs, which could induce nuclear winter and the end of most life on Earth.

HG: When the United States ratified the Non-Proliferation Treaty in 1970, one of the things they ratified was Article 6, which committed the established nuclear powers to negotiate, in good faith, ending the arms race and eliminating all nuclear weapons. In 1970 they agreed to a prompt cessation of the nuclear arms program. I don't think many people would think that waiting until 1992 to end nuclear testing was a prompt cessation of the nuclear arms race. Increasingly I think people from countries that don't have nuclear weapons are getting impatient with the United States especially, but all the nuclear powers, wondering when they're going to get serious about honoring their obligations under Article 6. The United States is busy proposing sanctions against Iran, which is enriching uranium. There are innocent and less innocent reasons for enriching uranium. Iran is allowed under the terms of the treaty to enrich uranium for nuclear energy plants. But the United States is proposing sanctions on Iran for violating the Non-Proliferation Treaty when I think any detached, objective observer would say that by far the largest violators of the treaty must have been the Russians and the Americans for sitting on these enormous stockpiles in spite of Article 6 commitments.

I found, in the late 1980s and early 1990s, most people in the nuclear weapons labs were unaware of Article 6 of the Nuclear

Non-Proliferation Treaty. I remember having conversations with very well-educated nuclear warhead designers, and one of them told me, flat out, I was wrong in saying that the United States and Russia had any commitment under the Nuclear Non-Proliferation treaty to end the arms race. I was so angry that I went home and Xeroxed the treaty and mailed it to him. Those commitments under the treaty have been much better reported by the U.S. press more recently. In the last five or six years knowledgeable Americans have become more aware of how the rest of the world feels about them. I also, as an anthropologist, find it particularly offensive when you talk to weapons scientists, or to other kinds of nuclear weapons professionals, that there's a uniform assumption that Americans are the only people who can be uniquely trusted with nuclear weapons in a way that black and brown people, non-Christians in particular, cannot. You hear people say openly that you can't trust Muslims with nuclear weapons, they're maniacs. That Muslims don't value their own lives, and all they care about is Allah, or that they'd be quite happy to blow up their own countries. You hear it said that only Americans and Europeans have the strength required of people to have nuclear weapons. Some people think this is racist, and it flies in the face of the evidence since the United States is the only country ever to abuse weapons.

HC: Is this the projection of the dark side by these Americans onto others?

HG: All of this is a struggle with our unconscious persona that we find difficult to come to terms with, and then project onto other people. It's been well established by psychologists as part of the process that makes it possible to wage war on other people. You don't have to go to a nuclear weapons lab to find this kind of casual racism. You can open the opinion page of any American newspaper and find it there at least once a week, about Iraq or Iran or North Korea. It's become something not even necessary to justify.

There's also an interesting process in which, when a country crosses the nuclear threshold, there's this panic about how they're going to behave with nuclear weapons. Then gradually over the decades they become normalized and accepted. If you look at the 1940s, the American reaction to Stalin testing a nuclear weapon was hysterical. By the 1970s the Russians were being treated as a reliable partner—a ritualized enmity. The Chinese were talked about this way and eventually were treated as responsible. I think we're seeing the same thing with the Indians right now, they're being normalized. When they tested their weapons in 1998 there were startling racist comments about Indians with nuclear weapons on the opinion pages of U.S. newspapers. Now the same commentators are busy pushing for the India-U.S. nuclear deal so the United States would be able to sell them uranium and make a huge profit.

HC: There's a lot of pathology. I'm fascinated by how the Department of Energy recruits anthropologists to work out what to do with the radioactive waste, huge amounts, and what scientists have put on the waste to warn future generations not to go near or they'll develop cancers or die of acute illness.

HG: Many years ago the Department of Energy did sponsor a competition for signs. The problem is that nuclear waste has a half-life of thousands and thousands of years. If you go back fifty thousand years, we don't have a very good ability to understand the remains of languages that were being used then, so the question is, What would you put on the sign? Would a skull and crossbones intuitively warn any human being that there was something dangerous there, so you shouldn't dig? Some anthropologists went for the money, tried to think what the signs might be, but the consensus is that it's an impossible task. It's impossible to predict how human beings we can't visualize, fifty thousand, one hundred thousand years from now, might interpret a particular sign. The skull and crossbones: we've been conditioned to see it as a sign of danger. But there's no reason objectively why someone who's never seen that sign before has to interpret it that way.

HC: Politicians, as they accept a nuclear country, say, Well, their politicians are safe, and it's okay that they have uranium, but when you fix uranium in reactors you make plutonium, which lasts for half a million years, the fuel for nuclear weapons. There's no discussion about the stability or instability of those societies as they proceed into the future. Mad politicians can arise, and that issue is never addressed.

HG: If you talk to nuclear weapons scientists, there is this stunted imagination about the political context into which their weapons are inserted. There's an assumption that the political reality we live in now should be our benchmark. The political scientists in security studies don't have a strong historical sense of how the international system keeps changing, so they encourage these weapons professionals to think about the current international reality as if it's somehow frozen indefinitely. But international systems change all the time. Some of your older listeners will remember a time when the United Nations didn't exist. There never used to be an international court of human rights.

HC: And that could change too.

HG: The news isn't all bleak. We seem to be making good progress rolling back North Korea's nuclear weapons program. There have been countries that have acquired nuclear weapons and then given them up. South Africa had a small number of nuclear weapons under the white minority government, and they decided to abolish them when they handed over the keys to the country to Nelson Mandela. They destroyed all the plans for how to make them, all the facilities that we use in designing and making them. When the Soviet Union split apart, Ukraine, Kazakhstan, and Belarus acquired nuclear weapons overnight. They were persuaded to give them up. North Korea may join that list. There have been countries that were pretty far down the road toward nuclear weapons and were induced to turn back: Taiwan in the 1970s; Brazil; and Argentina. So although it's part of the common sense of weapons scientists that you couldn't put the genie back in the bottle, I don't think that's true.

One of the things I find particularly interesting about the moment we're in right now is that there is a new movement to abolish nuclear weapons. There has long been a movement on the left of America to completely abolish nuclear weapons. It's been dismissed by people from the rest of the spectrum as naive and idealistic, but in the last years a very powerful, influential group of right-wing abolitionists appeared: Henry Kissinger, former Reagan secretary of state George Schultz, Sam Nunn, the former chair of the Senate arms committee, a conservative Democrat. They've written opinion pieces in the *Wall Street Journal* calling for the abolition of nuclear weapons. Three former British secretaries of defense wrote a piece for the *Times* of London. These hard-bitten realists are making a case for abolishing nuclear weapons. I think they're terrified by the prospect of nuclear weapons spreading to subnational groups, to terrorist groups that cannot be deterred because they have no territory against which retaliation can be threatened. Faced with the prospect of a nuclear-armed Al Qaeda, they've decided that it's time to abolish the weapons completely before they leak into the wrong hands.

HC: You mentioned the question of whether anthropologists should cooperate in counterinsurgency.

HG: The former U.S. secretary of defense, Robert Gates, decided that the key to victory in counterinsurgence campaigns in Iraq and Afghanistan is cultural knowledge. He came to the realization, I think an accurate realization, that American troops in Iraq and Afghanistan have generated opposition to themselves; they've made their lives more difficult with their own cultural insensitivity and their own cloddishness. They don't know the difference between a Sunni and a Shiite, or how you treat local women; they often don't know that you don't show the soles of your feet to local people; it's an insult. So the Department of Defense has decided they have to train troops to behave in culturally appropriate ways and figure out what's going on in the minds of the local population, so they know which ones to kill, which ones might be on their side, and how to do a smoother occupation. The people who understand culture are anthropologists.

There's been a big push by the Pentagon in the last two years to recruit anthropologists. The project that particularly concerned me is called Human Terrain Teams. The idea is that every brigade in Iraq and Afghanistan would have attached to it a Human Terrain Team of five people, two of whom would be social scientists, preferably anthropologists. It would be their job to go out to local communities, talk to village leaders, collect intelligence about what is going on in a local terrain, and feed that back to military commanders. If you're an anthropologist, this is a very troubling development. I hope that my colleagues in anthropology would be troubled by this even if they support the wars. Because the prime directive in anthropology is that you do no harm to your human subjects, the people you study. I could have used what I learned about weapons scientists to try to do them in, to try and do great harm to the nuclear weapons labs and institutions. Although my politics are such that I don't really support the nuclear weapons labs' mission, I would never do that, because I think it would be a breach of anthropological ethics to study people and then use the knowledge you've learned from and about people against them, to subjugate and destroy their villages, to help them be occupied. Most American anthropologists have been troubled by the Human Terrain Team system, and the American Anthropological Association has issued a statement condemning the teams and strongly discouraging anthropologists from participating in them. I, along with ten other anthropologists, established the Network of Concerned Anthropologists; the NCA has now gathered signatures from about one thousand anthropologists pledging not to be involved in counterinsurgency work in any way. If there's a small minority of anthropologists busy working for intelligence or for the Pentagon, trying to subjugate other people, all anthropologists everywhere will be suspected of doing this. You can talk to any anthropologist who's worked abroad anywhere, and they will always tell you that there comes a point in their field research where someone will say, Come on, tell us you're working for the CIA, and that's why you're doing this study. We often have to work quite hard to get people to trust us.

HC: How many anthropologists are there in the United States?

HG: The Anthropological Association has over ten thousand members. So getting them to sign this pledge is really quite something. It was a contentious, hot topic. And as I speak the anthropology association is embroiled in a struggle over the rewriting of its ethics code. In the midst of the Vietnam War in 1971 the association adopted a very strongly worded ethics code that forbade clandestine research of any kind. Any knowledge gathered about people should be shared with the people about whom it was concerned. It couldn't be given to the sponsors of the research and not to the people the reports were written about. In the mid-1980s that was watered down. At last year's anthropology meeting there was a motion to restore the much stronger wording from 1971.

HC: It seems to me that anthropologists, looking at it broadly, have a responsibility, and an opportunity, to go in directions that it hasn't thought about before.

HG: The study of anthropology is a sort of exercise in imagination. It's an expanding discipline. You grow up in a society in which you take it for granted that one man has one wife, then suddenly you find out there's societies where one woman has four husbands or one man has several wives. You can repeat this sort of shock of the encounter with cultural difference, with religion, folklore, origin myths. Anthropology really is a sort of opening of the imagination to all sorts of different possibilities that might be undreamed-of if you live within parochial life. But to go to where we began, understanding people, an anthropologist learns about people by moving in with them. If you study people through archival sources, you don't have the same kind of moral obligation to them as when you live with them in their homes. If they learn to trust you, if they tell you their most intimate thoughts, you write these thoughts down in notes in which you disguise their identities, so if the notes fall into the wrong hands, what they say can't be used against them. Anthropologists have this really unique ethical obligation toward people who make it possible for us to know things. That's why we are the last who should be helping the Pentagon to subjugate the people we work with. Because they trusted us, we shouldn't betray their trust. ～

CHRIS HEDGES

C hris Hedges is an American journalist, author,
and former war correspondent specializing in
American and Middle East politics and societies. His
most recent book is *The World As It Is: Dispatches on
the Myth of Human Progress*. He is also the author of
War Is a Force That Gives Us Meaning, a finalist for the
U.S. National Book Critics Circle Award. He is a senior fellow at the Nation Institute in New York City,
has reported from more than fifty countries, and worked
for the *New York Times* as a foreign correspondent for
fifteen years. In 2002 Hedges was part of a team of reporters at the *Times* awarded the Pulitzer Prize for its
coverage of global terrorism. He currently writes a column for the website Truthdig.

———

HELEN CALDICOTT: Did you get turned on so many issues when
you were a war journalist? Which countries were you covering for
the *New York Times*?

CHRIS HEDGES: I would trace my awareness of the duplicitous and
murderous effects of power to my childhood. My father was a vet-
eran of World War II. He'd been in North Africa as a sergeant for

the U.S. Army, came back from the war disgusted with the military, war, and violence, became a Presbyterian minister, and was very outspoken throughout my childhood. We grew up in a small farm town in upstate New York. No people of color. My father, from the pulpit, supported the civil rights movement in the early 1960s. I was a small child, but I remember people walking out of his sermons. This was a time when, in rural white enclaves, Martin Luther King was one of the most hated men in America. My father took a strong stance against the war, again very unpopular during the early years of the Vietnam War. And he was a very outspoken supporter of gay rights. His youngest brother was gay and lived with his partner in Greenwich Village. My father had a particular sensitivity to the pain of being a gay man in America in the 1950s and 1960s. Of all the stances he took in the church, that was the most controversial. He was pushed out of congregations. I watched my dad pay a price for a moral stance. Inevitably, as a child, that makes you ask questions that perhaps other children are not asking.

I went on to college, and when I graduated I went to seminary to be a minister like my father but lived in a housing project in the black and Hispanic inner-city section of Boston known as Roxbury for two and a half years. I had a trajectory that led me into pockets of poverty, violence, and deprivation. I think it all stems from the upbringing that I had and the issues I was forced to confront at a very early age, including why so many people didn't like my father. I first went to Latin America to cover the war in El Salvador for five years as a freelancer. Then I went from there to the Middle East. I took a sabbatical to study Arabic, was there for seven years, hired by the *New York Times*, and went on to cover the first Gulf War. I was in Basra during the Shiite uprising, where I was taken prisoner by the Iraqi Republican Guard for eight days. I went on to Yugoslavia, and in between these foreign assignments—I was overseas for almost twenty years—I was inevitably sent off to cover other conflicts, from the Punjab to the civil war in Yemen, the civil war in Algeria, and the civil war in Sudan. I was in southern Sudan for weeks with the SPLA [Sudan People's Liberation Army] rebels at the high end of the war. Outside of Asia there weren't many major conflicts that I missed from the period of the early eighties until roughly the attacks on 9/11.

HC: Did you have a family at the time?

CH: Yes. They were based in Cairo. I was of course traveling throughout the Middle East. When I covered the war in the former Yugoslavia, I was in Sarajevo and my family was in Zagreb, Croatia.

HC: Was your father recognized at any stage of his life for the outstanding positions that he took on the most controversial issues of the time?

CH: No. I think, in fact, that that was a really important lesson for me. I understood that you were not rewarded for taking a moral stance—that virtue was its own reward. The world outside was not going to reward you. I think that was a very comforting realization. I measure my own life by the standards that my father set. I went to Colgate University. My father by then had a church in Syracuse, which wasn't far away. When my dad found out there was no gay and lesbian organization at Colgate he brought gay and lesbian speakers to the university, and would have meetings with students to promote a kind of understanding for other ways of being. This eventually lead to gays and lesbians confiding to my father that they were too uncomfortable in that environment to come out publicly and found a gay and lesbian alliance. So my dad told me, although I wasn't gay, that I had to found it. So I founded the gay and lesbian alliance at Colgate. I used to go into the dining hall, and the guy would take my card and hand it back and go, "Faggot." I made it my undergraduate mission to seduce his girlfriend.

HC: Ha! Did you do it?

CH: I didn't think it was worth it.

Back to later events: I had a very acrimonious split with the *New York Times* in 2003. I had been the Middle East bureau chief, and I was publicly denouncing the Bush Jr. calls for the invasion of Iraq. Like most Arabists, I speak Arabic, and I understood that we would not be greeted as liberators, that democracy was not going to be implanted in Baghdad and emanate out across the Middle East. The oil revenues were not going to pay for the reconstruction. But that public stance cost me my career. I knew when I was doing it what the price was. After I was booed off the commencement stage at Rockford College, the paper issued me a formal reprimand. And we were guild, or unionized, so the reprimand began the process whereby the next time I spoke out about the war I would be fired. I can remember going into the *Times* office at 229 West Forty-third Street in New York. I can't pretend that was an easy moment, but as I sat there and received this reprimand, I understood that I had a choice. I could muzzle myself and pay fealty to my career, but to do so would be to betray my dad. I couldn't do that. I remember walking out of the building and realizing that the gift my father had given me was freedom. At that moment I understood the legacy that I'd been handed, and the beauty of that legacy.

HC: Did he die a broken man or a proud, upstanding man, knowing that he'd done the right thing all his life?

CH: He did not die a broken man. He died a man of tremendous dignity and pride who just saw, in the struggle of gays and lesbians, the struggle of his own brother. His brother was disowned by the family, and the only relationship left within the family was between my father and his brother. Jamie was incorporated into our family along with his partner. My father had that amazing capacity not to particularize injustice but to see in the injustice that had been visited upon someone that he loved very dearly the injustice visited on all who are marginalized and oppressed. I think you finally only teach by example, not by lectures. To this day my father stands as a kind of invisible witness to everything I do. He sets the standards by which I carry out my own life. When I denounced this war in Iraq in a very public way, it's the only time, in the United States, that I've ever received death threats. It was a very lonely position. People forget the cheerleading that went on, even among so-called liberals, in the United States, for this war. But I was fortified in everything I did by understanding that I remained true to the values that my father had imparted to me. That gave me a tremendous amount of self-satisfaction, dignity, and independence, and saved me from needing the acclamation of the herd.

HC: Your father really walked in the shoes of the fishermen.

CH: It's important to remember that when you take a moral stance, there's always a cost. There are certain moral issues that after the fact become accepted within the broad mainstream, and people will use those stances to paint themselves as moral. But go back to the prophets: Amos, Isaiah, Jeremiah, those who carry that banner of justice are often lonely and reviled figures.

HC: What did you say at that commencement address that caused you to be booed?

CH: I denounced the war. They cut my microphone twice. At one point the crowd stood up and started singing "God Bless America"; many people were weeping. Toward the end of my eighteen minutes two young men in their graduation gowns tried to push me off the podium. Security had to push them back. I was escorted off of the platform by campus security before the awarding of diplomas. I'd had my jacket in the president's office, and they said, "We'll mail it to you." They took me down to my hotel, stood with me while I packed my bag, drove with me down to the bus station, and put me on a bus to Chicago. Here's how I began the address:

> I want to speak to you today about war and empire. The killing, or at least the worst of it, is over in Iraq, although it [blood] will continue

to spill. Theirs and ours. Be prepared for this. For we are embarking on an occupation that, if history is any guide, will be as damaging to our souls as it will be to our prestige, power, and security. But this will come later, as our empire expands. And in all this we become pariahs, tyrants to others weaker than ourselves. Isolation always impairs judgment, and we are very isolated now. We have forfeited the goodwill, the empathy the world felt for us after 9/11. We have folded in on ourselves. We have severely weakened the international coalitions and alliances that are vital in maintaining and promoting peace. And we are part now of a dubious troika in the war against terror, with Vladimir Putin and Ariel Sharon, two leaders who do not shrink in Palestine or Chechnya from carrying out gratuitous and senseless acts of violence. We have become the company we keep.

HC: What year was that?

CH: Two thousand and three. Bush had landed in that photo op on the aircraft carrier with the "Mission Accomplished" banner behind him two weeks before I gave that address. And the mood of the country was thick, triumphant, and filled with militarized rhetoric about power and force.

HC: I had to address forty thousand people in Foxboro, Massachusetts, during the first Gulf invasion. I followed Jesse Jackson. I didn't know what I was going to say. I stood and I said, "You don't kill children for oil." The whole crowd stood up and booed me for about five minutes. I felt like someone who'd been in Nazi Germany telling the Germans that Hitler was wicked. And I felt really profoundly good.

You wrote an article titled "War Is a Hate Crime," and you just described how war and vengeance brings a nation together in a sort of tribalistic immorality. People who are enemies or don't like their next-door neighbors can unite under the banner of hatred of another sort of tribe. Do you think that's a sociobiological phenomenon?

CH: I think there's a deep attraction to the crowd, and wars are crowd phenomena. The power of war is that, especially to people alienated and atomized within modern society, it can look and feel like love, which is the chief emotion that war destroys. But it feels like love, because suddenly it's a false connection, but you believe that you have connected with everyone around you. There's a kind of egalitarianism that comes with having a common enemy. Nationalism is in essence about self-exaltation. The flip side of nationalism is always racism. The elevation of ourselves and the denigration of the other. If you watch, on American cable news shows, when you go to war it's a raw, naked celebration of our weaponry and by extension of our own power. This is very appealing to people who feel disconnected, and it's why social critics and intellectuals are often just as enticed by this poison as everyone else. I think it comes from an emotional and psychological impoverishment. It's repeated in war after war. People forget that even at the inception of World War I you had brilliant intellectuals like Freud and Thomas Mann writing. They changed eventually, but in the first few months of World War I—one of the most senseless slaughters in human history— they were writing about how this would be a cleansing of European society. It's amazing to me the numbers of people throughout intellectual and economic classes that get seduced by this. It requires an emotional fortitude, the ability to sort of stand alone, which is a kind of rare characteristic when you have an external enemy, fictitious or otherwise. There is a kind of retreat into the crowd for security and safety. The whole engine of permanent war is based on fear; the systems of mass propaganda have done a very good job of this since the end of World War I. Whether it's the communist or the Islamic terrorist, if you keep people afraid you disempower them politically. But more importantly, you ensure that ability to herd the country. And that is what has destroyed American democracy.

HC: Just as George the First was going to invade Iraq the first time I was invited to speak by a man who ran Barclays Bank in Sydney.

I started to describe, as a physician, the medical perspective of war. The hostility they showed me was as if they already had the scent of blood in their nostrils. There was nothing I could say to these men—and they were all men; a few women sat on the side—about babies being torn apart by shrapnel that would change their minds. I often wondered, when it happened, did they think, She might have been right.

CH: I think that's extremely interesting and terrifying. The visceral hatred—it's precisely what I invoked in my denunciations of the plans to invade Iraq. And let me be clear: I'd spent months of my life in Iraq. I've been in far more conflicts than most people in the military. That is exactly what I evoked. I had come into the office of the *New York Times* and I was stunned at the deep rage. People leaving messages about how I should be annihilated, how I was a traitor. People would leave anonymous phone messages, or I would be mailed anonymous death threats. I wrote a book about the Christian right that was pretty brutal called *American Fascists: The Christian Right and the War on America.* I never received death threats for that. It was death threats for denouncing the drumbeats of war. I think that what that rage stemmed from, at a critic such as myself challenging the sanctity of this conflict, was a fusion of violence with virtue, that because we have the capacity to wage war somehow we have the right to wage war. In an environment like that, for people who are otherwise disenfranchised emotionally, economically, who are invited to participate in this crowd phenomena, and who find a temporary sense of empowerment, a critic such as myself is threatening to push them back into those marginalized corners of society. The war phenomenon has given them the illusion that they've been brought into the fold. I was stunned at the level of hatred that my criticisms brought. These were criticisms based on deep personal experience with Iraq itself. It was a very lonely time. And the liberal class in this country was once again bankrupt. It was only after the war went sour that they found the moral courage to say what they should have said a couple of years earlier.

HC: Tell us about Basra. Were you aware that radioactive weapons were being used at the time?

CH: I was in Basra during the Shiite uprising. There was a lot of fighting, and then I was taken prisoner for about sixteen hours by a light armored battalion that was trying to punch its way through northern Baghdad. We were ambushed north of Basra. I stayed on in the Middle East after I was released. In Basra, there were craters from depleted uranium weapons—munitions that emit less radiation, but whose long-term health effects are unknown—and you could identify them because nothing grew there. It killed all the plant life. I've seen the highway of death, that road leading north of Kuwait City into Iraq, where you had a long file of Iraqi troops that were bombed from the air, just vehicle after vehicle a charred wreck. It was seven miles long, and it was a gruesome sight. The blood and bodies still sitting in the cabs, or bodies that had obviously been on fire then had tried to flee a few feet.

HC: The Americans bombed them?

CH: Yes. They were fleeing to Iraq. It was a total act of murder. Massive slaughter. They had obviously used depleted uranium weapons, because there was this grayish powder that had been left behind on the charred vehicles. Many of the soldiers who came down with Gulf War syndrome had been used to clean up the highway of death. My guess is that they kicked up this dust and ingested it. When I went into occupied Kuwait, I went in with a Marine Corps with primitive counters that measured radiation. The counters would sort of flip up into the red zone without any noticeable sign of a change in the landscape. There was clearly radioactive material in the atmosphere being picked up. And that dust, I know it's deadly because of what I saw in Bosnia, and as you correctly point out, the residue of this seeps out into groundwater and aquifers.

HC: And into food chains and children. Have you been following the medical reports from Basra?

CH: I have heard that there's a huge increase . . .

HC: . . . in childhood cancer. The half-life of uranium 238 happens to be 4.5 billion years. So they've decimated the cradle of civilization, in a certain way. I read that you became a vegetarian after seeing war and seeing so much flesh and body parts. Can you describe to us what you did see?

CH: When I was in Sarajevo it was being hit with about two thousand shells a day. These were massive pieces of ordnance: 90mm tank rounds, 155 howitzers, Katyusha rockets, and . . .

HC: These are American weapons?

CH: No, most of them were Soviet weapons. It was the Serb forces surrounding the city, and Katyushas are actually Russian rockets fired in bursts of a dozen or twenty-four. You literally hear them wash overhead in the city. They can take down a five-story apartment building in a matter of seconds, killing everyone in sight. These 155 howitzers are larger than watermelons. We're talking about huge shells. The explosive power of these ordnances is staggering. There was no running water, only about a dozen or so UN water taps where people had to go to get water, so the Serb gunners knew just where they were. They would fire these shells into crowds, and it was those explosions that just ripped bodies in half. Entrails coming out of people's stomachs, legs blown off. Unfortunately, I know from personal experience that you can have your legs blown off and survive for six hours as you bleed to death. It was seeing that kind of mangled flesh . . . I couldn't eat red meat after that.

HC: I've got another of your essays, and I'll read a little bit.

Our military which swallows half of the federal budget is enormously popular, as if it is not part of the government. The military values of hypermasculinity, blind obedience, and violence are an electrical current that run through reality television and trash talk programs, where contestants endure pain while they betray and manipulate those around them, in a ruthless world of competition. Friendship and passion are banished. This hypermasculinity is the core of pornography, with its fusion of violence and eroticism, as well as its physical and emotional degradation of women. It's an expression of the corporate state, where human beings are reduced to commodities and companies have become protofascist enclaves devoted to maximizing profit. Militarism crashes the capacity for moral authority in defense.

I'd like you to talk about the hypermasculinity and how it's used to get men to kill.

CH: The way military units speak about the sexual act is to reduce it to something that is crude and minimalist. It almost becomes an act equal to defecation. All of the words that are used to describe sexual activity are words of violence and degradation toward women. A language that eschews the possibility that anybody who is speaking about sexual relations could have felt tender, or gentle, or in love. And smut and porn are very effective weapons against the capacity of sexual relations to expose a kind of human vulnerability. The longest chapter in *Empire of Illusion* is on the porn industry. I interviewed a lot of women who had worked or currently worked in the industry. And porn has evolved into an attempt to eroticize violence. It's not simulated violence; these women finish these shoots completely black and blue. They have to take painkillers before they go on the set; they are constantly going in for reconstructive surgery of vaginal and anal tears. The first woman I interviewed, who had left the porn industry and was a well-known porn actress, I'm about three or four minutes into the interview and I stop. I recognized all of the symptoms of post-traumatic stress disorder, having suffered it myself. The access to porn through the Internet is within the click of a mouse. When you sit and watch this stuff, it's frightening. The still photographs from Abu Ghraib look like stills from a gonzo porn shoot. The bodies piled on top of each other, the figures with their hands tied and the hoods, it's all out of the porn industry.

HC: Really?

CH: Oh, yeah. I think there's a deep sickness that infects all imperial societies; ancient Rome was a prime example. Cicero wrote about it. Freud had it. There are two powerful engines in human existence, Eros and Thanatos, Eros being a capacity to nurture, preserve, and protect life, and Thanatos, which calls for the annihilation of all living things, including, finally, the annihilation of ourselves. In philosophical or religious terms, imperial powers become forces of death. I don't mean just in terms of what they do with their military power, but internally, what they do morally to the societies that become enamored of imperial violence. That goes back to Thucydides, who wrote that what killed Athenian democracy was that Athens became a tyrant abroad and a tyrant at home. The tyranny Athens imposed on others it imposed on itself. I think American empire now . . . we're in the very late stages of committing collective suicide.

HC: I'm reading a fascinating book right now, *The Female Brain*, and it describes the two emotions that trigger the release of powerful morphinelike substances in the midbrain. One is sex and the other one is violence. In the male brain they are side by side, the violence and sexual neurofibers that stimulate the release of this incredibly powerful hormone.

CH: Having spent a lot of time in combat, I can tell you that they are intimately related.

HC: I suppose that's how you brainwash young men to kill.

CH: The great dividing line is often between those who have

children and those who don't. It's not accidental that the only person at the My Lai massacre to try to stop the slaughter of several hundred Vietnamese women and children was a twenty-year-old helicopter pilot who had children. What you do in a culture of war is turn human beings into objects to either gratify or destroy or both. So by the time somebody's immersed in the culture of war they have a kind of godlike power to revoke another person's charter to live on this Earth. We used to say, "Hand a nineteen-year-old kid an automatic weapon, and it takes them four days to become God." Killing is part of war, taking the life of somebody who does have the capacity to do you harm. But murder is always part of war. The killing of somebody who has no capacity to hurt you.

HC: All war is murder, Chris.

CH: Murder is always part of war. But there is a distinction between killing and murder.

HC: Which is what?

CH: If somebody is carrying a weapon and is shooting at you, then shooting back is one act. If you walk into a village, and there are women and children, and you gun them down, then that is another act. These acts become fused together and take place at the same time. Watching crazed units go in with that intoxication and destroy people who are utterly defenseless was always the hardest thing to have to witness, especially children.

HC: And these men, and women now too, but these men never really recover. Fifty percent now have post-traumatic stress syndrome and never can fit back into their families, into society.

CH: You can't feel. I went through this.

HC: Did you?

CH: You can't sleep; it's revisitation of trauma night after night. You get up in the morning, and even just to shave becomes a sort of Herculean task. Dostoyevsky said, "Hell is the inability to love." And that's what PTSD is. It's very hard to reconnect, even with the people you love the most. If you can't reestablish that connection, you're finished. You commit suicide one way or another.

HC: I've been through severe depression after my mother died, when I couldn't love. Even my children. Was yours post-Sarajevo?

CH: I did the war in Kosovo after Sarajevo, so I sort of broke down in Kosovo.

HC: How long did it take for you to recover?

CH: It took me three years to put myself together. And even then it always will come back with a fury at night. Not like it used to, but it never goes away. ∾

DIANE
CURRAN

Diane Curran, a partner in the firm Harmon, Curran, Spielberg and Eisenberg in Washington, D.C., since 1981, has represented citizen groups, state and local governments, and individuals in licensing and enforcement cases relating to nuclear power plants, factories, and waste storage and disposal sites. In her thirty years as an environmental lawyer Diane has raised safety and environmental concerns in many Nuclear Regulatory Commission (NRC) cases. In the aftermath of the September 11 attacks, Diane's work has focused on security issues. In 2006, on behalf of the San Luis Obispo Mothers for Peace, Diane won a groundbreaking U.S. Court of Appeals decision requiring the NRC to consider the environmental impacts of attacks on a proposed spent nuclear fuels storage facility.

———◆◆◆———

HELEN CALDICOTT: You've been in this for thirty years—how did you get involved in the first place?

DIANE CURRAN: When I got out of college there was controversy about the Seabrook nuclear plant. I started paying attention to that. Then, while in law school I was on a camping trip with my fiancé out in the mountains in West Virginia, the Three Mile Island meltdown accident happened. I got back to town and that was a real crisis of confidence in nuclear power. I was looking for a job as a law clerk and went to work at Harmon and Weiss, which was representing the Union of Concerned Scientists in the case about restarting the Three Mile Island plant. I got very interested in the issues and just kept going. The first case I worked on was the Seabrook case, ironically, which I worked on for about ten years. These cases tend to last a long time.

HC: I remember the first march, on a cold spring April day in New Hampshire, to the Seabrook site, at that time a rubbish dump. I stood on the rubbish dump with a megaphone and talked about the medical effects of plutonium. There was a huge movement against Seabrook, and the Clamshell Alliance started. They went ahead and built the blasted things anyway. What sort of case were you involved in against them?

DC: The main issue at Seabrook in the 1980s was that, during the construction permit phase, members of the public and state officials raised concerns that a plant could never be safely evacuated, because the site was across a little bay from a barrier beach, next to the ocean. The barrier beach is chockablock with hotels and people all summer long, so if ever there were an accident at the plant, all these people would have to evacuate on little narrow roads. The NRC had said they wouldn't allow them to operate if it wasn't safe. The case went on for ten years, about the safety of evacuating the site. In the end, the NRC gutted the emergency planning rules that had been tasked in response to Three Mile Island, so they could license the plant.

HC: I've been there. There are thousands of people on that beach in the summer. It's ridiculous. What were the safety rules enacted after the Three Mile Island accident that they then gutted?

DC: The regulation required a demonstration that evacuation will be conducted safely in the event of an accident. When the state of Massachusetts refused to do their own emergency plan, because they didn't want to go along with the charade, the NRC allowed the Public Service of New Hampshire to do a plan for evacuating the seacoast that the state would implement. The state never bought into the emergency planning process. The NRC said, We're going to assume you'll implement it. Then when it came to looking at the actual doses of radiation that people would get during an accident, and whether the evacuation could be done safely, there were assumptions made about sheltering that undercut the fact that you could not get people out of there safely. It was a real lesson for me about the regulatory process, how it can fail unless the public is vigilant. Once these reactor projects get going, there's a lot of pressure to license them.

HC: The whole thing is corrupt. Let's be frank. If there's a meltdown like at Three Mile Island or Chernobyl, nobody knows for a while. The people at the plant are so anxious, not knowing what's happening, that they don't tell anyone, especially the officials. By the time there is an announcement, the radioactive cloud has passed over the public, and they've been severely irradiated. Most of them would die within a week or two, with their hair falling out, vomiting, and bleeding to death. Then the cloud could move. From Three Mile Island in Harrisburg, Pennsylvania, the radiation reached all the way up to Boston. We look at Chernobyl, and the radiation covered Europe. It's fallacious to talk about evacuation plans in the first place.

DC: It is difficult to see how you could evacuate safely in most places. There's usually some serious problem that goes with the site.

HC: My point was that by the time the evacuation order is signed, it's too late, because the people have already been irradiated. In my book *Nuclear Power Is Not the Answer* I described a report from the Union of Concerned Scientists about a meltdown at Indian

Point. People would be trapped, in gridlocked traffic, irradiated in their cars. How do they get their children from the kindergarten, their spouses from work? Their old mothers and fathers? The whole thing is an absolute farce. What worries me is that all the principles are based on lies. There's an assumption that people can be evacuated, and the truth is that they can't. Is there any way to challenge these principles upon which the laws are based?

DC: It's very difficult to challenge the regulations that they come up with. You can do it, but from my perspective, the neighbors don't have a lot of choice when a facility is proposed or operating in their neighborhood but to engage in the process. It's a way of improving the safety of the operation. If the neighbors are vigilant over the facility, it does get more attention from the regulators.

HC: We come down to basic human behavior, very complex systems designed by man, and faults that can occur in complex systems. For instance, the space shuttle exploded because there was an O ring made of rubber that froze at the very cold temperatures at Cape Canaveral that morning. They didn't compute that eventuality in their calculations, and hence lives were lost in a very complex system. As a physician, knowing the abnormalities and frailties in human behavior, plus the systems they design, we're battling uphill to make a basically unsafe system safe.

DC: I'm very concerned that the level of secrecy the government now requires over the operation of nuclear facilities is so extreme in comparison to how it was before September 11. It's very difficult for people who live near these facilities, or for scientists who are critics of the facilities, to get the kind of information that they need in order to make a meaningful criticism. For instance, NFS, Nuclear Fuel Services in Tennessee, had a spill of highly enriched uranium. That was kept a secret for over a year. Finally, Commissioner Gregory B. Jaczko of the NRC said, "This isn't the kind of thing that's supposed to be a secret. This is just embarrassing information." But the idea that it would be kept secret from the public, that a licensee responsible for the most dangerous material in the world could not take care of it, is astounding.

HC: How did the spill happen and what areas were affected?

DC: My understanding of how it was discovered was that someone was walking down a hallway and saw a yellow puddle of liquid leaking out from under a door. And lo and behold, it was highly enriched uranium that could have caused a criticality accident, a runaway chain reaction.

HC: Did the government keep it a secret?

DC: The U.S. Navy asked the NRC to keep it a secret, but because of this one commissioner it came to light. He noticed this piece of information buried and brought it to light.

HC: Isn't Jaczko now the chief of the NRC?

DC: He's the chairman of the Commission.

HC: He's an excellent man, with integrity. I had him at one of my symposia in the past. Tell us about how and why all things nuclear have become so secret since 9/11.

DC: Nuclear facilities are attractive targets for anyone who wants to do harm, because if you attack them you can cause great damage. The NRC does not want to put information into the public domain that could be used by people who would attack these facilities to do harm. But if nobody has information about the designs of these facilities, then it's not possible to criticize the designs from the standpoint of making them safer or resolving problems. A good example is spent-fuel pools, where spent fuel from nuclear reactors is stored.

HC: How many reactors are there in the U.S.?

DC: A little over a hundred, and each one has a pool filled with the used reactor fuel that needs to be disposed of, but there isn't any place to put it yet.

HC: It's highly radioactive. When you put uranium in a reactor it becomes one billion times more radioactive than the original uranium after the fissioning process. That's the spent radioactive fuel.

DC: It's different from the fuel that's fresh inside the reactor. It's got more cesium in it. Cesium doesn't kill you right away, but it contaminates the environment. People must be relocated. The main radioactive component from the Chernobyl accident was cesium. They had to kill reindeer herds in Lapland that were highly contaminated. It is a very serious contaminant.

The hazard posed by high-density pool storage of spent reactor fuel has increased over the years as the inventory of spent fuel has mounted at each operating reactor. Originally, the nuclear industry planned to reprocess spent fuel and therefore did not anticipate that large quantities of spent fuel would need to be stored. Back when Gerald Ford and Jimmy Carter were presidents, however, they both canceled the reprocessing program in the United States. They thought reprocessing was too vulnerable because it produced pure plutonium, which could lead to the proliferation of nuclear weapons.

HC: Can you explain reprocessing?

DC: In reprocessing, fissile uranium is removed from spent fuel and it is processed into nuclear plant fuel again. But significant quantities of radioactive waste are produced in the process, including plutonium. You have to take out the plutonium. In some cases, plutonium is used to make the new fuel, but it has to be separated out from the spent fuel. That's the reason why Carter and Ford canceled the reprocessing program.

The spent fuel had to be stored in pools. When the nuclear industry was young, the pools had very little spent fuel in them. But as the amount of spent fuel increased over the years, licensees had to do something to allow the radioactive spent fuel rods to be packed closer together. They had to put more boron in the water to prevent a runaway criticality reaction. Eventually the industry came up with a design that involved the construction of vertical metal sleeves that were impregnated with boron; each assembly would be put into a sleeve. Each sleeve had holes in the bottom and holes in the top, so that the water would go in the bottom holes, go up over the fuel assembly, being heated as it went up, and come out the top holes. Then it would go through a heat exchanger, cool off, and the water would be circulated over and over again.

In the early days, the analysis that the NRC did of the risk of a fire assumed that the most severe case would be if the fuel was completely uncovered in a catastrophic earthquake, and all of a sudden all the water is gone from the pool and only air is circulating over the spent-fuel assemblies. The NRC analyzed that situation and said only relatively fresh fuel is going to burn under these circumstances. If it's aged a couple of years, you don't have to worry. Various scientists were saying, What if the cooling function is disrupted? What if air can't circulate over the spent-fuel assemblies? What if there's half water in the bottom of the pool and air in the top of the pool, so the bottom holes in these sleeves are covered with water and the top is covered with air? The NRC ignored that. But twenty-five years later the NRC had to admit that in that situation, the fuel would burn. You'd have a catastrophic fire. Some time in 2001, after twenty-five years of denying this, the NRC admitted it.

Then September 11 happened, and most of the information relating to how the NRC has addressed this very serious problem has been taken off the public record and is now treated as classified information. So if you're a neighbor who's concerned about whether the licensee at your local nuclear plant has done a good job of reducing the risk of a catastrophic pool fire at your neighborhood nuclear plant, there's no way to get enough information to satisfy yourself that it's been done. This is the situation for an agency that for twenty-five years ignored evidence that they had a serious problem. It doesn't build your confidence to know that now all this information is a secret, and no one can look at it besides the NRC and the industry, which has a vested interest in minimizing the cost of safety measures.

HC: How on earth can we get this extremely important information out into the American public? If you are on the Bill O'Reilly show, you would have an audience of millions, and there could be awakened a huge citizens' movement for safety for themselves and their children.

DC: All of the groups I work with are very serious about working with the press to get their message out. The Mothers for Peace really appreciated the opportunity to go on your radio show. They're constantly sending out news releases. Public information is very important.

HC: About the cesium from the Chernobyl plant: at the moment there are hundreds of wild boars running through Germany that are so full of cesium that they have to be killed and disposed of in a special site. And that's only Germany. Things are pretty grim, and in a nuclear power plant the size of Diablo Canyon there's as much long-lived radiation as is released by a thousand Hiroshima bombs. In the fuel pools where the spent fuel is stored, there's two to thirty times more radiation than in the reactor itself. In a sense, a meltdown in a fuel pool is more serious by orders of magnitude than a Chernobyl-type explosion.

DC: The ironic thing is that this risk of a catastrophic fire in a fuel pool could be eliminated if the licensees, the reactor owners, went back to low-density pool storage of fuel and put it in dry cask storage on the site, which is a method of fuel storage that uses passive air cooling. You would want an adequately robust kind of storage container to prevent that from being vulnerable to an attack or accident, but you would dramatically reduce the risk of these fires. Why not say to the public, we have eliminated this risk? If you want to attack this facility, don't bother. Why not do something you can publicize and talk about with everybody instead of doing some half-baked thing and making it a secret?

HC: Let's get to the root cause of the problem. The Nuclear Regulatory Commission, a federal government body, is financially supported almost 100 percent by the nuclear industry itself.

DC: It is true that the costs of regulation have passed through to the licensees. The taxpayers aren't paying for it. But in every regulatory agency that becomes a captive of the industry it's regulating, the regulated industry has all the access, the money to lobby Congress, which oversees the NRC. There's a tremendous amount of pressure from the regulated industry on the agency, and the public does not have those resources or access to the information.

HC: The other thing that worries me is that most politicians are scientifically illiterate. They have no idea about the dangers of radiation. We're being governed by people who, on the whole, have absolutely no idea of what we're talking about.

DC: Mostly I deal with the NRC. I think you're raising a good point: you have a technology used to generate electricity; that's the purpose. But it's extremely dangerous, very complicated, and much of that important information is kept a secret. And here we are, at a crossroads where we must do something to reduce our dependence on fossil fuels. We must change our whole electricity production scheme. *Why* should we invest taxpayer dollars in supporting a technology that has so many disadvantages, so many risks, when there are other technologies that will accomplish the same thing with fewer risks? They are easier to understand and don't have to be kept a secret. It's an enormously important question.

HC: What do you think the answer to that question is?

DC: We should be investing money in solar energy, geothermal, wind, and research. The last president to spend any significant amount of money on research into energy alternatives was Jimmy Carter. We have a big catch-up game to play, but the big push now in Congress is money for nuclear power. We just saw this with the Calvert Cliffs Nuclear Power Plant, where the government offered a loan guarantee with very generous terms. The company didn't want it, because it didn't require the taxpayers to completely back the project. It's crazy to ask taxpayers to pay for this kind of thing without offering us a choice of whether we would prefer something less dangerous.

HC: Why do you think the Congress and Senate are so in love with nuclear power? Is it a particularly male attribute?

DC: I don't know [*laughter*]. The nuclear industry has a tremendous amount of money they can spend on lobbyists to try to persuade Congress of their point of view. I'm not sure the other energy technologies are as well supported.

HC: Nuclear power is socialized electricity. Because as you pointed out, it's well covered by the taxpayers.

DC: It's true. The Price-Anderson Act, passed when the industry was in its infancy, is a law that limits the liability of the industry for a nuclear accident. Once they pay up to that limit, the taxpayers take over the rest, because no company could get enough liability insurance for the kind of accident a nuclear plant could cause. And we've been subsidizing the industry through research and development grants, and now we have the loan guarantees for this new generation of nuclear reactors.

HC: The other thing to note is that the nuclear industry is a prodigal son of the weapons industry. The weapons industry is totally paid for, a socialized industry. The nuclear power industry has inherited that philosophy, and it goes along unimpeded. Europe is peppered with nuclear power plants, as is the United States. That makes war obsolete. If World War II were fought today, Europe would be un-inhabitable for the rest of time. Most of those reactors would have melted down.

The other thing is that one big hydrogen bomb exploded in space above the states could wipe out the power supply and eliminate six western states of the United States. That means a huge electro-magnetic pulse knocks out the electricity supply, which will induce meltdowns, because all nuclear power plants need external electric-ity. We don't talk about these things. Tell me about your work with Diablo Canyon and the Mothers for Peace.

DC: The San Luis Obispo Mothers for Peace is an amazing organi-zation that started in the 1970s as a peace group and turned their attention to the Diablo Canyon nuclear plant. It's an all-volunteer group. They fought the construction permit, the operating license, and when the plant was licensed, they set about monitoring the op-eration of the plant. They've participated in several hearings since the plant was licensed. They're in the middle of a case now that started in 2002 involving a proposed dry spent-fuel storage facil-ity on the site. Dry storage is a better way to store spent fuel, but it has drawbacks. This particular facility was to some degree designed to withstand an attack, but the NRC did not go through the full process to make this facility better protected from a terrorist attack. The Mothers for Peace was concerned that neither PG&E, Pacific Gas and Electric, nor the NRC had taken into consideration things like putting these casks in a bunker, so if anyone shot a weapon they couldn't hit them. Or scattering the casks over the site, so they couldn't constitute one focused target. We brought a lawsuit to try to get them to do it. The NRC said that they don't have to comply with this environmental law if it has any relation to security issues. We took the NRC to court and we won. The federal appellate court decision said there's no exception for security issues. So the NRC did a really quick job. Something like a ten-page study that said there can be no impact from a terrorist attack on this facility.

We were astounded, because it's obvious that you could do significant environmental damage if you set the fuel on fire. The really dangerous thing is that the cladding that surrounds the spent-fuel assemblies is flammable.

HC: Zirconium.

DC: We asked why they didn't look at the potential for setting a fire, and they said, We're not going to talk about it; it's classified. So we asked for a closed hearing, which we are entitled to under the Atomic Energy Act. The NRC said, We only do closed hearings for other issues, not environmental issues. We're back in court trying to get a closed hearing in which, even if we can't discuss all the issues publicly, at least we can have our technical experts look at what the NRC did and critique it. We think they've overlooked the most significant environmental risk that's posed by this facility.*

HC: I wish you luck. Is the spent fuel pool on the roof of Diablo Canyon?

DC: I believe the spent fuel pools are in the ground.

HC: If they're on the roof, and many are, they're open to terrorist attack. One shoulder-held missile going into a spent-fuel pool will drain the water out and produce meltdown. There are two other things: it's very close to a major earthquake fault, number one. Number two, as the oceans rise because of global warming, there could be a rogue storm that could flood the control mechanism of Diablo Canyon and cause a meltdown. Have those considerations been taken into account by Mothers for Peace or by the NRC?

DC: Recently PG&E applied for a twenty- to forty-year renewal of its license.

---

* Mothers for Peace eventually lost the case after the court ruled that the NRC was permitted by law to refuse to hold a closed hearing.

HC: How old is the plant?

DC: It started operating in the eighties. They've applied fourteen years in advance of the expiration date of their license. We're concerned that they've applied so far ahead of time. A new earthquake fault was discovered, and the fault runs right through the site. It's called the Shoreline Fault. PG&E and the United States Geological Survey are studying this fault. The Mothers for Peace have requested a hearing on why this plant should get its license renewed before there's better information about this fault. So we're contesting the issuance of the renewed license, because there isn't enough information about what risk this fault poses.

HC: The Shoreline Fault could be related to the San Andreas fault. You can't predict what the Earth is going to do.

DC: Nuclear plants are all designed to meet what's called the design basis earthquake, but that doesn't account for a really severe earthquake. You want to have as much information as you can about that, but PG & E is rushing ahead with their license renewal application.

HC: What's the matter with these people?

DC: It does seem like they're playing roulette.

HC: If you lived in San Luis Obispo with the current problems with this reactor, which is not very far away, would you stay there if you had children? What would you do?

DC: I represent people who stay. One of the things I admire about the Mothers for Peace is that they stay and fight. They feel it's their community and they're going to fight for it. They're not going to take assurances of "trust us, we'll take care of you"—they want to know. They really exemplify the kind of commitment that people need to have to where they live, to the Earth, and to their communities.

HC: You work for them for free, don't you?

DC: I donate a fair amount of my time. It's a real honor to work for them.

HC: Has sea-level rise been considered at any of the reactors that are placed at ocean level around the United States?

DC: It may have come up in lower-lying coastal areas, but I'm not sure.

HC: The predictions are pretty vast. They're talking about one to two meters [about one to two yards] by the end of the century. But that's not the only thing. There's going to be catastrophic storms, so together with the sea-level rises, it's quite possible that this reactor could be flooded, or a tsunami could occur because of the earthquakes off the coast of California.

DC: If you look at how several accidents happen, it's often in the context of off-site power loss, systems go down, and then you get a severe accident. If only for that reason, the storm activity is going to play a role in the risk of accidents at nuclear reactors.

HC: Is there anything else we haven't covered that you would like to bring out now in this interview?

DC: I really appreciate the opportunity to talk to you and to try to get the message out to the public how important it is to be aware, be educated, don't take "trust us" for an answer, and participate. ∾

VINI GAUTAM KHURANA

D r. Vini Gautam Khurana is a senior staff specialist neurosurgeon at the Canberra Hospital in Australia and an associate professor of neurosurgery at the Australian National University Medical School. After graduating with medical and research degrees in Australia in 1995, he moved to the United States for ten years, where he received advanced specialist training at the world renowned Mayo Clinic in Rochester, MN. Dr. Khurana has become well-known for his research on electromagnetic radiation from cell phones. He is the author of two books: *Brain Surgery: A Comprehensive and Practical Resource for Brain Surgery Patients, Their Families, and Physicians* and *The Brain Aneurysm* (with Robert F. Spetzler).

———

HELEN CALDICOTT: How did you, as a neurosurgeon, become interested in this area of cell phones and electromagnetic radiation?

VINI GAUTAM KHURANA: I had no specific interest in this field until 2006, when a close friend of mine, a renowned professor of surgery here, Professor Chris O'Brien, developed a malignant brain tumor, and in my opinion, he was a heavy cell phone user. The tumor was located immediately underneath the ear at which he held his cell phone. That got me thinking about this. In that same year I'd heard of a cancer cluster that occurred on the top floors of the Royal Melbourne Institute of Technology building. On the roof of that building was a telecommunications tower. Several people who worked in that building on the top two floors developed brain tumors. I started a long and very rewarding journey academically into reading about electromagnetic radiation and cell phones, communication systems based on cellular telephony, and came up with a report that received worldwide attention in early 2008.

HC: Can you summarize the results?

VK: The initial report was a very comprehensive review of many papers, journal articles, and resources such as the BioInitiative Report—a 2007 report that documents bioeffects, adverse health effects, and public health concerns about impacts of nonionizing radiation. My review looked at the issues fairly openly, and then put all the facts together as best as I could understand them. The conclusion that I came to was that a lot of studies out there do suggest that prolonged usage of cell phones or exposure at close proximity to cell phone masts—these transmission towers for cellular telephony—can have adverse health effects. My conclusion was that there was a lot of evidence out there, and it was quite surprising that governments, industries, and societies themselves hadn't quite comprehended or taken this as seriously as one should, because of the number of people using them, including young children.

When that report came out it was not peer-reviewed, and subsequent to that a very arduous task of peer review was undertaken. It was then published in the journal *Surgical Neurology*, which is one of the premier neurosurgical journals.

HC: What sort of reception did it receive?

VK: The report was initially reviewed in the local media in

Canberra. It caught the attention of the UK media, *The Independent*. Then it became a focus of global attention. It was aired in the United States and throughout the world, eventually on interviews given on *Larry King Live* as well as *60 Minutes* and other programs. It was quite broadly received. Overall the feedback that I got was tremendously supportive. There were certainly elements of sharp criticism from industry and scientists who are associated with the industry. But overall I had engineers, people who had worked in the cell phone industry, many in the general public, and some of my colleagues as well write to me and commend me on actually bringing attention to this with some degree of credibility. I tried to point out that mine wasn't original research, just a review of what I regard as credible information out there internationally. Overall I felt it was very well received. One of the criticisms that I took heed of was that if you're going to say something like this you really need to have it peer-reviewed, and you need to have this published. I did that with co-authors, some of whom had done the original research that brought attention to this area, particularly Professor Lennart Hardell and Professor Michael Kundi in Europe.

HC: A lot of work has been done in Sweden, has it not, on cell phones?

VK: Sweden was the country that really started off the cell phone revolution, and a lot of the data that had come out of Sweden from Professor Hardell's group were the seminal data that brought attention to the fact that there's a cancer risk associated with prolonged cell phone usage.

HC: Did Dr. O'Brien, that wonderful head and neck cancer surgeon who inspired so many people in Sydney, Australia, think that his brain tumor was caused by his cell phone?

VK: He had a fairly equivocal point of view on that. When he was diagnosed, the first thing that his wife, Gail, told him was that she thought it was his cell phone. His neurosurgeon, Dr. Charles Teo, said the same thing. When I heard about his diagnosis I also said the same thing. The three of us said it independently. Chris didn't feel that it was necessarily a cause. He mentions it in his autobiography, *Never Say Die*, which is a wonderful book. He mentions the fact that the three of us told him about our concern.

HC: How much did he use his cell phone?

VK: Whenever I visited him, when I returned yearly from the United States, I would make it a point as often as I could to visit him. On those visits what I witnessed was that he used it quite heavily. When you're in a vehicle, and a cell phone mast is trying to track you, your phone puts out the most energy in order to keep that signal faithful, because you're no longer standing still. It's tracking you as your car is moving. He used it quite a bit in the car, he told me that, and that's when it's at its peak output. Or in days gone by, when you were in a building, because of the interference from the structure of the building, the phone's output is automatically adjusted.

HC: I have a cell phone, and I've got a little plug-in microphone so I can drive and have this thing in my ear. I've heard that my head then becomes the antenna, and it doesn't stop the radiation getting to my brain.

VK: That was my understanding initially, that the head was converted into an antenna. Subsequently I appeared on a panel on *Larry King* where there was a very respected group of people from both camps, and the consensus was that the use of a wired earpiece was a lot safer than holding up the cell phone to your head. The *wireless* earpiece is still debated in terms of its safety.

HC: What's the wireless earpiece—the thing that people walk around with in airports attached to their ear?

VK: The Bluetooth. Obviously, it's convenient.

HC: And it goes straight into their brains?

VK: An engineer wrote to me saying that when he was one of the developers of the wireless technology for Bluetooth technology, they developed it so that the pulse of radiation is constant even when it's not in direct use and communicating, because it needs to be tracked by the cell phone, which is usually at the hip. That regular pulse of radiation was designed for maximal penetration into a gel-like substance.

HC: Which is the brain! Why did they do that?

VK: Obviously to maintain a very clear signal, to maintain a faithful audio. I imagine that's why they wanted to keep that signal that would register into the hearing nerve, and then register into the brain.

HC: There are some wired microphones that you can plug into your phone that are designed to block out the electromagnetic radiation.

VK: The U.S. military is supplied by a company called Aegis that has earpieces that have an intervening area over an air-containing tube, so that the wire itself stops before it reaches the head, and the rest of that signal—the oscillatory sound—is conducted through that air tube. They're referred to as air tube headsets, or tube headsets. I imagine that there must be a reason for producing that sort of thing for the military.

HC: I've tried, and it's almost impossible to get one. How do we—scientists, medical scientists, and biologists—think that electromagnetic radiation can induce cancer?

VK: Let's begin by saying that cell phone–related electromagnetic radiation can cause cancer. But you must look at it broadly. Electromagnetic radiation is a spectrum. At the very low end of that spectrum are the low-intensity waves, what are referred to as having a longer wavelength, like radio waves. As you move up that spectrum, to the more high-energy side, you get to the microwave region where cell phones and microwave ovens sit side by side. Then you move up toward ultraviolet light, such as solariums, then into the X-ray end of the spectrum, ionizing radiation.

So cell phones and microwaves, but particularly cell phones, are thought to be emitters of nonionizing radiation. They're thought, by that definition, not to emit radiation strong enough to break molecular bonds and cause DNA damage, mutations. Whereas at the higher end, the ionizing radiation—such as X-rays, ultraviolet radiation, nuclear bombs, all of those things—cause cancer. We all know that, it's well accepted by governments and the World Health Organization. But the nonionizing cell phone radiation is thought not to cause it. So how does this conjecture arise when we're saying that there's evidence for an association?

In the journal *Science*, one of the leading scientific journals of the world, I published a letter in which I clarified some misinformation about this issue. Numerous independent laboratories throughout the world have suggested that even though we're talking about nonionizing radiation, DNA damage is in fact observed with radiation such as cell phone– and microwave-type radiation. The mechanism of that is certainly not known, but there are theories.

HC: Can you see DNA breakage?

VK: Yes you can, damaged DNA and breakage. *Science* [journal] actually acknowledged in their response to my letter that they are now aware of other papers that have in fact cited that. A Centre of Research Excellence under the National Health and Medical Research Council of Australia published an article in which they have exposed human sperm to cell phone radiation and observed DNA damage. That has been published, and they proposed a mechanism as well in that paper. The point is that even though we call this nonionizing, I think we need to be thinking about the possibility that it promotes cancers—it doesn't have to directly break DNA, although there's evidence for that. But it may contribute to cancer through other mechanisms apart from DNA breakage.

HC: But is the DNA breakage related to microwave and electromagnetic radiation?

VK: I don't know for sure if there's a dose response. But if you think about electromagnetic radiation in terms of dose intensity, as you go up the scale, from the low frequencies to the very high frequencies along that spectrum, you start observing cancer. So microwave seems to be right at the borderline. On one side you've got the dangerous UV and atomic, and on the other side you've got radio waves.

HC: It seems fairly clear that what we call the etiology, or the cause of a disease, could well be related to electromagnetic radiation and cancer. Have you observed people who have developed brain tumors on the same side that they use their cell phones?

VK: I have, but I can't prove anything based on observation. Those who are concerned about this issue do see a number of younger patients with malignant tumors than would be expected. A number of them have exposures such as prolonged cell phone use on that side. Not all, but one has to think about where these cancers are originating from. Does it have to be on the same side? These malignant tumors appear to be associated with the very center part of the brain, where the human brain stem cells are present in what's known as the periventricular zone, the center of the brain.

HC: Is that where they seem to originate?

VK: When we see brain cancers, the majority of them, radiologically at least, appear to taper down into that perioventricular zone at the center of the brain. So if it's in the center, does it have to necessarily lateralize to one side in relationship to the exposure or the instigating insult? We do have some information from the United States that there is an increasing incidence, from the Central Brain Tumor Registry of the United States. It is not completely clear at this time what's causing that. In our publication, a graph shows it is increasing. The latest report from the United States Central Brain Tumor Registry only goes back as far as 2005. We have seen a 36 percent increase in primary brain tumor incidence between 1995 and that 2004 to 2005 period. Certainly there are many possible reasons, but it's something that we need to keep track of.

HC: And when did cell phone use become common in the Western world?

VK: In Europe, cell phone use started to proliferate in the mid-nineties. The United States and Australia picked up on it later.

HC: Do cell phones emit radiation when they're not in use, and what about when they're roaming?

VK: If cell phones are in sleep mode, but not switched off or the battery removed, they are emitting electromagnetic radiation. When they're on, when you're talking, obviously they are, and when you're not speaking it is sending a signal at regular intervals to a mast that could be kilometers away to let that mast know where the phone is in space. They are emitting unless they are switched off or have their batteries removed.

When they're not switched off, and they're in your waist pocket or your breast pocket, they are continuously sending a signal to the mast that constitutes the cellular network in order for that mast to know where the phone is.

HC: How far away from the body should a cell phone be so that the body receives no electromagnetic radiation?

VK: It's based on what's referred to as the inverse square law. As you move the emitter away from the body, there is an exponential decrease in the radiation received by the body. A safe distance would be around twenty centimeters [eight inches]. This is published in the manuals and online by the company. I use an Apple iPhone for my work. I use it in speakerphone mode; I don't hold it to my ear.

But if you read the manual that comes with the phone, or look it up online, the company actually recommends that the phone be held at least five eighths of an inch away from the body. It should not be held less than five eighths of an inch next to the ear, and they say in their manual that if you're holding it around the waist, it should be at least five eighths of an inch away from the body. No physical contact. That's an interesting thing to state in a manual. They state clearly that the farther you hold it away, the safer it becomes. A rather interesting comment to make.

HC: So if people walk around with them in their breast pocket, the breast is being irradiated, be it male or female breast. If they walk around with it in their pants pocket, the testicles could be being irradiated.

VK: It's not a matter of could; they are. We know these things produce radiation; it's defined as nonionizing; we know it's low intensity, low energy, but just like when a bomb goes off, there's that mushroom cloud. This thing has its own plume. There's a field around it. Anything within that field technically will be irradiated; high energy or low energy is another matter.

HC: Let's talk about children and cell phones. The kids walk around with them glued to their ears, or they're texting, and constantly using their cell phones. Little children are getting cell phones now.

VK: The exposure of children is my single greatest concern. A child who's handed a cell phone doesn't think about exposures. It's just a glossy-looking, fantastic toy that they can show their friends. There's a certain amount of innocence there that's different from an adult who's handed a phone or a cigarette.

The other thing that concerns me is that a child's anatomy and physiology are different from an adult's. A young child has a thin scalp, a thinner skull. If something is going to penetrate into their brains, it will do so much more effectively—particularly when we're dealing with radiation—into a child's head than into an adult's. The second issue is that the volume of a young child's head and brain is significantly less than that of an adult's. If you hold the same emitter up to an adult's brain and a child's brain, you know that the emitter, the plume of that emission, will penetrate farther across the child's head and brain, owing to its lower volume. A child's brain contains relatively more water, which is a conductor of currents. A child's brain is much more plastic. It is in a mode of flourishing, where connections are forming rapidly. There are connections, disconnections, etc. It's happening in a very energized space compared to an adult's.

HC: Cells are rapidly dividing in mitosis.

VK: Absolutely. Rapid cell division is possibly an event in which things can be equally disturbed. I've read review articles that have modeled mathematically the exposure of a child's skull and brain relative to that of an adult's; those articles have stated that, compared to an adult, penetration from electromagnetic radiation of cell phones is 20 percent to 120 percent higher in getting into a child's head. This is peer-reviewed, published data. The health authorities in Ireland, followed more recently by England, have declared that there is no reason to be concerned about children. This has been passed on to me by colleagues in the United Kingdom. I can't understand how you could make that statement and what data that must be based on. I'd be very happy to look at that data, because what I've read would suggest that precautionary principles should still be in place.

HC: Children are ten to twenty times more sensitive to ionizing radiation than adults, and fetuses are thousands of times more sensitive to ionizing radiation, because their cells are so actively dividing. Are your colleagues seeing more brain tumors in younger people now?

VK: Some of my colleagues, who are looking out for that, are saying so. Many are not commenting. There are colleagues of mine who say that the last guy I operated on had ten brain tumors. To me that immediately raises the question, Why are you seeing so many tumors? But of course, not everyone asks the question. They're just contributing positively to society by helping those very unfortunate people. We need to determine that in an objective not anecdotal way. There could be many reasons for it. We need to be able to determine that objectively by going in at the grassroots level to the places that these brain tumor specimens are sent to. Talk to our registries about what they're actually seeing and how they're collating their data. It's only at that point that we can make more objective statements. Regardless of what the trend is, we need to know that information moving into the future.

HC: Is the trend more in malignant gliomas—that is, astrocytomas—and/or meningiomas, which are benign brain tumors?

VK: The Central Brain Tumor Registry of the United States has reported an increase in certain benign tumors and in certain groups of astrocytomas, so there's both. The interesting thing about acoustic neuroma, a tumor on the hearing nerve, is that that data is somehow being clouded, because those tumors are now mostly being treated nonsurgically by radiation. Certainly those with the larger ones are still being sent to surgeons, but the smaller ones are being treated by radiation. So the incidence of those particular tumors may seem to be decreasing falsely, simply because pathologists and surgeons are not seeing the actual specimens anymore. The data on whether a tumor is increasing or decreasing in incidence comes from the number of pathological specimens.

HC: I thought we had to register cancers when they occur, even if they get healed or cured.

VK: Yes, but certain tumors associated with prolonged cell phone use are not defined as cancers. Acoustic neuroma, which we've shown from our meta-analysis to be significantly increased in terms of incidence with long-term cell phone usage, is defined as a benign cancer.

HC: If you get a tumor in the brain, be it benign or malignant, it takes up volume, and as the brain is in a fixed box, it can compress the brain to such an extent that the patient can die.

VK: You can speak to many people who have had so-called benign tumors removed and see how the treatments of those tumors can affect them. Here's an example: acoustic neuroma is one of those that is not defined as a cancer, and another one, glioma, can be defined as a precancerous tumor, and therefore not necessarily reportable. There's a lot of nonuniformity about what we're calling cancers and noncancers. I think we really need to look at that in a very systematic way.

HC: Are you planning to start doing this epidemiological work?

VK: It's already being done.*

HC: Are you looking at only Australian data or at United States and Europe as well?

VK: I'm monitoring the United States data but looking at the Australian data as well.

HC: How are you going to get the data for benign tumors, like eighth-nerve neuromas and meningiomas and the like, that aren't classified as actual cancers?

VK: We are trying to do that through pathology units in a multicenter manner.

HC: There are other areas where electromagnetic radiation is produced in everyday life, like electric blankets, computers, and all

---

*These studies have now been published in the peer-review literature; see www.brain-surgery.us/mobilephone. html.

the electronic equipment that we have in our houses. I know people who have got instruments to measure electromagnetic radiation. They went into a library through a scanning mechanism, and found that what the women at the desk were exposed to was really high-level electromagnetic radiation.

VK: I share this concern. I have done those measurements with the assistance of professionals who do this day after day. I have grounds for those concerns. Our prime minister told us publicly that if Australians live to the age of eighty-five up to one in two of them will experience cancer. Cancer is not going away. The mortality has decreased, because we have some better treatments; the best solution for cancer is prevention. I'm concerned for children who play for hours a day on floors that have baseboard heating with electrical wiring, which is found in many day cares and homes in Australia, people who sleep all night with electric blankets, people who sit for hours a day right next to their laptop computers. There's a report that investigated the incidence of brain tumors among the offspring of women who sit professionally for hours a day at electrical sewing machines. They have found a significantly increased rate of brain tumor incidence in the offspring of those women. That is a seminal kind of statement. Not any proof, but it lends substance to the concern you and I share: could these things be part and parcel of the increasing cancer rates we are seeing?

HC: What about laptops? Do they give off a lot of electromagnetic radiation?

VK: Those measurements have been made, there are publications of those measurements, and it has been advised that the last place that a laptop should be is on your lap.

HC: What about if it's on a desk about two feet away?

VK: That's a lot safer. It remains to be determined, but it's a paradigm shift in the way we're thinking. You remember smoking, you remember X-rays when they came out, ultraviolet tanning booths—all these things were well accepted, thought to be safe, approved by industries and governments. I remember doctors in their white gowns with cigarettes promoting them on advertisements. Just look at how this paradigm shift has taken place within the last few decades. We may be entering such a phase with electromagnetic radiation. We can't take away things like natural sunlight, of course, and no one is saying, throw your cell phones or electronics away, but think of them as a potential health risk that is worthy of exploration.

HC: Television sets also emit gamma radiation, because they have thorium in them. That's ionizing radiation.

VK: Those measurements seem to be high when one is close up to the set. I think it's something that will become more topical.

HC: Everyone should know that, be it ionizing or electromagnetic radiation, ultraviolet radiation . . . the dose you get decreases with the square of the distance.

VK: Based on that inverse square law, based on the fact that a laptop itself doesn't generate large amounts of energy, two feet sounds like a very safe distance. But I think within ten to twenty centimeters [four to eight inches] it would be rather safe.

HC: What really worries me is that there are 3 billion people using cell phones worldwide.

VK: Four billion now.

HC: There's a huge amount of money to be made with people selling these cell phones. Obviously people who work for the industry would want to negate what you're talking about. We're up against highly financed people who have a conflict of interest.

VK: I think it requires, as best as one can, a balanced approach. Being aggressively militant about this cell phone issue is not a long-term solution. The purpose of my report was to make people aware. I had to take a fairly strong view, because I was flabbergasted when I read so much work that suggested that there is a meritorious scientific basis for such a concern. So what am I going to do? Part of these things is already happening. In the United States, [former] Senator Arlen Specter chaired a U.S. Senate inquiry into the health effects of cell phones, a landmark move. The European parliament debated the health effects of electromagnetic radiation, and in a landslide vote, voted toward getting this on the table and really looking at the risks with all the new epidemiologic data in mind.

HC: And all the electrical appliances we are surrounded with both in our offices and at home . . .

VK: We are totally immersed and addicted as a species to cell phones. We need objective data. If there is a greatly increasing incidence of brain tumors or other cancers, and we have postulated this as being a possible cause, after a while you won't be able to hide that fact no matter how much money you have. Some epidemiological studies need to be done soundly on a number of fronts. Governments need to recognize that money is important, but human health is more important. And we need to make sure that we can preserve that human health. There's enough to know a definitive answer.

I'm absolutely not saying throw away your cell phones. They are life-saving tools. Sometimes we know that cell phones are life-endangering tools, as when they're used in cars. I'm saying that cell phone usage should be modified to make it safer. The way to make it safer is, instead of holding it to your ear, keep it in a speakerphone mode. The reason I use the iPhone is that it has such a clear speakerphone. I keep it at least twenty centimeters [eight inches] away from my head when I'm using it in speakerphone mode. If a privacy issue arises, then a wired earpiece can be used, or defer the conversation if possible to a landline. A hands-free car kit is safer than actually holding it to your ear, because the roof of the car is actually acting as the antenna. Overall I think the preference should be to use a landline, like we used to.

HC: What about landlines that you walk around with like a cell phone?

VK: Those are cordless handsets. They have an antenna and emit electromagnetic radiation at a lower intensity than that of a cell phone, but we tend to use them for much longer. Professor Hardell's studies from Sweden show that prolonged usage of those cordless handsets is also significantly associated with increased tumor rates. They are a problem. How does my family do it? I told you how I use it, and my wife uses it the same way. Our children do not use cell phones, and when they use the cordless phone, it's used in limited amounts. I restrict the time of usage, but always in a speakerphone mode. We don't keep the base station of the cordless unit anywhere near our heads.

HC: It's like when I began studying medicine in 1956. We already knew that smoking caused cancer, but it took decades to infiltrate that into the public consciousness because of the tobacco companies putting out the propaganda.

VK: As you hear the spin doctors in these various areas say, when they put the data together, there is what they call the weight of the evidence. How do you create the weight of the evidence? What you do is basically flood the literature with papers and letters that have some roots in industry. You say, Look, here's ten papers, and eight of them say there's no problem, and these two say there is a problem. Therefore, the weight of the evidence says there's no problem. When you start looking into where those papers come from you realize.

HC: I'm a pediatrician, you're a neurosurgeon—I think from a medical point of view that governments should ban these companies from putting out their propaganda either on smoking, asbestos, cell phones, or nuclear power.

VK: Anyone who generates an opinion, be it a doctor, a scientist, whoever, must declare any conflicts of interest with full transparency. Then somebody who is reading this can openly make up their own mind. If I debate somebody, and I have no conflict of interest, it's a pure health concern. But if we debate someone who is being funded directly or indirectly by a party that is the concern of the debate, that should be openly declared. I think publications, journals, and scientific conferences now require conflicts of interest to be openly declared. That is the first step, then let the public decide. ∽

DAVID KRIEGER

D avid Krieger is a founder and president of the Nuclear Age Peace Foundation, which has initiated many innovative projects for building peace, strengthening international law, abolishing nuclear weapons, and empowering a new generation of peace leaders. Dr. Krieger has lectured throughout the United States, Europe, and Asia, and is chair of the executive committee of the International Network of Engineers and Scientists for Global Responsibility. He is a founding member of the Abolition 2000 Global Council, a global network of over two thousand organizations and municipalities committed to the elimination of nuclear weapons. He is also a councilor on the World Future Council.

HELEN CALDICOTT: Let's go back to the beginning. How did you get involved emotionally and intellectually with the issue of nuclear weapons?

DAVID KRIEGER: I studied political science in graduate school, working on issues related to international relations. I was most interested in issues of disarmament because I felt that war was a terrible waste of lives and resources and undermined human decency. I came to realize that nuclear disarmament was *the* great issue of our time. Far too few people recognize that it has only been in the last sixty-five years of the nuclear age that we've been faced with this existential threat to the future. I believe it's the responsibility of all of those alive on the planet today to work for a world without nuclear weapons. So my impetus, my inspiration, and my belief is that we must achieve that world and pass on a world without nuclear weapons to future generations.

HC: Did you come from a family that had a reverence for life and had integrity?

DK: I did come from such a family, although they weren't engaged constantly in such issues. My father was a pediatrician. I remember vividly one evening when I was about twelve years old, sitting around the dinner table with my parents. We were talking about bomb shelters, which were much in the news in those days. I remember my mother saying that she would rather die than have to live in a bomb shelter and use weapons to keep neighbors out, that she would prefer death to that. I was surprised to hear her say that. I respect her position and her humanity.

HC: How old are you now, and how many years have you been working on the concept of nuclear disarmament?

DK: I'm sixty-eight now, and I've been working on nuclear disarmament for most of my adult life. From the time I was about twenty-five.

HC: What do you think you've achieved in that time? That's a very big question, and it's hard to answer, but why don't you tell us what you think you've achieved with the Nuclear Age Peace Foundation.

DK: Perhaps the most important thing I've done, along with others who have worked on this issue, including you, has been to be a voice of conscience on the issue, to not let the issue go away. To not let those who have pursued nuclear weapons do so without an opposing perspective. I think being a voice of conscience has been significant.

Along with some other individuals, I founded the Nuclear Age Peace Foundation in 1982. I think we've done some fairly remarkable things since then. The foundation itself has been a voice of conscience. We've reached out to young people throughout the United States and throughout the world. We have a wonderful peace leadership program now that is going on every day in which young people are being trained to have skills as peace leaders and be advocates for nuclear disarmament. We've shined a light on peace leadership and given awards to many amazing people, including you. We've constantly stayed true to our focus and worked for a world without nuclear weapons, the strengthening of international law, and the creation and empowerment of new peace leaders.

HC: If people want to learn about how to create peace, and go to some of your classes, how would they do that?

DK: Our website is wagingpeace.org. We're all about waging peace. We think that peace has to be as active and dynamic and engaged as the waging of war.

HC: Why are we moving so slowly toward the abolition of nuclear weapons, and where's the sense of urgency in general?

DK: That is a critical question. It's been sixty-five years since nuclear weapons were used in war, and I think many people don't believe that those weapons will ever be used again. But the threat exists each day. Complacency is detrimental to the human future. Unless we can awaken and engage people in this issue we'll continue to move slowly. We have to overcome ignorance and apathy.

A second reason we've moved slowly is that many people believe that they're protected by nuclear weapons. I think nothing could be further from the truth. Nuclear weapons cannot defend against other nuclear weapons. All that can be done with them is to threaten retaliation, based upon the theory of nuclear deterrence. The theory is, if you threaten another country with nuclear retaliation, it won't attack you. But the theory requires that the other side believe you are really willing to do that. It also requires that the so-called enemy be locatable and not be suicidal. Those elements—being locatable and not being suicidal—don't apply to terrorist groups, so you could never have effective deterrence against a terrorist organization in possession of nuclear weapons. It won't work.

The theory of nuclear deterrence is just that—a theory—and we should not bet our lives and the future of the world on it. It's not realistic, and even people like Henry Kissinger and other former Cold Warriors are coming to that conclusion.

HC: I've got a list from your website of a number of ways, and there are fifteen, that a global nuclear war could be triggered. I will read them out and you comment. Number one: "False Alarm: A false alarm triggers a decision to launch a nuclear attack." How would a false alarm occur?

DK: False alarms have occurred a number of times. A flock of geese picked up by radar has triggered the alarm that a country was under a nuclear attack. A false alarm occurred in 1995. The Russians were told that the United States and Norway were launching a weather satellite from Norway, but somehow that message didn't get through the chain of command in Russia. When they picked up the launch in Russia, the military thought that a U.S. missile was headed toward Moscow. They awakened the president, Boris Yeltsin. They opened the Russian black box with the code to launch, and fortunately Yeltsin said words to the effect of "Let's not be too hasty here." He had his wits about him. He did wait, and they realized that the missile wasn't headed toward Russia.

Yeltsin was given only a few minutes to decide. And this is a man who had a reputation for drinking a lot. Imagine if he had been awakened and been in a stupor and unable to think clearly. . . . We were very fortunate.

HC: Where can people look up a list of false alarms that have occurred in the North American early warning system, NORAD?

DK: We have a list of false alarms, and also accidents, at a second website that we have, called NuclearFiles.org. It is an educational website that tries to maintain the memory of the nuclear age and to not let accidents, near-accidents, and false alarms be forgotten over time.

HC: The next argument against complacency: "Unauthorized Launch: Launch codes are obtained by hackers, espionage agents or coercion and used to launch high alert forces. This could involve the physical takeover of a mobile missile, which the Russians have, or the use of codes obtained via predelegation." Explain how that could work.

DK: Human systems are not foolproof. Designers try to make systems for launching nuclear weapons as foolproof as possible. But the capacity to make them foolproof depends on where the weapons are located and under whose control. Nine countries have nuclear weapons. Some are more capable than others. The possibility exists for the codes to be stolen or fall into the hands of terrorist leaders or opposition groups, as well as for a weapon to be stolen and for the possessors to figure out a way to actually detonate that weapon.

We've heard the story that the Russians created suitcase bombs, and we don't know where they are. I don't know to what extent that story is true or apocryphal, but there's no such thing as a foolproof system. We have to understand that there are groups that, if they could, would like to have possession of nuclear weapons, and would use them.

HC: How many weapons do Russia and America have that are ready to be launched by Putin or Obama?

DK: I believe the latest figures that the experts agree upon are under two thousand deployed strategic nuclear weapons each, with about a thousand each on hair-trigger alert. Considering the current relationship that the United States and Russia have with each other, which is largely friendly, there's absolutely no reason to have these weapons poised for attack on a few minutes' notice, placing the future of humanity in jeopardy. An accidental launch could occur because somehow the computer system was wrongly configured and launches without human intervention. We've had instances in the past of airplanes losing control of their nuclear weapons and dropping them. One case like that took place over Palomares, Spain, when a United States plane carrying nuclear weapons dropped them accidentally during a refueling operation. On one of the bombs, five of six safety devices failed. It was only that sixth redundant safety device that prevented a nuclear explosion in Spain.

HC: Then there's "Control and Communications Failure: A rogue field commander or submarine commander falls out or deliberately puts himself out of communications with his central command and launches a nuclear attack on his own authority." How could that happen?

DK: The United States has a delegation of authority to commanders in the field with little understanding of what that actually means. Imagine that there are nuclear weapons at various bases in India or Pakistan, as an example, and a commander decides on his own authority that it's appropriate to use them, without control from the central authorities. He goes ahead and uses them and instigates a nuclear war.

HC: If one is used, no one would know what was happening, and it could trigger the whole thing to go off, right?

DK: Once a nuclear weapon is used, the side that's been attacked has no idea, initially at least, whether it's purposeful or accidental.

I think the assumption in every case would be that the use was purposeful. Even if the assumption were that it was accidental, there'd still be a dilemma in terms of how to respond to it.

HC: It's like 9/11. In that situation, because no one knew what was happening, the Strategic Air Command went down to the second-highest stage of nuclear alert—just before launching. The next one is "'Dr. Strangelove' Nuclear War," and that brings us to "the launch of a nuclear attack by a rogue field or submarine commander leads to a retaliatory strike that escalates into nuclear war."

DK: In the movie *Dr. Strangelove*, they couldn't recall a bomber with nuclear arms beyond a certain point. The president of the United States was bargaining, in the movie, with the premier of the Soviet Union and talking about exchanging Moscow for New York. They were actually negotiating what kind of retaliation would be appropriate once the bomb was dropped on Moscow. But it's a scenario that cannot be ruled out with certainty in today's world.

HC: The next one is "A Terrorist Bomb: A terrorist group obtains nuclear materials and creates an unsophisticated nuclear device or obtains a bomb and succeeds in detonating it in a large city."

DK: We know that terrorists are seeking nuclear devices. We know that the information on how to make nuclear weapons is available; there are many, many scientists who could advise on how to make a nuclear weapon. That is the example of A.Q. Khan from Pakistan, who was selling nuclear weapons. It may be difficult for terrorists to actually create a nuclear weapon. But it cannot be ruled out. If we continue on the path we're on, with more nuclear proliferation, and we fail to get adequate control of nuclear weapons materials throughout the world, it's going to be an increasingly likely possibility. There's no way to deter terrorists from using nuclear weapons by threat of retaliation. So it could result in the loss of a major city somewhere in the world.

HC: Then there's "Preemptive Attack: Believing one's country to be under nuclear attack." And that can come about by computer error or, as you said, a flock of geese triggering the early-warning system. About to be under such attack, a leader of a nuclear weapons state launches a preemptive nuclear attack, which is what Yeltsin almost did when America launched a weather rocket in Norway.

DK: That's exactly the case. If NORAD were to pick up a flock of geese on the horizon and think that the United States was under nuclear attack, then there'd be a very tough choice for the president of the United States and the commanders who are working under him. Does the United States just wait for the attack to occur or does it launch on warning, even though it may be a false warning?

HC: And that's the policy as we speak?

DK: Our policy is to launch on warning. Steven Starr, director of the clinical laboratory sciences program at the University of Missouri and an expert on the environmental consequences of nuclear war, has been very outspoken in calling for a change in that policy, away from launch on warning so you don't run the risk of initiating a preemptive attack based on false information.

HC: The next one is "Preventive Nuclear War: A nuclear weapons state launches an unprovoked nuclear attack against another country perceived to pose a future threat. An example would be the use by Israel of a small tactical nuclear weapon against deeply buried nuclear facilities in Iran."

DK: I'd like to think that this is not a scenario that any leader or country would even consider, but as we know, it has been talked about and considered in some countries. There's a great deal of concern and hostility coming from Israel and the United States about the possibility of Iran developing a nuclear weapons capability. I certainly do not advocate that Iran or any other country become a nuclear weapons state. It would only add to the problems that currently exist. But to contemplate a preventive nuclear attack would never pass the minimal test of human decency.

HC: Human decency. Let me read from an article that was published by Physicians for Social Responsibility about the possibility of Israel attacking the two nuclear facilities in Iran. They would use three B61-11 nuclear weapons, each 340 kilotons, so that is thirty times larger than the Hiroshima bomb. You'd have three 340 kiloton weapons on Isfahan and Natanz, and they calculated what that would mean:

> From our map we can see that within 48 hours, fallout would cover most of Iran, most of Afghanistan, and spread on into Pakistan and India. Fallout from the use of a burrowing weapon such as the B61-11 would be worse than from a surface or airburst weapon, due to the extra radioactive dust and debris ejected from the blast site. In the immediate area of the two attacks, our calculations show that within 48 hours, an estimated 2.6 million people would die.

That's forty-eight hours.

> About two thirds of those would die from radiation-related causes, either prompt casualties from the immediate radiation effects of the bomb, or from localized fallout. Over one million people would suffer immediate injuries, including thermal and flesh burns, radiation sickness, broken limbs, lacerations, blindness, crush injuries, burst eardrums, and other traumas. In the wider region, over 10.5 million people would be exposed to significant radiation from fallout . . . leading to radiation sickness, future excess cancer deaths, genetic abnormalities in future generations, as well as high rates of stillbirths, miscarriages, malignancies, and hypothyroidism. Most if not all medical facilities near the two attack sites would be destroyed, or located within the radiation "hot zone," and thus unusable. Little or no medical care would be available to the injured in the aftermath of an attack, leading to many avoidable deaths.

That's a scenario which is actually being contemplated as we speak.

DK: Even the possibility of causing that kind of death and suffering is almost beyond our capacity to grasp. But we must grasp it, because as long as nuclear weapons exist in the hands of any country, that possibility exists. Our responsibility is to close the door on that kind of possibility, and the only way to do that effectively is to eliminate nuclear weapons wherever they exist by negotiated agreement—not by physical attack.

HC: The next urgent reason we need to get rid of nuclear weapons is "Escalation of Conventional War: India and Pakistan, for example, engage in further conventional war over Kashmir" and the conflict escalates into a nuclear one. A small nuclear war could escalate to a global nuclear holocaust between Russia and America, right?

DK: The main point with that particular scenario is that you could have a conventional war spiral out of control, and, if one side feels it's losing and doesn't see any other possibility, it escalates to the use of a nuclear weapon or many nuclear weapons. The other side then retaliates in kind, and before you know it, you have a situation that, even without Russia and the United States coming in, could lead to the deaths of hundreds of millions. Obviously that's an incredibly serious situation.

HC: Now the next issue is "Military Parity: In a conventional war, Russia defaults to nuclear weapons due to its deteriorating conventional military capability."

DK: It's actually the opposite of the situation that existed through most of the Cold War, when the United States and Europe thought that they were in an inferior position vis-à-vis Soviet conventional forces. Now Russia perceives its conventional forces to be far weaker than those of the United States and the West in general. Should we get back into a situation of conflict with the Russians, and war were to break out, the Russians might feel compelled to rely upon nuclear weapons to protect themselves. Obviously, it is not a very effective means of protection, but an imbalance in conventional forces creates an impetus to rely on nuclear weapons so long as they exist.

HC: The next one is an "Irrational Leader: An unstable and paranoid leader, fearing attack and/or regime change, launches an attack against perceived adversaries. There are no democratic controls."

DK: That is something that is always possible. If we look around at the leadership of nuclear weapon states throughout the nuclear age, their leaders are not all rational. You'd be hard-pressed to find Richard Nixon, for example, to have been a rational leader, particularly when under serious stress while he was being impeached. For people who might think we're picking on the United States with examples, you also have the leadership of North Korea. But rationality, an absolute prerequisite for nuclear deterrence, is not always there.

HC: The other thing is that plutonium, which is made in nuclear reactors, lasts for half a million years; it is the fuel for nuclear weapons. You only need ten pounds to make yourself a bomb. So we may let countries under the nonproliferation treaty have nuclear power plants, and there may be rational leaders there, but you never know in the next generation. Look at Iran, for instance. They had Mossadegh, who BP and other oil companies deposed, and then they got the shah of Iran, who was less than rational, wanting to build nuclear power plants, and America was arming him with weapons of mass destruction. Then they got the ayatollah, who conducted a revolution against the shah, and so we go on. To suggest that, for half a million years, these countries, which now have access to plutonium, will always have rational leaders, stands in the way of rational thinking.

DK: It's very difficult for us to think in terms of that kind of a long timeline, which we should be doing. Even if you restrict that timeline to one or two generations, we have no guarantees that there will be rational leaders, or even that leaders who appear rational today won't become irrational under certain conditions or stress. I think that most leaders are rational at most times, but that's not good enough. And foolproof systems aren't good enough, because such systems would require rationality, a key element of deterrence. But rather than rely upon what we think are foolproof systems, which are beyond our capacity to create, we need to abolish the weapons to end the potential for annihilation.

HC: The next one is a "Rational Leader: A leader, making what he or she deems to be rational calculations, launches a nuclear attack against perceived adversaries to assure the survival of his country. There are no democratic controls."

DK: People understand that irrational leaders pose a serious problem in trying to create a foolproof system against a nuclear attack. It also is true that a rational leader could make a decision, believing his or her country is endangered to the point where its survival is at stake, to bring out its last trump card—its nuclear arsenal—and use it. The result could potentially be millions if not hundreds of millions of deaths as a result of that calculation.

HC: Let's go to the next one. "Prompt Global Strike: The U.S. proceeds with plans to place conventional weapons on some of its intercontinental ballistic missiles. During the launch of one of these missiles, it is mistaken for a nuclear-armed missile, resulting in a retaliatory nuclear attack."

DK: This whole idea of prompt global strike, which is part of the U.S. program for developing its offensive capabilities, opens up some serious concerns for nuclear weapons use. The idea is to take a missile that formerly carried a nuclear warhead and exchange that warhead for a conventional one. You would then have the capacity to strike anywhere on the globe within thirty or forty minutes and take out a very precise target, and to do that with a conventional, rather than nuclear, warhead.

Other countries are never going to be certain about what kind of warhead is on that missile. Once a prompt global strike is initiated, another country might well believe that, under the guise of prompt global strike a nuclear attack has been launched, and then decide to launch a retaliatory nuclear attack and to launch on warning. I don't rule out that danger. I think it's an extremely foolish move on the part of the United States to consider arming ICBMs with conventional warheads.

HC: Wouldn't you call that in itself irrational?

DK: I think it's a systemically irrational move. The United States has become increasingly reliant on using technology to assassinate terrorist leaders, and perhaps others, in other parts of the world. I think more serious discussion needs to take place about this. I don't like nuclear weapons, but I also don't like using predator drones, which are operated like video games. The difference is the drones actually kill people. Of course, you're putting no American citizens directly at risk because nobody's piloting the planes. Ultimately, to do this you have to have a policy of assassination and approve such a policy. And you've got to believe that this kind of technology is reasonable and won't be setting a precedent by which many other countries, or perhaps every country in the world, will be developing this kind of drone technology.

HC: They're using unarmed drones now on the Mexican border. They're using them in Afghanistan and Pakistan to assassinate people, and America's not even at war with Pakistan. There are officers sitting at consoles in Nevada pressing buttons to kill people. It's almost beyond imagination.

DK: The predator drones at the U.S.-Mexican border may be only for surveillance.

HC: Now the last one is "Intentional Nuclear War: Tensions and conflict between major nuclear powers mount, leading to an international nuclear war. Civilization is destroyed and complex life on earth is ended."

DK: Often, when we talk about the possibilities of using nuclear weapons, that one is left out—the idea that anybody would use nuclear weapons intentionally. I don't think it can be ignored. As long as these weapons exist, there may be somebody who believes that an intentional nuclear war is the right thing to do. They would be crazy, but perhaps without appearing so; they simply launch a nuclear attack, and that triggers a much larger war that could destroy civilization. That danger is always with us. So long as the weapons are with us, that possibility will exist.

HC: I've been reading *The Sociopath Next Door*, which says that one in twenty-five people are sociopaths. Very charming, highly intelligent people, extremely successful in their careers, but they have absolutely no moral conscience. In the area of politics, the most powerful people rise to the top, and often I think they're sociopaths, like Rumsfeld, Cheney, Wolfowitz, Richard Perle, you can name them. They may seem superficially to be rational, but underneath they're really disturbed. I think that it's time we start looking at the *cause* of war.

And as we have talked, it's felt like we've been talking about really primitive man. Since we've lived in caves, men have always fought for various reasons: to kill marauding tribes, or destroy saber-toothed tigers to protect their women and babies in the caves. That instinct in our reptilian midbrain is still there. And we've moved on from spears, stones, and clubs, to nuclear weapons that can destroy the planet. It seems to me that without actually analyzing and criticizing with a clear rational mind what causes these men to want to kill—and to use this incredibly rational language to justify it—that we'll get nowhere.

DK: I think what you're saying is right. I would imagine that, if it were looked at closely, sociopathic behavior is more concentrated in political leaders than in the general population. I think that has to do with the drive for power and a high level of conformity to national security policy. National leaders tend to promote national security. One of the most important issues of our time is that powerful technologies, including our nuclear weapons technology, have made it necessary to move from national security to global security. I don't think most leaders have made that necessary evolutionary leap. I talk about it in terms of moving from MAD—which I see as either Mutually Assured Destruction, or perhaps more appropriately today as Mutually Assured Delusions—to a new acronym, PASS: Planetary Assured Security and Survival. We need to choose national leaders who recognize our current dilemma and who understand that national security isn't any longer possible in a world with nuclear weapons—weapons that undermine *planetary* security and survival. That's the kind of transformational leap that needs to be made now. ∼

CAROLE GALLAGHER

Carole Gallagher achieved much success as a photographer with exhibitions at the Castelli Gallery in 1978 and 1981. She exhibited in museums and galleries nationally and internationally before moving to Utah in 1983. There she began work on a documentary book on the effects of nuclear testing in Nevada, *American Ground Zero: The Secret Nuclear War*, which was published in 1993. In 1997 Carole Gallagher began work on a documentary about the sickened veterans of the first Gulf War. After seven years of work, she was disabled in an accident and had to put aside this documentary project. For the last several years she's been alternating between writing and recovering.

———

HELEN CALDICOTT: Your book, *American Ground Zero: The Secret Nuclear War*, is full of the most extraordinary photographs. What these people endured as the nuclear testing occurred is also extraordinary. I want to read from the foreword by Keith Schneider:

> Over the next 12 years, [from 1951 in the United States], the government's nuclear cold warriors detonated 126 atomic bombs into the atmosphere at the 1,350-square-mile Nevada Test Site. Each

of the pink clouds that drifted across the flat mesas and forbidden valleys of the atomic proving grounds contained levels of radiation comparable to the amount released after the explosion in 1986 of the Soviet nuclear reactor at Chernobyl.

I'll repeat that: each of the bombs exploded at the Nevada test site contained amounts of radiation comparable to that released at the explosion in 1986 of Chernobyl. There's a map in the book of areas of the continental United States crossed by more than one nuclear cloud from aboveground detonations: one nuclear cloud equals one Chernobyl explosion, which contaminated 40 percent of Europe for hundreds of thousands of years. Virtually the whole of the United States is covered with fallout. Many of these clouds intersected and combined right over to the East Coast. New York got a lot.

CAROLE GALLAGHER: That's right.

HC: I think this book should become compulsory reading for every child in secondary school, and every American citizen. I know a lot about radiation, but these people were exposed to experimentation and were lied to again and again. Thousands died of leukemia and cancer. What got you to start documenting what happened in Utah, Nevada, and South Dakota?

CG: I was a child in the fifties, and I remember that these explosions at the Nevada Test Site were viewed as making history. Walter Cronkite would report on television from News Nob, the place for the press to observe the detonations at the Nevada Test Site. It was made to sound awesome, and it was a macho-building exercise. This was a scientific program that was not necessary. Even Robert Oppenheimer said that testing was something that should never be done.

HC: Robert Oppenheimer was the father of atomic weapons, the director of the Manhattan Project, correct?

CG: Yes. And Edward Teller, a much less admirable character, the father of the H-bomb, stated that when it comes to nuclear power plants you must not build them unless you can build them five miles underground. These were scientists who knew the effects of fallout and of the radiation. They just decided to use it as a boondoggle, a scientific program of experimentation. By the end, when we were about to get a test ban treaty for aboveground tests in 1963, they were exploding a nuclear bomb a week just to get their inventory used. In the test site documents from the Atomic Energy Commission [AEC] they listed Alamogordo, the first nuclear test, and Trinity, the very first bomb exploded in New Mexico. Hiroshima and Nagasaki were also listed as tests. All of this can be found in a report from the Department of Energy, "Announced United States Nuclear Tests: July 1945 through December 1983," prepared by the Office of Public Affairs in cooperation with the Los Alamos National Laboratory, Lawrence Livermore National Laboratory, and Sandia National Laboratories. The tests in the Pacific became prohibitively expensive. They wanted a test site closer to Los Alamos and the other places where the bomb material was produced. They chose this test site north of Las Vegas.

HC: The tests in the Pacific, I believe, were mostly hydrogen bombs that were vastly bigger than the ones exploded at the Nevada Test Site. Over what period of time were the bombs tested in the Pacific?

CG: From 1945, right after Hiroshima and Nagasaki, through 1962. Our first tests in the Pacific were at Bikini Atoll in July 1946. The last were detonated over Johnston Island in November 1962. They were testing hydrogen bombs in the Pacific because they said they would never explode a hydrogen bomb on domestic soil, but they did. There was at least one hydrogen bomb exploded into the atmosphere at the Nevada Test Site.

HC: What was it called?

CG: That was Simon. It was a huge test.

HC: How many megatons?

CG: Simon was a test geared toward developing the TX-17/24 thermonuclear weapon design. The TX-17 and TX-24 were physically the largest and heaviest weapons, and among the highest yield weapons, ever deployed by the United States. The predicted yield was thirty-five to forty kilotons.*

HC: An atomic bomb is made of plutonium or enriched uranium. The ones that were first tested—Trinity, named after the father, son, and holy ghost, Hiroshima, meaning Little Boy, and Nagasaki, Fat Man—were small bombs, about thirteen kilotons. I think there's a hot place reserved in hell for Edward Teller, who designed the hydrogen bomb, which uses an atomic bomb only as a trigger mechanism. Some of them are fifty megatons, which is equivalent to 50 million tons of TNT. Most of the weapons in the arsenals of America and Russia now are hydrogen bombs. That's Teller's legacy.

What triggered you to be interested in this and be interested in these places?

CG: I was five years old in 1955, and the bombs were being tested. Nuclear weapons had been on earth for ten years. I lived in Brooklyn, New York, in a beautiful part named Bay Ridge. I asked my father how many miles we were from Times Square and, if a hydrogen bomb exploded in Times Square, whether we would survive. I was a little ahead of my time. It was seven miles away, and my father got this incredible look on his face. I sometimes think the looks tell it all. He said we'd be perfectly safe. The cloud would not be out as far as where we were living in Brooklyn.

I became interested in anything nuclear, including nuclear power. Later, I did reports on it in school.

---

* A kiloton (kt) is a unit that measures the explosive power of an atomic weapon. One kiloton is equal to the power of one thousand metric tons of TNT.

HC: But when you were five, how did you know about this?

CG: From television. Walter Cronkite was reporting from the test sites, and I was amazed that this killer bomb could be exploded again. Then I learned that they had been doing them in Nevada since I was one year old. I thought, What happens to the people in Nevada? The AEC said the West was relatively uninhabited. The people downwind started to call themselves "relative uninhabitants," because there were 250,000 people living within 250 miles of ground zero at the test site. A quarter of a million!

The fallout clouds would drift up into the Rocky Mountains, and the fallout would get in the snow. The Wasatch Front of the Rockies in Utah are famous for alpine skiing, very beautiful. People would be skiing in radioactive snow. The same was happening going up into South Dakota. Dr. John Willard Sr., a professor at the School of Mines in Rapid City, was working for the AEC. When he discovered that the puddles in the streets were radioactive, they sounded a civil defense alert in the town before informing the AEC. Dr. Willard was summoned down to the AEC headquarters in Nevada and was reprimanded. In many ways the testing program was secret, but it was also dangerous, well publicized, and it was a macho thing. It's still a macho thing for countries getting the bomb. It's as if you can't be a power on the planet unless you have a nuclear weapon.

HC: It's still a macho thing in the military. And the scientific community involved is still designing hydrogen bombs. The populations who were most intimately exposed time and time again are described in your book. What happened when the bombs exploded? I read that people were covered in a sort of dust and the children played in it thinking it was snow.

CG: Utah, parts of Nevada, and Idaho. The areas of the West around Salt Lake City are largely Mormon. Salt Lake City was the place where the Mormons escaped to. They walked across the plains with their belongings to escape religious persecution in the East.

Very brave, intrepid people. This was their land. They were people who believed that the government was divinely inspired, and that the Constitution was given to us directly by God, through revelation and other rather authoritarian-loving ideas. These were not people who were going to object. The church itself made a point in the weekly meetings to say that the atomic testing was a good thing and that they were participating in a moment of history. The schools had these road shows in which a general would come in and tell them how lucky they were to be living at this time in history. The schoolteachers would actually bring their classes out to watch the bombs go off.

Joanne Workman, a Utah resident, described children in a geology class who, after the cloud went over, were instructed to stay out for five hours to identify geology specimens. When Joanne Workman returned home to the town of St. George, there were police at the entry point washing off vehicles, because all the vehicles were loaded with radiation. By the time she got home, ran her fingers through her hair, and tried to brush out the fallout, her scalp was so badly burned that it just lifted right off in the hairbrush and never grew back. She had tremendous radiation burn. By the time she was in her forties she'd had five different types of cancer. She coped by moving to California to become part of an experiment in cancer treatment at Stanford University. In order to participate, she had to sign paperwork stating that she would never sue the government or the university for exposure to the atomic bomb.

HC: The regents of the University of California oversee the Lawrence Livermore labs and Los Alamos. So on one hand they're educating students to live a good and healthy life, and on the other they're working to blow up the students.

CG: The collaboration between the church being faithful to the government and all of that caused the University of Utah, a world-class institution now but a rather small, primarily agricultural college at the time, to get several very lucrative government contracts in the sciences. One was for a cancer study of leukemia, and another was for a study on thyroid cancer. There were whole wards of children with leukemia. There was a scientific program that involved going down to southern Utah to take out the bricks from people's houses and see how much radiation had penetrated the houses. From grants to build a tremendous computer lab, one of the best in the world, to the artificial heart—you name it. They got federal contracts and scientific awards to proceed with all sorts of experimentation.

HC: It leaves me feeling speechless. I want you to elucidate some of the case histories that particularly stick in your memory, from when you photographed these people and took their verbal recollections.

CG: Martha Bordoli Laird's family lived on a ranch just north of the test site. When they started to fire atomic bombs from cannons, they could actually see the cannons and the bombs go off from their front door. These are people living right due north of the test site, a huge area the size of Rhode Island. The fallout would come over their land—

HC: They were actually in a nuclear war.

CG: Everyone really was. It was just testing, testing, testing for what we [humans] could stand, health-wise and otherwise. The bomb going off shattered their windows. Every once in a while the AEC chap would come along and ask them how they were doing. One time one of them brought his daughter, and the daughter loved the ranch so much and the people living there that she wanted to stay. Of course, the owner of the ranch saw the AEC fellow's eyebrows go up into his forehead. He wasn't going to let his daughter stay there any longer than she had to.

Martha Laird's son, Butch, got leukemia by the time he was five, and her husband died of lung cancer at a very young age. She gave birth to a baby who was blackened in his body and shriveled from the waist down, and her two other daughters have had subcutaneous cancers. Finally she had to sell that ranch, and she moved to northwestern Nevada. She lost everything. The ranch wasn't worth anything, because it was near the test site. I photographed her in a barn. Her second husband was a hunter, and they had the heads of two slain deer hanging up to dry in the barn. In the photograph she is holding two photographs. One was of the one-room schoolhouse in that community, with the fallout cloud approaching it. The fallout cloud looked like a huge thunderhead, and she said she could stand on the mountain and see the thunderhead coming with the tail, the stem of the atomic bomb dragging behind it. Then she had another picture of the kids in the one-room schoolhouse. There were only about five or six students and their teacher. By that time they were all dead. There was so much constant radiation, and they were so close to it. It went on from 1951 to 1963.

HC: Is there an estimate of how many people died from malignancies in that quarter of a million population?

CG: There isn't because if somebody dies of cancer, the death record will not necessarily say they died of cancer. If they died of extenuating circumstances secondary to chemo, like pneumonia, then it would say they died of pneumonia.

HC: So the doctors were kind of like the Nazi doctors. They participated in this nuclear genocide.

CG: I can't go that far, because I don't understand the culture. I don't care to make judgments about it. But the truth was that there were tons of kids in those hospitals in Salt Lake, since there were no big hospitals in southern Utah that had leukemia treatment. As time went on people in their thirties and forties started to die. If they were treated with chemo and got an infection, the infection would be called the cause of death. This was not necessarily happening in other places.

HC: When you do a death certificate, you say the cause of death was pneumonia, but you always say, for example, secondary to carcinoma of the liver. Did they do that?

CG: No, they didn't do that.

HC: I have to say, as a medical doctor, these people, my colleagues, were participating in nuclear genocide. The fact that no one has the documentation or the epidemiology of the number of people who died, the doses of internal and external exposure to radiation, what cancers they died of, and how old they were, is a crime.

CG: It is criminal, but there is epidemiology going on at the University of Utah that is federally funded. I think if you take the king's penny, you do the king's bidding. There has been definite corroboration by people who worked on the studies that the numbers were being jiggled. A death certificate is one thing; maybe an underling does it and gets instructions. But I do know that the studies themselves far underrate the level of cancers that happened, both thyroid and leukemia. They would feel the nodules on the thyroids of people, but they wouldn't remove their thyroids necessarily. They would give palliative care, but not always surgical care.

HC: Why?

CG: They were watching over thirty years to see what the difference would be between a nodule from radioactive iodine and other kinds of thyroid cancers. The truth is, by the time baby boomers die, if they die in their eighties, everybody will have at least one thyroid cancer cell, because we all drank the milk. I had thyroid problems in 1964, shortly after that full year of exploding a bomb a week, because the radiation was going over the dairy country in upstate New York and I was drinking milk.

HC: The CDC [Centers for Disease Control] did a study on the fallout across America and the number of thyroid cancers specifically.

CG: In 1997 the National Cancer Institute, NCI, did that study with maps. They showed how many people and which counties experienced the worst exposure across the country.

HC: Was it ten thousand people they estimated had developed thyroid cancer?

CG: I'm not sure offhand of the precise number, but certainly it's going to increase. I have Hashimoto's disease, an immune disorder that has destroyed my thyroid. I went from having thyroid disease at fourteen to having Hashimoto's disease at fifty-seven.

The blood and bones develop cancers from radioactive cesium and strontium, because they're calcium imitators. The death estimate of people on planet Earth from all the nuclear tests is 6,290,000 people. Physicians for Social Responsibility estimated that number. If one in three people who get cancer die, then there's 12 or 13 million people who have gotten cancer from testing worldwide.

HC: Can you walk us through that reasoning? I thought one in three people would develop some type of cancer, not necessarily die of it.

CG: Of the people who get cancer, one in three die of it. We know for breast cancer that it's one in eight in the United States. For 6,290,000 people dying, a lot more people have gotten cancer and survived. So some people have survived cancer caused by fallout and radiation. We have no way of knowing, because these numbers are apparently not worth studying. You're not going to give a federal grant to find out that you've killed 6 million people or more.

HC: Did that figure come from John Gofman?

CG: Yes. He was the only doctor who worked on the Manhattan Project and came forth to speak out. He paid dearly for it, but he gave me most of the numbers before I published the book.

HC: He was my mentor. I read his book *Poisoned Power* in 1975.

I had never known anything about nuclear power, only that bombs vaporize people. It was my first introduction to the medical implications of nuclear power, nuclear fission, fallout, and the like. Your book, *American Ground Zero: The Secret Nuclear War*, is the most extraordinary book documenting the medical histories of these lovely and innocent people.

CG: Sweet people, really sweet people.

HC: They didn't even take the government on. Some of them got angry, but some of them remained patriotic until the end.

CG: They're fighting very hard now in northern Utah to have that part of the state compensated the way the southern part of the state was. I said to one of these activists, in the late 1980s, Do you actually think that there was a fence or a wall high enough to stop the radiation mid-state, so that Salt Lake City never got any radiation? She was allegedly a journalist, and you could see her eyes sort of popping open, because *she* had thyroid cancer. She was about thirty then, and her sister died of lupus. Now her other sister has multiple sclerosis. Everybody was told it was only southern Utah, because that area was so close to the Nevada Test Site.

HC: And they believed it?

CG: Yes. But we know that the fallout went across the country, which is why Richard Miller's map at the beginning of the book is so important. You can see a cloud here, there; it's over your hometown, your grandmother's hometown. We all got irradiated one way or another.

HC: For this project, how long were you in the West? How long did it take you to take all these photographs and oral histories?

CG: It took about ten years altogether. I lived there for seven years, and then the harassment got so intense that I had to get the police in on it. There were nightly death threats for many months by phone. I thought it wasn't worth losing my life over—I'd had cars totaled, my apartment had been broken into many times—so I figured I could commute for the next three years. I started being interested in 1979, and I moved to Utah in 1983. I left in 1990 and was very happy to leave. I published the book with The MIT Press in 1993.

HC: How were you received in Utah when you moved there to do the research?

CG: As a pariah. There are many sociological reasons. You have a state that's all one demographic; everybody's Mormon, everybody's blond, blue-eyed, and intermarried—and everybody knows everybody. It's a small state. There weren't more than a million people in the whole state at the time. Suddenly somebody new shows up. An outsider is not appreciated until she converts, and I wasn't going to convert. I'm brunette with brown eyes. People would come up to me and say, crinkling their noses, Are you Jewish? And I'd say no, I'm Irish and Italian and this is how it looks. I stopped saying I was from New York, because everybody hates New York in the West, in the heartland, and in other places. All they know about New York is what they see on television, a fantasy of some kind of sadistic place. I would say I was from the state historical society in Salt Lake City, which I was.

HC: On the other hand, you said that your naïveté and your innocence, in a way, allowed the people's trust in you to build. You must have impressed so many of these local people for them to tell you their most intimate stories.

CG: They were in a state of desperation and so was I. I was living on next to no money, and I had dropped about forty pounds from lack of food. It was a struggle. I didn't have money for gas, so I had to walk to the interviews with all my equipment. I think people could sense that. You know that saying, "Never let them see you sweat"? Well, I was sweating and they were sweating. Then they would begin to tell their story. They would start crying and I would start crying. It was impossible not to have an empathetic reaction to people who have told you these stories—stories that you could never dream in your worst nightmare. Children walking down the aisles of McDonald's with wigs on because they're being treated for leukemia. And not just the first generation, but the second and the third. People didn't even know that they had been exposed, people who may have lost sixteen people in their immediate family. The survivors would have children born with leukemia because the genetic makeup was changed by the radiation. The energy of the radiation would break the DNA, and you'd have a cancer-producing gene in three generations.

HC: And a lot of Down syndrome, mentally retarded children, and congenital anomalies.

CG: It's getting to the point where immune system diseases in baby boomers are becoming commonplace. It's like adding ten years of mileage to your car. When you're exposed to radiation like that, you're giving up ten years of your life.

HC: Were you harassed by the AEC and their people?

CG: No. I had mail tampering, but I don't know what that was about. There's no way I can prove anything. I realized when I was there that paranoia would be my worst enemy, so I ignored it. It turned out that the people who were making the nightly death threats—I had the police tap my phone to find out who it was—were part of a downwinders' group that was very upset that I had received a grant from the MacArthur Foundation. They started spreading slander that I kept them from getting any money from foundations. This kind of abuse has gone on now for more than twenty years. I'm fighting plagiarism cases, one that involves a woman writing a play based on my book without any attribution. She had a stalking injunction put out against me. I live in another state, I'm disabled, and I cannot fly or drive very far, but she said in legal papers that she feared for her life. It's called "the Long Arm of Utah Law." They had the sheriff come here to my house in Colorado to serve me with civil stalking injunction papers! These ruthless people have not given up, because I'm an "outsider." No matter how hard I've worked to see that they get justice.

HC: The people who killed their fellow countrymen knew damn well about radiation. I've read an article by Oppenheimer and he knew. They all knew. I worked with a lot of the fellows who were in the Manhattan Project, talking about the medical effects of nuclear weapons. They never talked about the downwinders. They were so guilt-ridden about Hiroshima, Nagasaki, and the arms race that they developed nuclear power to salve their consciences. But they knew about these downwinders.

CG: And the test site workers on site day after day. The atomic veterans. I've never had my heart broken so much as by the atomic veterans.

HC: Tell us what they told you.

CG: These were soldiers, either put in foxholes or told to stand on the side of a hill or just on plain level ground three miles from ground zero, some six miles, without protection at all. One man, Robert Carter, told me that they were on the mountainside, and he refused to put his hands over his eyes like they were told to because the soldiers would say they could see their skeletons. The light was that bright. All of a sudden his whole platoon is up in the air, thirty to forty feet, from the shock wave. They're like tin soldiers thrown in the air. Once they recovered from that, they're vomiting, put on a bus, and driven to ground zero to do military maneuvers right on the same spot where the bomb went off. What Robert Carter told me, and I had to get corroboration from other soldiers because it sounded too crazy to me, is that he saw people near ground zero in cages. People in hurricane-fence kinds of enclosures, handcuffed to the fences with what was left of their trousers on.

They were doing human experiments. I started looking into that. I interviewed the man in charge of the airplane that brought men from Panama *in cages* to the test site. I ran out of his house. I just didn't want to hear anymore. He was also involved in some of the chemical weapons experiments. He ripped open his shirt and showed me his chest, which was all scarred from chemical weapons tests at Fort Detrick, Maryland.

I've seen it all, and the major thing for any journalist is verification. I had to verify Robert Carter, and I got his story verified not only by other soldiers who had been there, but by the man who had actually brought the people to be experimented upon.

HC: They did this to see how humans could survive in a radioactive environment after a nuclear war, and how soldiers could operate. It was a military, scientific, and medical maneuver.

CG: It was psychological more than anything. All the victims say they were guinea pigs. They knew that these men would come down with terrible diseases. What they were really checking on at that point was what human beings could endure psychologically.

HC: Did they follow these men during their lives?

CG: Very briefly. Robert Carter, the man I mentioned who saw the people in the cages, was taken in by the AEC and questioned. When he said that he had seen that, they started medicating him and told him if he ever told anybody that he saw that, he would be court-martialed and they would go after his family. From what I know, they were not given any care for post-traumatic stress disorder [PTSD]. At the time, soldiers came back from World War II with shell shock. Vietnam vets were coming back with PTSD and other mental illnesses, and those soldiers were not taken care of either.

HC: Whistle-blowers in the nuclear power industry are often removed from their jobs and given psychiatric treatment. It sounds like Russia!

CG: [*sarcastically*] Well, whistle-blowing is not a good state of mind.

HC: How was *American Ground Zero* received by the people in Utah and Salt Lake City?

CG: There were pockets of intellectuals and academics at the University of Utah, and some in the art and literary circles in Salt Lake, who got really frightened. One reviewer said it was the most frightening thing he'd ever heard of in his life. People were getting seriously messed up in their heads about a project that had been published by a very serious publisher—MIT—that had exposed this for what it was. But then the Mormon Church took it off the bookshelves at Brigham Young University, saying it wasn't true. There was a demonstration of students who had lost parents and siblings and were saying, It is true, it is absolutely true.

That was Utah. The rest of the world embraced it, especially out-side of the United States. I had interviewers from Norway, France, and several other countries coming to my house. Somehow it seemed more believable to people who were not Americans. Why would Americans want to believe we could do this? It's the most horrifying thing that you could ever think of, doing nuclear experiments on your own people and essentially carrying out a nuclear war within the confines of your own country. Plus, the underground tests after 1963 leaked a lot of radiation as well.

HC: How many aboveground tests did they do in the Pacific and in America?

CG: There were 106 atmospheric nuclear weapons tests in the Pa-cific. I'll defer to the estimate of my friend Stephen Schwartz, au-thor of *Atomic Audit: The Costs and Consequences of U.S. Nuclear*

Weapons Since 1940. In the official U.S. testing history, from 1951 to 1992, there were a total of 904 U.S. tests at the Nevada Test Site [NTS]: 100 atmospheric and 804 underground. In addition, there were seven tests in Nevada outside the NTS: five at Nellis Air Force Range, one in Fallon, and one in central Nevada. And finally, there were twenty-four joint U.S.-U.K. underground nuclear tests at NTS.

In all, there were 935 nuclear tests in Nevada: 105 in the atmosphere and 830 underground. The total number of U.S. detonations is 1,054, but keep in mind that number includes Nevada, the Pacific, and everywhere else. It also includes the twenty-four joint U.S.-UK tests. Some tests involved more than one device, hence the discrepancy between total tests and detonations. The really big ones were in the Pacific. They thought they could move the people from their island; after all, they're savages who can just be moved to another palm tree island.

HC: Didn't someone compare them to mice?

CG: A quote I included in my book reads, "It's true they're savages, but they're more like us than mice."

HC: Who said that?

CG: One of the AEC fellows. It's amazing what can be done in the name of national security.

HC: Everyone should get an emotional understanding of how the nuclear age began.

CG: And how sweet these people were that met with me. The faces of these people, their kindness and their goodness . . . that's the part that reminds me of people being taken on the trains to the death camps. The sweet faces of people that couldn't believe what was happening. Trusting and encouraged to trust. I think the encouragement is what irked me the most. Who's encouraging these people to die? Who's telling them the big lie and saying this is a moment in history, and you should be grateful to be a part of it?

HC: As you said, Oppenheimer comes up smelling like roses and Edward Teller was the really wicked person who destroyed Oppenheimer. Oppenheimer died of lung cancer, a voracious smoker. But in fact Oppenheimer was part of this cover-up, and he liked to see the weapons tested. Who knows how many other scientists participated in this moral and medical outrage.

CG: It's not just the physicists; it's also the medical doctors and the people who examine people with skin peeling off and hair falling out, saying to women that they had housewife syndrome or that they were neurotic.

HC: They had acute radiation sickness. We knew that from the Hiroshima and Nagasaki data.

CG: I have a fresh admiration for the people of Utah and other Mormon areas of the country who had the guts to come forward and speak up when they were encouraged not to. Many were pushed almost to the point of excommunication if they spoke up against the bomb, and yet they did. They had a moral sense. A religion can give you a moral sense and it also can do evil things. The evil part is any kind of collaboration that could allow people to be murdered.

JONATHAN SCHELL

Jonathan Schell has been writing and speaking about the global nuclear situation for more than twenty years. He is the Doris M. Shaffer Fellow at The Nation Institute, the peace and disarmament correspondent for *The Nation* magazine, and a visiting lecturer at Yale University, where he teaches one course on the nuclear dilemma and another on nonviolent political action. Jonathan Schell began his career at the *New Yorker* as a staff writer in 1967 and published *The Fate of the Earth* in 1982. He has published over a dozen books and is frequently consulted by members of Congress and the media. His articles on the nuclear question include essays in *Foreign Affairs* and *Harper's*, of which he has become a contributing editor.

———◇◇◇———

HELEN CALDICOTT: Your book *The Fate of the Earth* for me was a turning point. It summed up where I stood and my fears at the time in a lovely philosophical way. I think we need to proceed from that book, where you talked about the fact that the Earth could be annihilated by nuclear war, to the present time. It's twenty-seven years. Do you want to summarize from there to now?

JONATHAN SCHELL: Let me talk a bit first about the surrounding context. In 1945, when the bomb was born into the world, it became quickly apparent to certain people, certainly to all scientists, that this was an invention that could put an end to the human species if we built enough of those weapons. We went ahead during the Cold War. At that time people became acutely aware of living under the shadow of extinction. But that problem existed in a kind of weird and lonely isolation from other issues. For one thing, it was so inconceivably huge that it bore no relation to the kind of historical issue that it agitated in previous centuries, so it was really sort of incomprehensible to many people. By the way—that admiration runs two ways, from me to you regarding your wonderful activities in the eighties and thereafter on this issue. But it came in kind of a boom and a bust, in terms of attention to the issue. One of the issues was that we had no context for it. I think there is a proper context since then that has emerged, and that is really the broader ecological threat to the ecosphere of the Earth that comes in many forms.

Scientists are saying that as many as 50 percent of existing species could be extinct at the end of this century if we could continue on the present path. Then, as we're so acutely aware these days, global warming has the capacity, like nuclear war, to change the conditions of life on the planet to drastically mutilate and whittle back the resources of life on a global basis. To me it's as if the nuclear question was a sort of Mount Everest in the midst of a Himalayan range that hadn't risen out of the plain yet. Now we see the rest of the mountain range rising up, and so we're in a position to understand that we're in a much broader crisis.

Crisis is a funny word to use, because this is one for the ages, extending over decades and centuries. We think of a crisis as something sharp and short and something we have to deal with tomorrow. But in any case, I think we have to see the nuclear question in that broader context, which is only now occurring.

HC: But we've lived with this threat for so long, haven't we? In the eighties there was an acute anxiety. But I think that we moved on and developed what Robert Jay Lifton termed "psychic numbing" to other more immediate effects that our psyches could encompass. Like the Iraq War and the World Trade Center towers. We can easily understand that. While the nuclear threat, hovering over us like a sort of death cloud, disappeared over the horizon.

JS: It's absolutely true that if one was speaking of it, as you and I were in the year 1995, we were really talking to empty bleachers. Less so today; we want to acknowledge that the end of the Cold War did remove the chief political motivation that might have led to a full-scale nuclear holocaust. People, and certainly I was one of them, heaved a huge sigh of relief and thought, Well, we've come out of the end of that nightmare, but the great mistake that people made was to have thought that nuclear danger was coeval with the Cold War. That the two were really one and the same, and if the Cold War ended, nuclear danger had also ended. But really what was happening was that it was about to change shape. And the change in shape took the form of proliferation.

HC: Not just that. It was the fact that America and Russia maintained their arsenals on hair-trigger alert. I was always worried, not so much that these weapons would be launched at a time of political crisis, but about accidents and computers malfunctioning and human beings malfunctioning. That did not change.

JS: One of the great illusions of our period is that nuclear danger emanates from proliferation alone, because on the one hand there's fresh danger, whereas on the other hand the nuclear arsenals of the Cold War were reduced in likelihood of use. But—and this was the mute key in my mind in the development of the nuclear age—it's been very much including proliferation in that silence, in that period of declaring or imagining that the nuclear danger was over. Russia and the United States and the other powers held onto their arsenals, so they were removed from view but not removed from reality. They stayed there and exercised a kind of hidden malign influence. So we managed this concealment of our own arsenals from ourselves, and weirdly including even the Russian arsenal, although that's pointed right at our noses here in the United States. That concealment prevented us from understanding proliferation. Not until you see your own arsenal can you understand the reasons other countries are going to get that stuff.

HC: Israel has, they say, from two hundred to four hundred hydrogen bombs. It's a model prototype for other countries in the Middle East. Why shouldn't they get bombs if Israel does? It's the same with the rest of the world. Russia and America still have vast nuclear arsenals ready to launch by either President Putin or now Obama. It's a model for leaders of other countries. You put it beautifully in your essay in *The Nation* very recently when you said that the attitude is, "Well, we've got nuclear weapons and you can't have any, because you're inconsequential and we're the boss." I never can get away from the fact that it's Russia and America that threaten life on Earth, still, as they have for so many years. So, if Iran—I don't think it's going to build a nuclear weapon from all evidence—builds one bomb, it could blow up a city. But Russia and America could destroy almost all life on Earth, and I think proliferation could provoke that exchange between Russia and America. If Pakistan used some against India, and vice versa, that could trigger a global nuclear war. Do you agree?

JS: Yes I do. One of the immense mistakes of the whole nuclear age, which we are in now, is to try to partition this danger into various segments and just look at one or the other. You just described the attempt to speak as if proliferation alone is the danger, whereas we know the motherlode of nuclear weapons, upward of 95 percent of them, are in the hands of Russia and the United States, still on hairtrigger alert, and serving as a motivation for proliferation. That goes back to 1945. If you recall, at that time the United States was the only country that had the atomic bomb, and the dominant opinion was that the United States could hold that monopoly for ten or twenty years. Of course, Russia got it in 1949, and ever since then a steadily expanding club of nuclear powers have thought, "Okay, we can draw the line here, we can draw the line with us." Not understanding the prime maxim of the nuclear age, which is that as long as any country has nuclear weapons, other countries will try to get them. So to state what's so blindingly obvious: the key to stopping proliferation is full nuclear disarmament. And the cost of stopping proliferation is getting rid of your own nuclear weapons. That's an axiom of the nuclear age. Maybe this time we can learn it; there have been a few promising signs.

HC: It's funny, isn't it, the psychological attraction that scientists in the nuclear sphere have to these weapons. When I interviewed Ted Taylor, the man who invented the suitcase hydrogen bomb but became violently opposed to nuclear weapons, he started describing the explosion of a hydrogen bomb, and he got so excited. I said, "You're addicted to these explosions, aren't you?" He said, "Yes, I am." Have you thought about that from a male point of view?

JS: I'll tell you my theory about gender and war. Warfare certainly is a way of doing things that is attractive to men. You have to disregard all of history to deny that. Call it culture, call it nurture, call it genes. Boys . . . men have an attraction to this feuding and all the rest that we see in video games. That whole way of doing things has obviously become dysfunctional, and worse. The nuclear weapon is a key to that, because you can't go on doing it. Before, you could win some wars, and some people would survive, but with nuclear war it's not so. So my thought on this crisis is that this way of doing things has become bankrupt in its own terms, as well as morally. Nature had another gender up her sleeve that conceivably could step forward and maybe do things in a different way. Of course, we get into discussions of whether women are going to do what men did or whether there's going to be something new that's brought into the picture as women move into seeing this as their responsibility. The jury's still out, but I still have the hope that as women break barriers, another instinct will be brought to bear and have a calming influence.

HC: In that context of women and men, in a laboratory in Los Angeles a woman scientist was researching sex hormones, and she noticed that when there was an argument in the lab, the men would go into their rooms, shut the door, and fume, and the women would come in the next day, clean the benches, and make coffee and talk. She thought, "That's really interesting," and she measured the hormone levels in such a situation. The testosterone in the men went sky high. There's a hormone in women called oxytocin, which is produced in labor, and it's the nurturing hormone. And oxytocin went right up. Women, physiologically and psychologically, are the peacemakers. We're not necessarily talking about Indira Gandhi or Golda Meir or Margaret Thatcher, but most women. It's oxytocin time.

JS: Maybe there's a biological basis here.

HC: Let's move on. The *Times* reported that the Obama administration wants to move with Russia quite rapidly toward nuclear disarmament. One thousand weapons on each side instead of ten thousand or five thousand. They're also reconsidering the missile shield in Czechoslovakia and Poland, an idea that has been sold to Russia.

JS: Both of those things, from my point of view, are insufficient but welcome. They are what these two places need: a modest reduction in flat-out insanity. I'm sitting at Yale University, where I still teach that course on the nuclear dilemma.

HC: Is it popular?

JS: I have eighty to a hundred students each year, which is quite a few. There seems to be a reviving curiosity among a generation that really has had no education from the school system or the media. They're saying, "What is this?" It's a desire to know about it again.

HC: Are they worried?

JS: They are worried. And they're getting their minds around it, is my feeling. I try not to propagandize in the classroom and to give them the wherewithal to find their own way through the maze. Maybe they'll find their way to solutions I can't think of. I was going to mention a talk by Jack Matlock, Ronald Reagan's ambassador to the Soviet Union and a supporter of Reagan's idea of abolishing nuclear weapons. One of those political curveballs that we all try to get our minds around. He was saying that Russia and the United States have nothing to fire a pistol over, yet they are still sitting here threatening our existential being. What is that about? It's some dumb momentum carried on from the Cold War, because we just didn't bring the garbage trucks in time to get rid of this garbage.

HC: A kind of psychotic madness, a split between reality and perception of reality. Everyone walks around being totally unaware.

JS: They're not thinking about it, which is one of the great mysteries of this whole age.

HC: I want to talk about Obama now, and the major issues he needs to confront. The economic crisis, the shortage of natural resources as we use more and more and pollute the planet by using them, and the spread of nuclear arms, which we addressed. There is another crisis, the ecological one, which is global warming, and wholesale, human-caused annihilation of species, population growth, water and land shortages, and much else. And last, the failure of the American bid for global empire and the consequent decline of American influence abroad, with Obama. I don't know where it's going. Let's address the decline of the American empire, and what's happened.

JS: I use this phrase "American empire," but I have to add a great big asterisk to that, which is, if there is an American empire, it's radically different from what Rome was, or the Ottoman Empire or the Russian or British empires. In a certain way the whole thing has been a tremendous flop from the start. It's three-quarters a mirage. For example, George Bush decided to reach out and decide what was going to happen in Iraq and Afghanistan and occupy those countries. It looks like neither of those things is going to be possible. Traditionally, when you've had an empire, there's been some countries you've been able to push around and get your way. So the United States has ended up spending a couple of trillion dollars and has been unable to do this in some of the weakest countries in the world. I mean, the British really did run India for a couple hundred years. We do not run Iraq or Afghanistan, in my opinion, any more than we were able to run Vietnam.

HC: But will the United States get the oil?

JS: On the one hand, you get the oil in the sense that that oil is not useful to anybody in Iraq unless they sell it, and we want to buy it. You don't really need a war for oil.

HC: But will your oil companies take over the oil from the Iraqi people?

JS: They would adore doing that, but those projects are not very popular. If you look at Venezuela or Bolivia and their natural resources, the idea that foreigners are going to come in and walk off with the lion's share, even in Saudi Arabia—I don't think that way of doing things is popular. We live in a pretty nationalistic world, one where people have taken over their own countries. I'm not so sure it's going to be easy for the big oil companies to push around other countries.

HC: Globalization is really mostly about American companies but also some European companies, saying, These are our resources. It's happening in Africa, the Congo, and other places full of natural resources that the developed world wants. Do you think the American people are willing to concede that they're not the greatest country on Earth!? Although they have the greatest number of nuclear weapons, would they say, We are part of the family of nations, and we'll work together at the United Nations and elsewhere for the benefit of the majority of the people of the world, and not use up a lot of the world's natural resources—do you think that they can get to that stage?

JS: That's the question that hangs over the Obama administration. Unquestionably a different group of people has come to power. They have, in my opinion, much better instincts. And they're backed by people whose instincts are better still. I don't know whether you were able to take in any of the inauguration, but there was a wonderful concert at the Lincoln Memorial the day before the inauguration. Bruce Springsteen was there, Cat Stevens, and Stevie Wonder. There were black and white people singing together with Lincoln sort of brooding in the background and a wonderful chorus. And of all people, which was really a bold stroke I thought, at the very end they brought out Pete Seeger. Everybody sang "This Land Is Your Land."

HC: I would have wept.

JS: That whole concert, the Obama family was sitting outdoors and taking it all in and sort of nodding to the beat. I have to say that I was very moved by that. It's hard to tell how deep this goes or how broad that spirit is in the United States, but a different America crystallized there, cultural as well as political. That doesn't mean that that spirit is going to be translated into action and prevail, but at least there's the chance of that. I think it's moving and very heartening, even for someone like me who casts a very watchful eye on the whole thing and really wants to see the results as the proof of the pudding.

HC: I think that you put it beautifully in this paragraph in *The Nation*:

> "Reality" has bifurcated in a manner confusing to politicians and citizens alike. On the one side it is political reality, which by definition means centrist, mainstream opinion. On the other side is the reality of events, heading in quite a different direction. If Obama makes mainstream choices, he is called "pragmatic." And it may well be so in political terms, as the poll results attest. But political pragmatism in current circumstances may be real folly, as it was on the evening of the Iraq War and in the years of the finance bubble preceding the crash. Smooth sailing down the middle of the Niagara River carries you over Niagara Falls. The danger is not that Obama's move into the mainstream will offend a tribe called "the left," or his "base" but that by adjusting to a center that is out of touch, he will fail to address the crises adequately and will lose his effectiveness as president.

JS: The premise behind that paragraph is that we've been living at a remove from what is real, certainly in the last eight years, and in many ways for many more years than that. Look at the delusion that we have bought. Weapons of mass destruction in Iraq; imagining that these financial derivatives that Wall Street was putting together had any value behind them. That's a huge bubble that popped. That global warming wasn't real—that's the biggest of these delusions. That we could exploit the world's resources indefinitely. Even with global warming, when a majority of the public probably accepted the reality of it the government was acting in a different way. One of the things that has to happen is, we have to get real. Our major institutions were just lying to us on many of these issues, or deceiving themselves and us, leading us down a garden path in the Bush years and also in the Clinton years. The problem for Obama is that if he adjusts to that mainstream, and he feels that temptation to do things together with Republicans, he may detach himself from what's real out there in the world—from the icebergs that we're heading toward. I want him to be bold and lead.

HC: We've been in a kind of psychosis, particularly in the Bush years. And you write about it beautifully: "The largest government, business, military and media organizations, as if obedient to a single command, began to tell lies to themselves and others in pursuit of or subservience to wealth and power." Then you talk about how these huge bureaucracies, banks, hedge funds, regulatory agencies, intelligence organizations, the White House, the Pentagon and news organizations "can grind inconvenient truth to dust, layer by bureaucratic layer, until the convenient lies that have been wanted all along are presented to the satisfied money- or war-hungry decision-makers at the top."

JS: One question in my mind is, Why did this happen? And why all at once did so many institutions start to lie to themselves? I can't help thinking that you can't reduce every problem to one problem. I begin the article with a quote from Euripides, which I would mangle—maybe you have it?

HC: "I see the work of the gods who pile tower-high the pride of those who were nothing and dash present grandeur down." I think lying to yourself is something that happens when you go after power and glory that is not reachable. This is the old story, to use the now cliché of hubris; these problems don't originate in external threats like an enemy but have germs in your own behavior and your own conception of yourself in regard to the mass of the universe. Regarding the financial, the United States succumbed to the allure of the idea that we were really history's commander. For the globe as a whole this was not only morally, but ethically, as it so often is, a delusion. When you've become enchanted with your own power you're less likely to have a grip on what's real. I think something like that happened to the United States, starting with the end of the Cold War, and the neocons getting together and writing out the amazing documents that really said, We're the leaders now, and that's it. You put it well: "One group of nations, led by the United States, lays claim to the lion's share of the world's wealth, to an exclusive right to possess nuclear weapons, to a disproportionate right to pollute the environment and even to a dominant position in world councils, while everyone else is expected to accept second-class status." Then you say, "Since solutions to all the crises must be global to succeed, and global agreement can only be based on equity, the path to success is cut off."

JS: We do have globalization, and to a certain extent it's irreversible. I don't mean that the economic system can't be drastically changed, but we have the Internet, the global environment. And when you have problems on a global basis, then we need the cooperation of everybody to solve those. But to get that cooperation you need what was so visibly lacking in our impoverished world, which is equity, or justice. Justice is something that's morally desirable, but it's also, in such a world that we live in, an absolute, practical necessity.

HC: At the moment you're expecting your first grandbaby, which is an amazing thing. In that context I want to read this paragraph.

> All the crises (but especially those that are endangering the ecosphere) involve theft by the living from their posterity. It's often said that revolutions, like the god Saturn, devour their children. We are committing a slow-motion, cross-generational equivalent of this offense. My generation, the baby boomers—ominously nicknamed "the boomers"—has been cannibalizing the future to provision the present. Though we are not killing our children directly, we *are* spending their money, eating their food, cutting down their cherry orchards.

JS: That's the new reality, because we're cutting into a level of life support that used to be taken for granted. That is the broad ecological crisis, part of which is the nuclear threat. We really are wrecking the planet for our children. We haven't yet invented the political, the journalistic, even the spiritual correlate of such a situation. It's as if we're confined in a narrow labyrinth and can't fight our way out of it to the bigger world in which we're actually living. And I don't know what those new ideas are, but I know they're needed.

HC: When we had a really seriously ill patient in the past, we used to put leeches on them and do bloodletting. And now we can, with modern medicine, cure many ills previously incurable. When you think about it, what we need is a new philosophy. A new spiritual guidance.

JS: Some of the most compelling figures are the great advocates of nonviolence, including Martin Luther King Jr. in our own country, who really draws the connections. Way back in the beginning of this century Mahatma Gandhi was crossing the borders in a certain way, between politics and such matters as diet and sometimes art, but what's interesting is, he wasn't confining himself to the arena that politics has stayed in before. I think some of this is needed, and these solutions that may be foundational for fixing our predicament now could be discovered in the actors and writers of the twentieth century.

HC: When I've been lost in the past I've read Gandhi. It's been very inspirational. He was a revolutionary. He practiced asymmetry in that he went back to India not with a uniform and a gun to take on the British but almost stark naked and leading a salt march. I'm not sure what the asymmetrical approach is at this point with the planet.

JS: I'm not either. When a response comes on the scale that's needed, we're guaranteed to be surprised by it. Just think of the fall of the Soviet Union, that great repressive creature people thought was there for their lives, and for their great-grandchildren's lives. No one had a clue that it would all dismantle itself and fall apart like a sandcastle in the face of the waves. And it was an internal process. With Gorbachev there was a process that was off our charts, and still is off our charts.

HC: I think the world was in such shock after the Soviet Union collapsed. No one knew what the new reality was. I don't think people have adjusted to that in a major way.

JS: And they tried to say that we won the Cold War, as if it had been a military defeat. I'm actually ready to concede that at points in the Cold War there was some wisdom, at least the aspect of restraint, in America's Cold War policy. I think George Kennan, who was prophetic, by the way, said, Stop them from expanding and let the internal process take over. It will go down with its own weight. He said these things back in 1944.

HC: Then there's Reagan, who started his presidency saying on a live mic that he didn't know was live, "The bombs are going to start falling." He frightens the bejesus out of everyone. Then he started to say, "A nuclear war cannot be won and must never be fought," and he ends up in Reykjavik with Gorbachev. And Gorbachev arrived with the most incredible agenda to eliminate nuclear weapons. They almost did it over a weekend, two mere mortals.

JS: It's an amazing story, which people are just beginning to absorb. Talk about the unexpected! Even today I've looked into it to try to figure out how and when Reagan developed what were unquestionably wise and also strongly moral feelings against nuclear weapons.

HC: I think all of us were responsible for that. I spent a lot of time with him alone during his time as president, more than many people. He was protected. He agreed to see me because he thought he should hear his daughter's point of view. He started seeing a different perspective, and probably was forced to by the gravity of the situation. Eighty percent of Americans were passionately opposed to the concept of nuclear war and to the nuclear arms race. I think we all should accept responsibility for that societal movement.

JS: You can demonstrate that the peace movement had a tremendous political effect on the administration. On the other hand, there are signs that Reagan had had that position back in 1982. There were speeches that startled everybody, and he was so out of character that they didn't include them in their picture of him. He makes a very intense objection to nuclear arms, expresses his disgust for them, and says it's the issue of our time. It's something that just surfaces now and again, but I don't know if we'll ever get to the bottom of it.

HC: Come back to our president Obama and this news that he wants to work with the Russians at getting down to a thousand weapons on each side. That isn't good enough, because it could still destroy most life on the planet. Presently there's enough in the arsenals of the world to overkill every person on Earth twelve times. Where should he go from a thousand on each side? We have to think clearly and work out what his next move should be, so we can pressure him and lead the public in a way of thinking.

JS: You know as well as I do, and every thinking person knows, that we have to go to zero. That's the solution to the big arsenals, and then we can really sleep safely in our beds. It's the solution to proliferation. The goal of getting to zero—which, by the way, is getting a lot of mainstream support, even from Henry Kissinger, the old reprobate—is getting a hearing in those quarters. There's wide acceptance among the public, for practical as well as ethical reasons, of the idea of going to zero. Bring that into the forefront of the negotiations. I can see two ways of going. One is you say, Okay, let's start along the weary path, and go to one station, and then the next, and let's see if we can get to the next. Then you wearily arrive at the destination, if you ever do. But if you start off at the beginning, and say, This is our destination, to get to zero, and we commit ourselves to that, then you can immediately go to potential proliferators and say,

Look, we're at a bargaining table here. We're staking our arsenals on that table. That's the biggest bargaining chip that anyone would have put on any table ever.

HC: I want to say all the options are on the table!

JS: Well, yes. We have the option of putting all our nukes on the table. My point is, the second you do that you develop a global consensus. Then every nation has a role, including the ones that have renounced nuclear weapons already, because they are the leaders in the race. They got to the finish line before everyone else, they are our models, the people to be emulated, and they should add their voices to the laggards and say, Come on, catch up with us!

HC: That's very exciting, I love that. So, how are we going to get to Obama?

JS: He did associate himself with the goal of getting rid of nuclear weapons. But he didn't make a big deal of it. On the other hand, there are people around him who've said, This is the way to go. Kissinger and that whole group is advocating this now. It's dormant, but it is there. The key would be to activate it. That's where we need to put our heads together.

HC: That's where we need to restart the grassroots movement. How do you get the media to discuss this so it comes to the front in people's minds again?

JS: My own feeling is that you can't get to the media until you're representing somebody. That's where the public and the grassroots movements come in, like during the freeze period.

HC: How do you get the grassroots movement going without getting to them through the media?

JS: Well, it involved the media, but I think that there was an energy there that the media had to respond to and respect. I would say in a sense it was like the civil rights movement.

HC: So we come full circle to where we were in the beginning.

JS: We always come back to that. But there are these hopeful elements, there is this change of opinion and goals, and there is Obama, who has signed on, so there are some good things. ∼

WILLIAM HARTUNG

William Hartung is director of the Arms and Security Project at the Center for International Policy and a senior research fellow at the New America Foundation, a nonpartisan policy institute that invests in new thinkers and ideas to address the next generation of challenges facing the United States. He is the author and editor of numerous books and studies, including *Prophets of War: Lockheed Martin and the Making of the Military-Industrial Complex*, *Lessons From Iraq: Avoiding the Next War* (edited with Miriam Pemberton), and *How Much Are You Making on the War, Daddy?* His articles have appeared in the *New York Times* and the *Washington Post* and on *Huffington Post*, and he has been a featured expert on NBC, CNN, and the BBC.

———

HELEN CALDICOTT: What's happening with the arms race and military spending in the United States under the new presidency?

WILLIAM HARTUNG: As a result of the Bush buildup, the United States is spending more than at any time since World War II. More than at the height of the Korean War, the Vietnam War, and more than the Reagan buildup. In recent years it's generally been over $700 billion counting the wars in Iraq and Afghanistan—per year.

HC: Does that include the black box items too?

WH: They're folded in there, but we don't know for sure. It doesn't include veterans' benefits and the interest on the debt that comes with militarism.

HC: What about money spent at NASA, which is now allied toward the space race and the arms race?

WH: That would be above the $700 billion in direct military spending. The Homeland Security Department has kind of insinuated itself into many parts beyond the Pentagon.

HC: How much has been spent on Homeland Security?

WH: It's been running $30 billion to $35 billion a year, and over $200 billion since September 11.

HC: We're probably nearly a trillion dollars, or over that.

WH: When they throw a trillion dollars at the banks to get out of a black hole, it makes these military numbers . . . not normal but in line with some other things the government's doing. Spending a trillion dollars a year on the military—unless we really stand up to that, it's going to happen year after year.

HC: How much did the Pentagon budget increase during the Bush administration?

WH: It almost doubled. But Clinton was no arms controller. Early on he came to the Pentagon and said he wouldn't lower the bar any further. Bush's father actually made deeper cuts to the military budget than Clinton. But under Bush Jr. it reached levels of obscenity.

HC: What are the drivers behind this obscenity?

WH: One is the extent that the executive branch, the Pentagon, and Congress to some degree, want the United States to be a global military power, with bases all over the world, and the ability to fight two wars, as they're doing now in Iraq and Afghanistan. But there's tens, probably hundreds of billions of dollars driven by the military-industrial complex. Companies want to build the F-22 fighter planes, the most expensive combat aircraft ever built at $350 million each. Even Secretary of Defense Robert Gates said we're not using this aircraft in Afghanistan or Iraq. Obama said we need to get rid of weapons we're not using, which seemed to be a signal that the F-22s would be eliminated. Lockheed Martin went into overdrive, putting pressure on members of Congress about jobs in their districts. It secured forty-four senators and two hundred members of the House of Representatives.

Even for a relatively modest change—cutting the F-22 would save roughly $4 billion a year out of close to a trillion that's spent on all the military spending—you've got a fight on your hands. You go up against this formidable military industry lobby that gives misleading figures about the numbers of jobs involved. It does not talk about the fact that there are much more constructive ways to employ people.

HC: It seems like a behemoth that is unstoppable. Most people are unaware of the amount of their tax dollars spent on this obscenity. Meanwhile people are suffering dreadfully from a lack of health care and poor education. Do you think Obama has the courage to take on this behemoth and challenge it head-on?

WH: He had talked about the need to eliminate nuclear weapons and he stopped requesting funding for one of the Pentagon's favorite warheads, the so-called reliable replacement warhead, which would have been put on all existing U.S. nuclear-delivery vehicles—

HC: That's a hydrogen bomb.

WH: Yes. It sounds very innocent when you talk about it in

antiseptic language. He eliminated the money for that in this recent budget and has given Hillary Clinton authorization to start talking about deeper cuts with Russia. He said he will push to get the United States to ratify the Comprehensive Nuclear-Test-Ban Treaty. He's put himself on record. It's going to be a fight. He's really the first president who's made that kind of commitment so early in his presidency.

HC: The model of Roosevelt's fireside chats—he's got the ability to do that, and he has permission as commander in chief.

WH: Well, he's certainly smart and articulate. He does better in that kind of format of nuts-and-bolts education. I think he would need to really be pushed in that direction. It's partly a question of which fight he's willing to pick. People are so relieved that George W. Bush is no longer president, that Dick Cheney is no longer vice president, there may have been a notion of, Let's give Obama a honeymoon and he'll take care of it. Now seeing how difficult the economic situation is, if we want him to focus on these other areas, there's really going to have to be significant public outcry and public pressure. We can't assume that Obama's going to do everything he promised, just because he said the right words.

HC: Well, he calls for his grassroots supporters, of which there are millions, to help him. When you look at the outrage about the bonuses given to AIG employees, and other bonuses, that's nothing compared to what Lockheed Martin, Northrop Grumman, Raytheon, and Boeing have done with people's tax dollars. If only we could work out some way to transfer the rage into the areas where there's massive stealing from the American people. How on earth can you educate people about what is going on behind the scenes?

WH: It's hard to get people to understand a trillion dollars.

HC: Why don't you explain what a trillion dollars really is?

WH: It's more than almost every other country in the world combined spends on military. It's more than half the discretionary budget in the United States. More than the government spends on everything else except for Medicare and Social Security—administration of justice, environmental protection, public housing, poverty, educating our kids. All the positive things our government does combined get less money than the Pentagon. Even locking up nuclear weapons around the world, which you could do for about $3 billion a year, is only the cost of a few days' war in Iraq. Likewise, for a day of the war you could double the budget of the International Atomic Energy Agency, which is the main organization that's trying to figure out where the bombs are and trying to keep new countries from developing them. The National Priorities Project, based in Massachusetts, breaks it down by program, by congressional district, how much your city's paying in taxes to support this. I did a thing called the Lockheed Martin tax. How much does it take to pay Lockheed Martin off? It comes to about $250 a year per household. People on top don't pay any taxes, the people on the lower levels can't afford to pay taxes, so it really hits a much smaller number of households. If you're paying taxes, probably $500 a year goes to supporting that one company, and if you add the whole military-industrial complex, you're talking thousands of dollars per year in tax dollars.

HC: Per household.

WH: Would you rather write a $2,000 check to Northrop Grumman or spend it on something else?

HC: People are unaware that their tax dollars go in this huge bag.

WH: Very few people grasp how enormous it is. The only thing that's communicated clearly, and the other side does this very effectively, is fear. It's a dangerous world. Therefore, just to be safe, let's throw more money at the military.

HC: It seems like this is the time to get people really stirred up.

WH: There are other threats to our existence. There's the economic crisis, climate change, things that we could do something about. A colleague of mine, Miriam Pemberton at the Institute for Policy Studies, did an analysis of how much the U.S. government spends directly to try to deal with global warming versus what's been spent on the military. It's an eighty-eight to one ratio: $88 to the military for every $1 trying to address climate change. It's an outrage, throwing money at things that are going to cause harm and neglecting things that could help us deal with one of the biggest crises in the history of the species.

HC: Let's talk about Gates; I think he's a fascinating character. He toed the line under Bush and Cheney, but he seems to be stepping out. What's your assessment of Gates as secretary of defense?

WH: The most hopeful interpretation is kind of a Nixon to China analogy. He's more of a realist in the Brent Scowcroft school rather than the Donald Rumsfeld school. He's not a peacenik, but he thinks that there's a lot of unnecessary spending by the Pentagon that could be used for something else. He also has talked about the State Department and its diplomatic efforts that are woefully underfunded. He gave one stark example: it takes more people to run a U.S. aircraft-carrier task force than there are trained diplomats in the entire U.S. Foreign Service. The fact that he pointed that out indicates that he's aware of that imbalance. I think where he's not going to be helpful is on the nuclear issue.

HC: Really?

WH: He's embraced this notion of the Reliable Replacement Warhead. He gave speeches about it and had an article in *Foreign Affairs* that dealt with that. The good news is, Obama's not going to buy into that.

HC: There are enough nuclear warheads in America alone to overkill everyone on Earth several times. The thinking is psychotic.

WH: This twisted logic is that the more you enter into it and act as if it's rational, the harder it is to extract yourself. They have this notion that they need a new warhead because you can't count on the current warheads to explode properly.

HC: And kill 2 million people.

WH: God forbid you try to end life as we know it and one of the weapons doesn't go off. It's such an absurd concept, and yet they go before Congress to talk about these things. They also are arguing that the warheads will be safer, and they won't use as many toxic materials; the workers will be safer; and it'll be harder for a terrorist to use them. So they make it sound like it's some sort of health program. Gates has bought into that argument, but on the other hand he may be helpful to Obama in blunting some of the conservative criticism and making it more normal to cut the military budget.

HC: I was interested in Obama's initiative to send huge numbers of diplomats to Afghanistan as well as soldiers.

WH: Right. I can't believe that Obama wants to go down the road of more and more troops in Afghanistan. You know they've been strafing the Afghanistan-Pakistan border in unmanned aerial vehicles.

HC: I want you to describe what an unmanned aerial vehicle is.

WH: It's a combination of a surveillance plane and a bomber, which has no pilot. The ones that I'm familiar with are for surveillance, and they have this huge wingspan, like a gigantic glider. In both the surveillance and strike versions there's a pod where the pilot would be, so it looks like some sort of praying mantis. It further depersonalizes the concept of war. Not only is there not a pilot at fifteen thousand feet to see the damage, as would happen with a manned aircraft, but they're not even in the same country.

HC: Well, how do they launch their weapons?

WH: The base could be in Florida or anywhere in the world, setting off bombs that are killing people in Afghanistan or Pakistan. Apparently, the dial and the controls for setting off the bombs are right next to the ones for self-destructing the weapons! If they are afraid that the weapon is going to be captured, they'll just blow it up. They sold these things on the idea that there's no pilot, so it's going to be cheaper. But they neglected to mention that it's quite expensive to have these ground control stations and the equivalent of the pilot.

HC: Someone sitting at a control board in Florida, because of the satellites and GPS system, can direct the targets from the drones onto a house in Afghanistan. I read that the people who'd launched the bombs at the control boards in Florida can see the actual destruction and body parts that they've created, and that that does them some sort of psychological trauma.

WH: There's going to be fewer people who want to do that sort of thing. Voting with their minds, in a way: That's not something I want to be involved in. They've had a shortage. Initially they were only using people who had been pilots. Now they're running thin, and they're going to start using people who aren't used to that quick reaction of a fighter pilot.

HC: In light of the present global financial crisis, do you think that the American people, the Congress, and Obama will wake up from this nightmarish dream that has cloaked America since 1945? The money spent on killing people, as we said just now, is nearly a trillion dollars a year. It's money being stolen that could be used to help recover from the financial crisis.

WH: I think we have the opportunity to make that case and to understand—probably the best opportunity since the end of the Cold War—that building more weapons not only doesn't protect us, but also causes more harm around the world, and therefore great harm to the reputation of the United States. Because of the financial crisis there's a sense of need. If all this money's being thrown at the banks, what's left for the rest of us? There's not going to be much left if we allow the Pentagon to continue to consume more than half of the discretionary budget. There have been some organizations, budget coalitions that work primarily on domestic needs, who during the Bush years just threw up their hands and said, Let's try to get money elsewhere. Now those groups are saying they'll join with arms control groups and the disarmament community to push for changes in the military budget, so we can put those resources to more constructive use. But I think there's a great opportunity here that we need to feed.

HC: In the Congress and the Senate? I know Lockheed Martin et al. say, You build an F-22 and parts of the plane are built in every congressional district, so every Congressperson is captive, because it means jobs in their district. Are you able, with others of your ilk, to get to congresspeople and senators?

WH: I did a little analysis of the Lockheed Martin claim that the F-22 will create 95,000 jobs all over America. I looked at how many jobs one billion dollars of military spending will create, and it looks like Lockheed Martin is overstating it by two to three times. It might be 30,000 or 35,000 jobs total for the program. In some states there might be some guy with a pencil and a pad, and that's the entire Lockheed Martin workforce. But they control the information. There was a reporter from *USA Today* who pointed out that, if it's in these states and these districts, and it's going to create this many jobs, they should share further details. And the Lockheed Martin spokesperson said, "That's confidential business information." So there's manipulation. We've been trying to educate some of the members of Congress that there are a lot more direct ways to help their districts. If you support the F-22 based on jobs in your district, you're trying to recruit a coalition. Somebody says, I'll support you on the F-22 if you support me on the F-18. And I'll support you on missile defense if you support me on nuclear weapons. Next thing you know, they've woven together this coalition of death. It's not just the cost of that one plane; it's the cost of doing business that way, allowing the Pentagon and its contractors to sort out the budget and the economy.

HC: The cost of mass death.

WH: There are members who've been speaking out. Dianne Feinstein of California used to be quite influenced by the military industry, and now she's come out well on some key issues. She's come out against the new nuclear warhead; she's come out for the ban on cluster bombs; she's spoken about the need to cut military spending, and also on this related issue of gun control. I think members can grow beyond that pork-barrel politics and that sort of narrow vision. In her case it was partly her experience of gun violence, including becoming mayor of San Francisco after the assassination of the mayor and Harvey Milk. I think people's personal experiences and their moral compass can be appealed to in order to trump the military-industrial juggernaut that's really based on a sort of crass consideration of dollars and cents.

HC: The one who interests me is Christopher Dodd, the senior senator from Connecticut. Connecticut's economy is based on the military-industrial complex, is it not?

WH: It's the biggest per-capita recipient of Pentagon money in the United States.

HC: That's where the Trident submarine is made.

WH: It's awash in a sea of military money.

HC: Dodd must receive a lot of money from these corporations.

WH: He has opposed military efforts in Latin America, but in other ways he's played the game as a spectator. He doesn't get a lot of attention when he does that. He's associated with his work related to banks and regulations. His work on behalf of the military companies is under this shroud. There's not a lot of transparency or public knowledge about that.

HC: It's under the table. Let's move on to the lovely Congressman Barney Frank from Massachusetts.

WH: He's in charge of the Financial Services Committee. He's right in the middle of the effort to figure out how to get back some of this money that's been thrown at the corporations and to hold them more accountable during this bailout process. He's been one of the more outspoken and articulate members during that whole fight. And thankfully he's made the connection with the military budget and said that at these record levels, we should be able to cut 25 percent from military spending. He's set a good tone for the beginning of the debate that needs to happen. We could cut more, but in terms of what he's spoken about in Congress in the last decade, it's quite a courageous stance. He's trying to build a coalition, working with activist groups and within the Congress, to make something real out of that pledge. Republicans tried to throw that back at the Democrats to show that they were soft on defense, soft on terrorism, that they didn't want to defend the country. Interestingly, those assertions didn't have a big impact. I hope that means that people are not as easily driven into fear mode by those kinds of outrageous claims that came in the wake of 9/11.

HC: I think he's in the driver's seat because of the financial crisis. Do you think people are with Barney now, on the 25 percent cut in the military budget?

WH: I think there's a lot of support. There still has to be education done, and a prominent member has made that part of the debate. But I think we almost benefit more from push back from the other side to elevate the visibility of the issue. If we got a real public debate, there's no question we would win that debate. If we could create political cover by having a big enough movement, then I think some of the others would come around.

HC: So the movement needs to expand enormously fast. The grass-roots movement—the people are starting to wake up and say, My God, the military spending is absolutely insane. We can't afford to pay our rent or our mortgages or get health care for the kids.

WH: I do think people are back on their heels because of the enormity of the economic crisis. The military budget is an obvious place to look for money that's not only being wasted but being used to cause destruction. And as you said, it threatens life as we know it. There are many benefits of going after that money: financial benefits, moral benefits, benefits in terms of being able to address real problems like climate change. And one thing that's almost taboo is the subject of poverty in the United States. A lot of what's been talked about in the debate is the middle class falling. People who were poor in the first place have not gotten a lot of attention. If middle-class families are feeling it, the people who were poor in the first place are feeling it by many multiples. I don't see politicians standing up and saying, We have to do something about this problem. A lot of poor people don't vote, and middle-class people have this idea that the welfare budget is one of the largest items in the federal budget. In fact, Lockheed Martin itself gets more money each year of our tax dollars than the largest federal welfare program. Corporate welfare is much larger than anything that benefits individuals.

HC: It's social welfare for the corporations.

WH: And capitalism for the rest of us.

HC: What percentage of the American people would you classify as poor now?

WH: The measure the government uses would put it at about one out of every eight. But when you look at the effects on children, it could be as much as one out of every four children in America. It's a huge problem, but a lot of people have this mythology that this is the wealthiest country in the world, and people envy our way of life without realizing that the problem of poverty is very close to home. It's in the cities of the United States also.

HC: If you drive through the back lots of Vermont, people are living in tar-paper shacks in the middle of winter. It is ubiquitous. I know that President Obama is conscious of this because of his own childhood and his own experiences.

WH: I think Obama has a visceral understanding of it. There's a political calculation: if he spoke honestly and offered a vigorous program, he would risk his majority. There was a lot of reaching out to conservatives, Republicans, the upper middle class. I think their logic is, if we don't have a majority, certain issues will have to be dealt with in ways that aren't really up to what's needed to solve them. Thirteen million people in his e-mail network are mobilized to do various things. Given the support he has in some areas, if he had a more ambitious agenda and did the job of public education in the way you mentioned before, he wouldn't need to be so timid on these issues. I think he could put the Republicans and the conservative Democrats on the defensive.

HC: I think he needs to come on full blast. Not this bipartisan stuff that failed during his last initiative, when he was trying to get his stimulus package through and the Republicans all rose up as one. He has so much more power than they do. He has the voice, and he's the commander in chief.

WH: I think they would have to understand that if they don't come around, they're not going to be in Congress next time around. That means mobilizing people in the states where these people get elected. He's capable of doing this, especially with the network that was built up during the campaign and with the help of other interested networks. It's a strategic decision for him; otherwise, it's death by a thousand cuts. You compromise and you compromise, and the next thing you know, the junior Republican senator from Maine is deciding the policy for the entire country.

HC: Exactly. Let's get on to NASA. Its propaganda is extraordinary. I've read a paper produced by Bruce Gagnon, who's one of the leading people opposing the arms race in space. It was decided under George W. Bush in late 2001 that all NASA missions would be dual use. That meant that every NASA space launch would be both military and civilian. The military would ride the NASA Trojan Horse and accelerate space weapons development without the public's knowledge. NASA would expand space nuclear power systems to help create new designs for weapons propulsion, permanent nuclear power bases on the Moon, Mars, etc. The International Space Station, originally scheduled to cost $10 billion, is now over $100 billion. All related to the military.

WH: The notion of weapons in space is quite frightening to people. When they're made aware that this is even a possibility you get quite strong opposition. The concept of hiding some of these programs within the NASA budget, which has a much more positive image in people's minds—Kennedy and the Moon launch, the heroic stature of astronauts like John Glenn, and so forth—makes sense, because a lot of the technologies do have overlap: launch technologies; power technologies; the abilities to put things in the proper orbit so they could be used as weapons. It sort of cries out for an exposé, and what Bruce Gagnon is saying needs to be plastered all over the front pages of every newspaper in the country, or at least all over the Web.

HC: What is occupying your time and emotional energy?

WH: I have a lot of ability to confront these things and feel optimistic about people being able to change what's going on. We're doing a piece on the cost of the plans to expand the nuclear-weapons complex. If we're going to get rid of nuclear weapons, we don't need this kind of complex. It sticks out like a sore thumb, and it stands in the way of getting other countries to reduce their weapons or forgo developing them.

HC: Describe the complex that they want to expand.

WH: There are major sites right here around the United States. There are weapons labs in New Mexico, Los Alamos, and Sandia, one of which is run by Lockheed Martin. Then there's Lawrence Livermore in California, and there's a plant in Kansas City. In South Carolina they generate tritium, which boosts the efficiency of a nuclear explosion. In the Pantex Plant in Amarillo, Texas, they do assembly and disassembly of nuclear weapons. Ideally we would keep them busy taking the weapons apart rather than putting them together. Then there's the Nevada Test Site, which at the moment is not doing nuclear testing but has been put in a state of readiness to resume.

HC: What are their plans?

WH: They want to build a new factory in Los Alamos that would make the plutonium triggers for the bombs and a factory in Kansas City that would make the nonnuclear parts of the bomb. They want a new uranium enrichment facility in Oak Ridge, Tennessee. These I mention are well over $10 billion of investment. There's a number of smaller things they're selling as an efficiency measure. These plants will be more energy-efficient and easier to guard and so forth. Again, they're not really addressing the question, If we're going to disarm, why do we need this in the first place? Not only shouldn't we modernize, we should be dismantling it.

HC: The point of modernizing is to build more weapons, right?

WH: They want to be in a position to build thousands of weapons if requested forevermore. Rather, if we're moving toward disarmament, then part of the good faith gesture or diplomacy of disarmament should be that we're going to get rid of our capability to build these things. Otherwise the arms race is just a stroke of the pen away from being restarted.

HC: How many hydrogen bombs does America currently hold in storage, on readiness alert?

WH: It's believed to be, if you count everything, it probably would be in the range of twelve to thirteen thousand. The Russians have a similar number, and then other countries have much smaller but equally dangerous amounts. About 95 percent of the nuclear weapons worldwide are controlled by the United States and Russia.

HC: Do you know how many weapons it would take to produce nuclear winter and the end of most life on Earth?

WH: I haven't looked at that in a while, but I don't believe it would take more than in the hundreds.

HC: That's right—about 250.

WH: The whole notion that these things protect anyone in any way is part of that psychosis that you talked about. The only way to be safe, and the only way to protect ourselves against nuclear weapons, is getting rid of all of them. There's this idea that some countries are responsible enough to have nuclear weapons and that other countries are irresponsible. In fact, nobody is responsible enough to have these things given what they can do. ～

MICHAEL T. KLARE

Michael T. Klare is a professor of peace and world security studies at the Five Colleges, Inc.: Amherst College, Hampshire College, Mount Holyoke College, Smith College, and the University of Massachusetts at Amherst. Before assuming his current post in 1985, Professor Klare served as a fellow and program director of the Institute for Policy Studies in Washington, D.C. He has written widely on U.S. foreign policy, the arms trade, and international resource politics. He is the author of *Resource Wars: The New Landscape of Global Conflict* (2001); *Blood and Oil: The Dangers and Consequences of America's Growing Petroleum Dependency* (2004); *Rising Powers, Shrinking Planet: The New Geopolitics of Energy* (2008); and *The Race for What's Left* (2012). Klare has written for many newspapers and journals, including *Current History, Foreign Affairs, Harper's, The Nation, Newsweek,* and *Scientific American.*

———

HELEN CALDICOTT: This is a subject emerging rapidly without the obvious consciousness of many people in the world. We're feeling it in Australia, but you describe China as the shopaholic of planet

Earth while the United States, because of the current recession, is staying at home.

MICHAEL KLARE: Everybody is very well aware of China's rise as a great economic power, and in its rise China is building up its industries and infrastructure and acquiring all that goes with that—new cities, expanding cities, highways, and railroads, and all this requires a tremendous amount of resources. It's acquiring the natural resources to make this happen: iron ore, coal, copper, and a lot of oil in particular, because China is now the world's largest automobile market and all those cars need oil. So China is scouring the world to acquire oil and all these other resources. Australia is one of those places where the Chinese have gone looking for minerals and natural gas. What I've been following is the degree to which China has used its accumulated wealth to buy these assets around the world to position itself with resource assets under its control. It's buying oil wells, natural gas fields, copper and iron mines in Asia, Africa, Latin America, and the Middle East. Everywhere. This is a matter of concern for the United States, because in many cases, these countries are formal allies or trading partners of the United States and its allies, places long in the Western orbit that are now moving into the Chinese orbit. This is the kind of thing that makes American leaders very nervous, especially when it's countries like Iran or Venezuela that have taken an anti-American position. We're talking not only about an economic issue—and this is part of the shift in economic power from West to East—but it also has geopolitical and military implications.

HC: Do you think that the leaders currently in the United States House and Senate and the White House are aware of this situation, or is this under their radar?

MK: Oh no, this is something that they're very aware of. The president has been preoccupied with domestic issues, but certainly senior members of his staff and the departments of State and Defense are very much concerned about the geopolitical implications of China's resource acquisitions around the world. A lot of what the State and Defense departments do is to seek alliance and diplomatic means of countering China's activities. To give one example: the United States as recently as 2008 created a new military command, the Africa Command. This is a reflection of America's dependence on African oil but also of concern about China's growing presence in Africa.

HC: It's very clear that Africa is a huge "resource commodity" and open to great exploitation. Obviously America would move in with its military power, in light of where China is at the moment.

MK: In their pursuit of these resource assets both the United States and China want to form very close relationships with the governments that control these assets, whether it's an oil-producing country or a major mineral producer, so they can count on getting access to those resources. Very often what those governments want, Sudan or Nigeria or Angola, is weaponry to help keep themselves in power, because very often these governments are contested by their own populations. As part of their efforts to cement ties with these resource-supplying countries, the United States and China offer them weapons. Not only weapons, but military training, military technological support, military intelligence support. This can become a competition in which the United States and China are both providing arms and military support to the same countries, as in Nigeria or Kazakhstan.

HC: Are many of the governments of these countries corrupt?

MK: Oil production is a natural invitation to corruption. A phrase for this in the academic literature is the resource curse; the wealth coming from the production of oil is called rents. You have individuals, royal families, cliques, or clans that seek to monopolize the collection of rents, enrich themselves, their relatives, and their cronies. They use the military and the police to remain in power. Corruption is almost always present when you have oil production in developing countries, where there is no other source of wealth.

HC: Let's take Myanmar, or Burma, as a classic example.

MK: Burma does have a lot of resources, a lot of natural gas that's of interest to foreign powers. It's in the Andaman Sea, off the shore of Burma. There was a great deal of interest by American companies in acquiring that, particularly the Unocal Corporation, which had the concession to acquire Burma's natural gas and build a pipeline across Burma to Thailand, where there was a market for it. Because this pipeline went through areas that were occupied by the Mon and Karen peoples, Unocal brought in the Burmese army; slave labor was used to support development in the region, and American corporations were accused of participating in egregious human rights practices. This was brought before American courts and they had to pay damages. Eventually Unocal's properties were acquired by Chevron, and it was exempted from some of the sanctions that were imposed on Burma. Now China wants to become a leading energy producer in Burma and is doing everything it possibly can to woo its leaders—providing arms, economic assistance. The Chinese are going to build a pipeline across Burma to bring oil from the Persian Gulf into China. There is a lot of Chinese investment now in Burma.

HC: When we look at the slaughter going on in Sudan and the Congo, and in many other countries of Africa, do you think that the main dynamic behind this is what you have just described: the race for resources; corrupt governments that keep their populations subdued; and the weapons and arms trade? Or is it about other things—tribal competition and the like?

MK: There are always ethnic differences involved, but I think those are manipulated by warlords, corporations, and other parties that seek to exploit the resource assets of these countries. Of course they will try to whip up ethnic differences as a way of recruiting people into warlord armies, to get foot soldiers for whatever conflicts are taking place. Historically there may have been ethnic clashes over the division of water supplies or something like that. But most of what we read about, in Africa or in the Middle East, have resources at the root of it, a competition for the control of the resources or the wealth that the resources generate—you have to distinguish between those two. Most of the oil, the diamonds, and the iron ore that's produced in Africa is not used by the people in Africa; they see no benefit from the diamonds. Warlords and corrupt governments all jockey for control over the distribution of these precious resources; they are the ones getting the wealth generated from the export of those materials to Europeans, Americans, Chinese, and Japanese.

HC: So there are three categories of resources, really. There's the fossil fuels: oil and natural gas. The minerals: iron, copper, uranium, aluminum, and the like. And then there is land and water. China began gobbling up foreign energy assets in Angola, Iran, Kazakhstan, Nigeria, Sudan, and Venezuela. These acquisitions were still dwarfed by those being made by giant Western firms like Exxon Mobil, Chevron, Royal Dutch Shell, and BP. But this is new—the growing Chinese presence in the universe that was once dominated by Western majors.

Do you think that America went into Iraq largely because it contains one third of the oil resources of the world?

MK: Iraq has about one tenth of the world's oil resources. But the region as a whole, the Persian Gulf region, has about two-thirds, and you can't separate one from the other. I think the United States went into Iraq because it's a key player in the region that has two thirds of the world's oil. It was a strategic or a geopolitical move. It is the declarative policy of the United States, known as the Carter

Doctrine, that says that the United States will not allow another power to rise in the Persian Gulf area that will threaten the flow of oil from there to the West. Saddam Hussein was viewed as a threat to American domination of the Persian Gulf and all of its oil. The United States invaded Iraq to ensure that no other rival to American dominance would ever arise. And that's the essence of the current U.S. crisis with Iran, because the Iranians are challenging American dominance in the Persian Gulf. I fear that this too will lead to a clash.

HC: So they're just using the uranium enrichment situation, which Israel is very worried about, to get at the resources of Iran and the Persian Gulf.

MK: Iran's persistence in nuclear enrichment is worrisome to the United States on several grounds. One, it raises Iran's profile in the region, and that makes everybody very worried; second, if Iran were to acquire nuclear weapons, it would make it much harder for the United States to invade and occupy Iran the way it did Iraq.

HC: Do you think the Pentagon is actually discussing invading Iran?

MK: I certainly think that that has been on the agenda in the past. When President George W. Bush spoke of the axis of evil, he mentioned Iran among the nations that were viewed as a threat to the United States. I think a war between the United States and Iran was being considered as what the military would call a contingency, not as an inevitability. They plan for all such contingencies.

HC: Australia is such a very ancient continent, and we have giant mountains of iron ore. We have huge amounts of bauxite, which is used for aluminum. We have 40 percent of the world's richest uranium. What we're observing, because of globalization and how the economics of the world operates, is that the Chinese are coming in and buying up shares in companies either owned by Australian corporations or by British and other corporations, and there is a feeling in government and among people who are aware that this is scary, because China, without having a war or occupying Australia, could end up owning much of Australian wealth and resources.

MK: One thing that concerns me is the degree to which the economy of Australia is becoming dependent on the exploitation of its natural resources as the driving factor in the economy. First of all, these resources are not going to last forever. Second, to what degree does this generate other economic activities? Or is Australia just becoming a third world country, a banana republic that's just a source of resources for China or somebody else? If I were an Australian, I would worry about the excessive dependence of the economy on raw-material exports. I'm an observer, so it may look different on the ground. I know that this has generated employment for Australians at a time when my country has 10 percent or more unemployment. That said, if I were Australian I would be concerned about the degree to which any single country was gaining control of so many of the natural resources that form such a large part of the economy.

HC: Would you discuss the huge land grabs developed countries are making in developing countries around the world? And the water resources?

MK: This is becoming a matter of extreme concern to many people, and not only in Africa, but also in the Philippines. I suspect in Indonesia as well. But it's not just developed countries that are acquiring these huge plots of land; some of the wealthier Middle Eastern countries, which aren't able to grow their own food like Saudi Arabia and Kuwait, are also buying large plots of land, in Ethiopia and Sudan, so that they will have exclusive rights to grow food there in order to supply their countries. This is troubling on many, many levels. The government comes in and says, This land is underused; therefore it's up for sale. But there are many people in those areas who say that they occupy that land, and they have for centuries. But these are places where there isn't the same kind of title that you would have in a more developed country, where deeds are recorded. There is some evidence of the Sudanese and the Ethiopian governments, for example, seizing land from the people and turning it over to these corporations. Then there's the whole issue of food being provided exclusively to foreign mouths when there is a high level of starvation in the exporting country. To think that food is being produced there and exported someplace else, where people have enough money to buy food from anywhere. I find this highly unethical.

HC: I can't really get my mind around these huge movements for acquisition of virtually entire countries and their natural resources. One, the resources of the world are finite, so we're going to run out of all the resources we've been talking about. Two, we've got a massive overpopulation problem; we've moved from one billion people two hundred years ago to now nearly 7 billion, an exponential growth in human beings. We've got China, who's joined the capitalist ethic with great enthusiasm and is unstoppable. We've got a huge military force in the United States that has the capacity to destroy most life on Earth through its nuclear weapons, and Russia too. Then there's global warming. We've just been talking about acquiring oil from all these countries; we haven't even mentioned coal. Australia is a huge exporter of coal, and actually a Chinese coal freighter that hit the Great Barrier Reef, one of wonders of the world, is spilling and threatening the coral and the fish.

But the two arguments don't seem to be conjoined. There's an argument about acquiring the world's fossil fuels for energy—for China, for Japan, for America, for all the countries—to keep their economies growing and growing. At the same time there are people like James Hanson and the scientists in the IPCC—the International Panel on Climate Change—warning that we are at the tipping point of global warming unless we stop burning coal and oil within fifty to a hundred years; if not, many of the world's species will become extinct, and we will be in dire straits as a species ourselves.

MK: Population growth, resource scarcity, world accumulation of weapons, and global climate change are all mixed together, and accelerating and exacerbating each other. It's hard to know even where to begin to talk about them. The big worry is our need to acquire and consume resources. The underlying force here is that, as a species, we keep on needing more of everything, and it has been our consumption of fossil fuels that's causing global climate change. It's in the pursuit of resources that we create armies. I see the nature of our consuming behaviors as the central issue. If you don't somehow bring that under control, none of the others will be solvable. If we don't reduce the consumption of fossil fuels, there is no hope of addressing global warming, and there is no hope of addressing the plunder of Africa and the other oil-producing countries. So the nature of our consuming behaviors, and the kinds of decisions that societies make about the consumption of resources, is the nub.

HC: How can we rejigger the global economy to be not dependent on growth, and on the growth of human populations?

MK: We have to imagine new ways of living. We have to rebuild the economy around new concepts of appropriate human living and modes of existence. I'm sorry if this sounds a little bit utopian, but this is what it's going to take for humans to survive on the planet. I'm very aware of that, because I live in the United States, and it's the so-called American way of life that is projected around the world through the media, through television and Hollywood, that is responsible for a lot of the problems we see. The American way of life is the most energy-intensive, resource-intensive life imaginable. Everybody has an automobile, at least one—in America most families have two or more—and a large house with air-conditioning and a swimming pool in the backyard and a million appliances.

That image of what people aspire to is spreading around the

world, and as people reach middle-class status in China, India, Brazil, and Mexico they try to duplicate it. This is unsustainable. The planet cannot survive that, so we really have to begin to think about a new image of the good way of living that is much more modest in its impact on the planet, and uses fewer resources, which nobody doubts must happen. There will be opportunities for entrepreneurs to develop new energy systems, new modes of transportation, new ways of living in cities that are much greener. There will be new opportunities, but it has to be based on energy-efficiency and low-consumption patterns.

HC: Last but not least is the consistent growth of the human population.

MK: All of the evidence is clear: when you provide more education and health care to young women, the population rate goes down, and there is no other way to do it. We have to provide additional health care and education to young women around the world, and that will bring the population down. But our problem is not primarily population growth per se. It is the increase in the population of automobiles and giant homes and other gas- and energy-guzzling appliances, and that has to be curbed first.

HC: The question is whether we're psychologically, spiritually, and intellectually smart enough to do this in time.

MK: Young people in my classes all know that this is something that has to occur. They may not know how or when, but they understand that this is necessary. So I'm hopeful that they will seize the reins when they can and make it happen. ∽

DANIEL ELLSBERG

D aniel Ellsberg is the subject of a documentary called *The Most Dangerous Man in America: Daniel Ellsberg and the Pentagon Papers*. The film won the audience award at the Sydney Film Festival in June 2010. In 1967 Ellsberg worked on the top-secret McNamara study of U.S. decision making in Vietnam, later known as the Pentagon Papers. He photocopied the seven-thousand-page study and gave it to the Senate Foreign Relations Committee, to the *New York Times*, the *Washington Post*, and seventeen other newspapers. His trial on twelve felony counts could have resulted in a sentence of 115 years, but it was dismissed in 1973 on the grounds of governmental misconduct against him, which figured in the impeachment proceedings against President Richard Nixon.

—◦◦◦—

HELEN CALDICOTT: How old were you in 1959, when you became a strategic analyst at the RAND Corporation?

DANIEL ELLSBERG: I was twenty-eight. I'm very impressed by twenty-two-year-old Bradley Manning, who's in jail for allegedly using the Internet to put out ninety thousand pages of reports. I put out seven thousand pages using Xerox. But I couldn't do what he's allegedly done. There's talk of another quarter of a million cables. He will be facing the same charges, threatening life imprisonment, that I was facing, and he has worse odds. The law has turned against him in recent decades. He's in a military court, so the cards are stacked. I was impressed to read that he was willing to go to prison for life, or even be executed, to get out this information, what he called horrible crimes. I feel great empathy for his state of mind, and I admire what he's done.

HC: Absolutely. But what compelled you to become a strategic analyst at the RAND Corporation in the first place, which was supporting the concept of nuclear war?

DE: They were a haven for people working on decision making under uncertainty, which was the subject of my PhD thesis at Harvard. Much of the abstract research on that comes from studies by mathematicians and economists there. I discovered that they were working to avert a surprise nuclear attack from the Soviet Union, which was supposed to be a crash effort to develop a first-strike capability against the United States. The only way to avert that would be to deter them by posing the ability to retaliate enormously. I accepted that framework, the top-secret assumption of all my colleagues. I really thought it was the most important problem in the world. Now it turned out that the notion of a missile gap favoring Soviets, or any large Soviet ICBM capability in the late fifties or early sixties, was as much of an illusion as the claims that Saddam Hussein had WMDs in 2003. He had nothing, and the Russians had four ICBMs.

HC: It was a lie propagated by JFK.

DE: I don't think JFK knew he was lying when he said that. He was going on intelligence estimates that were entirely false. It was the air force putting up that hoax, on very thin, controversial evidence.

HC: Why would the air force do that, Dan?

DE: The more ICBMs the Russians had, the stronger claim that the air force had for high-flying, fast-flying bombers, like the B-1 or the B-70. The whole basis for their missile program was the greatly inflated claims of what the Russians were doing. We were working very hard on an illusion. I was being paid well, but I would have worked for free or even paid to do it as a public service. The effect was that we contributed to the air force's construction of a doomsday machine, a system of missiles that could destroy hundreds of millions of people, and though we didn't know it at the time, could cause a nuclear winter that could destroy most life on Earth.

HC: And that system remains in place as we speak.

DE: On alert. The capability of causing nuclear winter would still be true after the reductions that President Obama and President Medvedev agreed to. If they go down to fifteen hundred warheads, that's still far more than is needed to cause the death of most people, most species on Earth. That's really inexcusable that this capability remains on alert, subject to false alarms and accidents and preemptions in a crisis.

HC: Did you meet McNamara when you worked on his top secret study of U.S. decision making in Vietnam?

DE: The last time I met him was in 1967, when I was starting on that study. I had a lot of questions, not all of which would have discredited him. But he was so enraged at my having released this information that he would never talk to me again. Earlier in my work on nuclear war, I felt that he was really appropriately opposed to employing it. Yet he was the instrument for building up this doomsday machine, and so was his boss, John Kennedy, who I believe also abhorred nuclear war. They were part of this system that led them to order an enormous buildup in our destructive capabilities.

HC: I got to know McNamara toward the end of his life. He said to me once, "Helen, you don't know how close we came in the Cuban Missile Crisis." He said it was within minutes.

DE: His book had a lot of shortcomings, but the major reason he had to write it was an appendix spelling out how close we'd come in the Cuban Missile Crisis. He wanted to spread that word. I've never seen a review of that book that paid any attention to that. He was very good at speaking about nuclear weapons, but in a way, it was too late for him; his voice had no impact.

HC: He also said to me, "I think people thought I did the wrong thing in Vietnam." I said, "Yes, you did."

DE: What'd he say to that?

HC: Nothing. He looked at me. He was admitting that he had done the wrong thing.

DE: You may be right. But at the time, and later, my impression is that he was so fixed on the notion that it was the president's sole responsibility for those decisions that he didn't feel a lot of personal guilt. I think he felt that the president had done this, and it was all a big mistake.

HC: No. I got quite close to him. He was racked by guilt.

DE: Whether he felt guilt or no guilt at all, it would have meant a lot more had he been willing to act against his loyalty to the president in 1967 or 1966. He knew that the war was hopeless; he was saying that to intimates. He figured that if he said what he really thought to President Johnson, he'd be fired. And when he did say it, he was fired. Even then it wasn't too late for him to tell the truth to the Senate. Instead, when he appeared for hearings on the Tonkin Gulf, he lied to the Senate, strongly, in his last months in office. I believe he could have gotten us into negotiations and ended the war even as late as that. It took him about twenty years to say anything about Vietnam.

HC: He was a very, very torn character.

DE: I don't doubt that.

HC: What were the dynamics personally that led you to release the Pentagon Papers?

DE: I'd been to Vietnam. I'd come to know people there, over the course of two years, and to care about what happened to them. They were real to me, and the prospect, which I knew from inside sources, that the war was going to get larger in the air was very anguishing. Going to prison for life—I wouldn't have thought of that as a possibility if it weren't for the example of young men who were going to prison to resist the draft. It was their statement against the war. I realized that I could do something comparable. I had access to information that might make a difference. My motives were very much what I observe for Bradley Manning now, releasing all these documents about the Afghan war. I would not have thought of doing it without the personal example of people who were going to prison. I imagine that there probably were influences for Bradley Manning of the same nature.

HC: I had death threats during my career working against nuclear weapons. Martin Luther King, and I'm paraphrasing him, said, If you don't have a cause that you're prepared to die for, then you're not really living. I feel that quite strongly.

DE: It's rather easy to mobilize humans to die for what their leaders tell them is in their country's interest; people in the service are risking their lives all the time in combat. But it doesn't occur to people that they might be called on to use the same courage with respect to their careers, or even their freedom, in civilian life, as officials or people in corporations or as citizens who are aware that lives are in danger by some process that is being wrongfully kept secret. And that they have in fact great power to save lives if they're willing to take a risk themselves.

HC: I wish someone would release the papers from the Pentagon about nuclear war that make the case for a straight, winnable nuclear war.

DE: I feel great regret that I did not release what I knew about nuclear war in the early sixties or the late fifties. Mikhail Gorbachev was the only world leader who really, rightly saw the urgency of this problem. And of course he presided over the Russian doomsday machine. If he'd stayed in office even a year longer, I believe he'd have extended his glasnost policy to nuclear weapons. There was a real chance that he was a person who could have thrown open his safes and said, Look, these are what our plans look like. I'm sure your American plans look just the same.

Let the world see how insane and immoral they are. This has to change. I think he would have been willing to take unilateral steps and call on the United States to do the same. There are people who could tell us the nature of their targeting, what the impact could be on humans if those plans were carried out. Every nuclear state, nine of them, has such nuclear plans right now. That's where humans, especially in organizations, don't on the whole take risks—of being ostracized, of possibly being punished in a terrible way—as individuals, in order to save hundreds of millions of lives. We're talking about life on Earth, and it seems to me people should be willing to pay the price or take that risk. That's why Bradley Manning is a hero of mine at the moment.

HC: Would you call people who are involved in planning the destruction of possibly the only life in universe cowards?

DE: I used to think that more. Are you talking about for not revealing?

HC: Yes.

DE: You're talking about people who have great misgivings about what they're doing. Wars, nuclear war, many people in the Bush administration were very opposed to torture. General Colin Powell, secretary of state, wrote strong memos against the use of torture under Bush. When he was overruled, he didn't reveal them to the public, to the Congress. If they confront the choice and they decide, No, I cannot take that risk. I cannot make that choice, it's partly cowardly, but it's also about their priorities.

An even broader phenomenon is people just don't confront the possibility—their obedience is so strong and their roles are to be people who are trustworthy. It doesn't occur to them to go against the interest of their bosses in secrecy, even those who are concealing crime. Or projects that could threaten life on Earth. Nevertheless, their loyalty to their bosses, which is to their career and to their sense of themselves, they're president's men, basically keeps them from even imagining that they could go against the president's wishes.

HC: Doesn't that take us back to the Nuremberg trials, that every person is morally responsible for what their country does?

DE: A lot of people don't believe in the Nuremberg principle. A man named Calley, an officer, carried out the My Lai massacre in Vietnam. He was actually convicted, and then his sentence reduced to house arrest by Nixon. One of the most popular things Nixon did was to commute his sentence. After that commutation of the sentence, Americans were asked, first, whether they thought civilians should be massacred like that. "No," they weren't agreeing with that. Second, "Should Calley have followed his orders to do it?" The answer from about 67 percent was "yes, he was right to follow orders." "What would you have done in that situation?" they were asked. Again, about two-thirds said, "I would have carried out the orders," even though they perceived them as bad orders. And then the real clincher, thirty years after Nuremberg: "Do you think German generals should have been convicted or punished for carrying out higher orders in the war?" What would you think the answer would be?

HC: I suppose they said, "Yes."

DE: They said, "No, they should not have been convicted." The Nuremberg trials had had a different answer. But the majority of Americans do not accept the idea that you're individually responsible for what you do. There's a very disconcerting book about this called *Crimes of Obedience*, by Herbert Kellman. His interpretation was that the general life attitude of the enlisted men and junior officers, is, "Our deal is, we do what you elites tell us to do, we follow your program. And in turn, you take the responsibility; it's not ours." They feel that Nixon had violated that by putting Calley on trial.

But it really goes back to my interpretation of McNamara. As secretary of defense he said many times, "I worked for the president, I did what the president said." When he talks about what he should have done differently, he says, "I should have told the president more forcefully in private what I really felt." The most effective thing he could have done was to split from the president.

HC: Yeah, resign.

DE: I don't want to seem entirely critical of McNamara. In *The Fog of War*, he alluded to the fact that there were people who wanted nuclear war. Even in *The Fog of War* he couldn't bring himself to name "Joint Chiefs of Staff." Even then, his instinct of not getting in a public fight with the military ruled. He had reason to believe, in his last years in office, that his role was to help the president keep both a lid on the violence of the Vietnam War and the Joint Chiefs from forcing President Johnson to invade North Vietnam, hit every target up to the Chinese border, possibly bringing in the Chinese, and if that happened, use nuclear weapons. I think he thought he was the only person who could have mastered the chiefs enough to keep that from happening. He could well have been right.

So he was very instrumental in the bombing and getting us into the war in 1964, for which he does or does not feel a lot of guilt. I think that's countered in his mind by his feeling that he was the person who kept the Joint Chiefs and Johnson from doing to North Vietnam and China what he had done under General Curtis when they were in the Second World War, which was to kill eighty thousand people—twenty thousand people in one night in Tokyo. In the movie *The Fog of War* he revealed for the first time that he had worked under General Curtis LeMay and recommended the firebombing of Tokyo, something of which he said, "We could have been tried as war criminals." That's not quite the same as saying, "We were war criminals." But he foresaw big escalation if he left office in 1966 and 1967. So he had a good justification in his mind for staying, and he gets no credit for this. Hardly anybody recognizes to this day that the Vietnam War could have been much larger and more violent. It could have killed millions more people in North Vietnam. You asked me why I gave over the Pentagon Papers. Really what was in my mind above all was the feeling that that kind of escalation still was a possibility. It turns out I was right. And McNamara was rightly concerned about that risk and did work to avert it.

HC: Were you privy to the plans about using nuclear weapons against Vietnam and China that the Joint Chiefs were postulating?

DE: I learned more about it later. In 1968, having gotten back from Vietnam, when I was in the Defense Department working on high-level policy, and I was aware that the Joint Chiefs were discussing the possible need to use nuclear weapons at Khe Sanh, a besieged marine outpost near the northern part of South Vietnam that was in danger of being overrun. That was very much in my mind when I made my first top secret leaks in March of 1968. Later I was told by Mort Halperin, who was working for Henry Kissinger, that the president was threatening major escalation if his demands were not met. I didn't understand those as being nuclear threats at the time, but I was worried Nixon would be threatening nuclear weapons.

That's why I wanted to get the Pentagon Papers out. At the very time I began copying them, Kissinger, through Nixon, was making explicit threats to use nuclear weapons to the North Vietnamese and conveying those also to the Russians and Chinese. And saying he would do it as early as November 1961, the very month I was copying the Pentagon Papers. If I had known that directly, I would have leaked that out rather than the Pentagon Papers. What kept Nixon from carrying that out at the time was that there were 2 million people in the streets on October 15, 1969, the largest collection of antiwar actions all in one day that had been held in this country, or perhaps in any country. Nixon decided it was not the time to carry out his ultimatum. People did not know that they were postponing the use of nuclear weapons.

HC: What's your take on Kissinger?

DE: He's a clever servant of power. Most people see him as a kind of demonic figure. I think he was doing pretty much what, Nixon, his boss wanted. If he'd had a different boss, I think he would have done that too. He has a lot of blood on his hands, and is a major war criminal, but as a subordinate to the president.

HC: It's amazing that he's still referred to and used by the media for opinion making.

DE: Well, he did get a Nobel Prize for ending a war that had not ended. It had two years to go. The other person who got it with him, his negotiating partner, Le Duc Tho, had the honor to refuse the prize. He said the war was not over. Kissinger took the money.

HC: Let's move now to the present time. With your huge experience with the Pentagon, the RAND Corporation, with nuclear weapons policy, I want you to give us a brief appraisal on where we stand today in terms of nuclear weapons doctrine, who is deciding, and where President Obama stands, as well as Putin.

DE: The Bush administration brought out into the open doctrines of first use of nuclear weapons, the right of the United States and the readiness of the United States to initiate nuclear war, when the president decides its use. That has not been repudiated by Obama. Nor has the notion of preemption. Obama has moderated the rhetoric of the Bush administration. But that says little about the policy side. Obama's policies seem unusually divorced from his rhetoric. I scarcely listen to him anymore, because you learn so little about what he's doing. I could talk about transparency, which he promised. He's totally reversed that; he's at least as secretive as the Bush administration in the field of national security. And on constitutional matters, he is as bad at civil liberties as the Bush administration. He has not addressed suspending habeas corpus in asserting the right of using indefinite detention of people who have not been charged, or who have been charged and convicted but who he intends to detain anyway, indefinitely. In these cases he's reversed some hundreds of years, going back to John the 1st, back to the Magna Carta, the notion basically of the rule of law and civil liberties.

In the field of nuclear weapons, the prospects are not much better. For all Obama's talk, he's another Nobel Prize winner who deserves it about as much as Henry Kissinger. He hasn't gotten as much guilt yet as Henry Kissinger, who for his Nobel Peace Prize had dropped 4.5 million tons of that explosive on Indochina. We dropped 2 million tons in World War II in all theaters. But Obama hasn't reached that level in high explosives, or even body count yet, but he has expanded a war very like Vietnam.

Coming right to your question on nuclear weapons: to reduce nuclear weapons from a level of, 1,750, by 250 warheads, to 1,500 is an absolutely meaningless and insignificant reduction. In recent years Gorbachev, and even Yeltsin, showed a willingness to go far below that if the United States had been willing to go down. Yeltsin had talked about a thousand, and even lower. But the United States was not willing to match him. Obama still isn't. One of the best things he did was to back away from the immediate plan to put the missile defenses in Czechoslovakia, and yet as usual with Obama he seems to have come full circle to continuing those defenses in Europe. Now does that really justify the Russians having fifteen hundred or more warheads? No, it doesn't. There's this roadblock here on major massive reduction. What's more egregious than that is that he's again rejected what every other president has rejected, a no-first-use agreement saying that the United States would never initiate the use of nuclear weapons. Obama has continued what every other major candidate in 2008 said, Republican and Democrat: that all options are on the table with respect to Iran. Keep in mind that Iran does not have nuclear weapons, and this is a threat against a nonnuclear state, a threat of initiating nuclear war, specifically against underground sites in Iran that might someday be used to produce nuclear weapons. That's not happening now, but it could happen in the future, and to prevent that he would initiate nuclear war. Obama is using his nuclear weapons right now in the way that you use a gun when you point it at somebody's head. Or put it on the table. When you put the gun on the table, as poker players did to keep everybody honest in Western films, you're using the weapon. You couldn't make that threat if you didn't have it. Every president, in many cases secretly, used those weapons. I would say that it's an absolute block to a real nonproliferation program.

Now what about preventing proliferation to other countries, to get other countries to forswear ever having nuclear weapons? We not only propose to keep thousands indefinitely, against our commitment in a nonproliferation treaty, but to continue to use them and assert our right to use them by threatening them. To say to another country, like Iran, "We're threatening you with nuclear weapons, but you don't have any right to acquire them yourself" to deter those threats is absurd. But the issue here is not whether it's logically coherent, or even legal or moral. The major issue is what the effects are going to be. You cannot get other countries to forswear the use of these weapons while we're setting that example, and we're threatening them.

HC: What do you think the risk of nuclear war is over the next ten years?

DE: I think it's very high. The smallest amount would be considered high, 1 percent or 2 percent. It's a lot more than that. The highest risk would be the use of nuclear weapons in the course of a war between Israel, Iran, and the United States. Israel or the United States may start in preemption of a nuclear attack, probably not starting with nuclear weapons, but possibly escalating to the use of them against Iranian underground sites. That's probably the most likely use of nuclear weapons since Hiroshima.

There's also the possibility of the use of weapons between India and Pakistan. But the possibility of a terrorist getting weapons is the one mostly focused on. The possibility of an all-out attack arising from a false alarm or an operation between the United States and Russia is quite low. But it is not zero. We have two doomsday machines, each capable of destroying all life on Earth, poised in readiness to go off in minutes. And both systems, especially the Russians', are subject to false alarms and fears that have come close to unleashing those machines in the past. So the risk, even if it's low, of all these events put together, lower probably than 50 percent in the next ten years, is nevertheless intolerable, unforgivable. It's the highest human priority to avert it. ∼

ANTONY LOEWENSTEIN

Antony Loewenstein is a Sydney-based journalist who has written for publications around the world, including *The Guardian*, *The Nation*, and the *Sydney Morning Herald*. His book *My Israel Question* is a dissenting Jewish view on the Israeli-Palestinian conflict. He has also authored *The Blogging Revolution*, a book about the Internet in repressive regimes. He is currently working on a book about disaster capitalism and speaks regularly for the campaign to defend WikiLeaks.

—∞—

HELEN CALDICOTT: This WikiLeaks thing is major. What do you think it really means? I see it as a revolution; governments now can't hide.

ANTONY LOEWENSTEIN: It changes the relationship between the states and the media. In the Australian press and globally there's a very cozy relationship between governments, officials, media spokespeople, and journalists. When most people in the media see so-called big stories on the front page of the paper, most of those stories are sanctioned leaks, basically some media adviser giving a journalist a story. Maybe it's a great scoop, mostly it's not; it's someone being soothed. What WikiLeaks does is change that, and challenge that. People often forget that Julian Assange, the founder of WikiLeaks, is not the leaker; he was allegedly given information by Bradley Manning, who is a low-level U.S. intelligence official from Iraq who's now sadly in jail in the United States. Julian Assange is an outsider, not a player. He's not someone who's spent many years working to make contacts in the media. He challenges that cozy relationship. Many in the media resent how WikiLeaks operates, because they didn't get the leaks, or they weren't the ones who had the relationship. So that's one change in the relationship between the media and the state. The other is the reality of how our government operates, which many people presumed, is now revealed very clearly in black and white.

HC: When you say "our government," you mean the Australian and U.S. governments?

AL: Many governments. In recent documents, Cablegate, there's information about countless countries—Southeast Asia, the United States, Australia, parts of Asia, the Middle East—many, many countries. It punctures the narrative of the American government and the West being benevolent, always striving for peace, looking for the best way forward for themselves or their people. You find countless examples, many of which have been in the press. A few examples: the reality of Shell operating in Nigeria, which has been known for years, essentially infiltrating the Nigerian government to make sure that it gets the best opportunities possible, and the United States being very aware of that. The reality of many of the Arab states—Jordan, Egypt, Saudi Arabia, all dictatorships—who are encouraging the United States, or Israel for that matter, to strike Iran militarily, which is seen as a regional threat to American and Israeli hegemony. You see, for example, Australian government ministers giving intimate information about their governing parties to the U.S. embassy in Canberra. When you see it in black and white it reveals very much how U.S. foreign policy works, and often it's not pretty; it needs to be exposed, and that's why many in the government, and many indeed in the press who feed off that relationship, are resentful.

HC: Michel Chossudovsky was pointing out that even though these WikiLeaks have come straight from government documents in the United States, they are being published by traditional media outlets. And that, for instance, the *New York Times* is checking with government sources all the time. He was setting up a query about whether this was all absolutely kosher. Could there be intrigue still between the traditional journalists who are very close to government agencies in the United States and the Pentagon, like David Sanger and many who write for the *New York Times*, or could this be absolutely independent?

AL: The *New York Times* has been very keen to check everything they've been doing with the government before they publish it. For the first three years since its birth in 2006, WikiLeaks refused to publish materials through the mainstream press. Julian Assange's ideology was: we're getting information; we're putting it on our website; people can access it, bloggers, journalists, whatever. But he got very frustrated with the fact that, in his view, it wasn't getting the kind of traction that it needed. So he decided before he released the Afghan and Iraq war logs, before the "cablegate" logs, to partner with *The Guardian*, the *New York Times*, and a few others to release them. There's no doubt that *The Guardian* and the *New York Times* have reported the information very differently. The *New York Times* was very keen to make sure the Obama administration was pleased, or not displeased, with the stuff they released. *The Guardian* did not do that, though the relationship with both outlets has collapsed. I think WikiLeaks has shown that simply releasing mass amounts of information without some analysis is very difficult. To its credit, *The Guardian* also released the cables at the same time. So people can look at those and make their own assessments.

HC: The uncensored cables.

AL: Indeed. The strengths, though, in my mind of what *The Guardian* did as opposed to the other press is that it reported the documents and essentially gave analysis, context. Some have argued that there were 250,000 cables released at the same time, but they were released gradually. WikiLeaks is essentially saying, We're not going to release them all at once, we're going to release them in staggered way, then the public can put them in whatever order they want. The mainstream press was selective in releasing information. The *New York Times* clearly is doing that. Lots of evidence suggests a lot of stories and angles they're doing sort of cover the embarrassment of the U.S. government. *The Guardian* is not taking that point of view. *The Guardian* has reported numerous examples. In Australia, one of the major news organizations has struck a deal with WikiLeaks, and the problem with their coverage, although much of it's been very interesting, is that a full week and a half after they released the documents to their papers, they didn't publish the cables themselves. The editors of the major papers in Australia that released it said, "We didn't want to give our rivals special advantage." They didn't want the cables to be seen by the wide public, or by media rivals, because the rivals may well have written stories based on them before they did. That really goes against the spirit of what WikiLeaks is doing.

HC: What if some of the cables start to reveal the truth about government thinking about 9/11?

AL: That's a very interesting question. Most of the documents that have been released are generally about the last decade. Some of the documents go back much further, stuff about Indonesia and East Timor in the 1970s. There may well be stuff about 9/11. Many people I know would like to find out about details on the runup to the Iraq War, the Afghan War, and potentially, as many of us fear, a war against Iran.

HC: If 9/11 documents were released, that would put the cat among the pigeons. There's a huge amount that we don't know, that was covered up and could have huge political ramifications in the United States.

Give us a little background about Julian Assange. His childhood, his philosophical attitude toward life, the media, the truth. Where's he coming from, and who is he?

AL: He's an Australian citizen; he was born in 1971. He came from a relatively broken home. He lived in Queensland, which is the northern part of Australia. He spent many years as a hacker. He was charged in Australia about fifteen years ago with hacking and ended up being released. He's written a number of manifestos. One book, *Underground*, looks at the way in which the state has a relationship with information. He comes from a position that many people in the hacking world do, that information should be far freer. There should be far less secrecy in government. And that it's our responsibility as citizens to demand information gets released. In 2006 he launched WikiLeaks. Back then it was a pretty small website. He approached a number of people, including me, to be on the board. I said yes. He was interested in finding individuals both in Australia and overseas to get information for WikiLeaks. Because one of the things he believed was that the press simply wasn't doing its job; the corporate press was far too close to the governments in power, and therefore you needed an outside force, a website, to be a check on government, but also on the media itself. So he started receiving information, large amounts of information. People often forget. Look back before these last years; WikiLeaks has really taken on a whole new life of its own globally, but they'd actually released mountains of stuff already. A few good examples: he released information about: guidelines for Guantánamo Bay, stolen elections in Kenya, torture in Iraq. This is well before 2010. He believes in challenging the corporate press, and I think he mostly dislikes the press. He's recently courted them, for reasons that people can applaud or criticize. I would argue correctly, probably, that he wants to get massive exposure for this kind of material, and the simple truth is, with all their faults, the corporate press still gets huge amounts of readership. If you can release information, and get it out in a way that he feels, and the organization feels, is transparent, then why not?

There's been criticism of Assange being rather egocentric; there's a danger both before his recent controversy, and now in making WikiLeaks all about one person. There's always a danger in having a cult figure. The current rape allegations in Sweden add a very complex level of difficulty to that situation. Without going into great detail, because it's complicated and we don't know all the specifics of the case, there's evidence that suggests the allegations are very politically motivated, but no one suggests, including me, that he should be above the law. Far from it. But I think we'll see a prolonged legal battle to avoid extradition, to avoid going to Sweden, to the United States. But ultimately that's a separate issue. Unfortunately, the press now, arguably what many governments would like, is taking up a lot of the time and space to talk about Assange's sex life as opposed to what WikiLeaks is actually doing. It's exactly what governments would want, to smear the messenger. And we know that the allegations against Assange and what he's doing are not directed at the press that are reporting it; there's been some calls in America for the *New York Times* to be prosecuted, because they've allegedly published information that is potentially treasonous. But much of the criticism of this recent leak has been directed at Assange, not at the press.

I wouldn't call him an information anarchist; I'm not sure that's the right term. But certainly he's very skeptical of how the corporate press does not keep checks on government power, and I would agree.

HC: Someone recently pointed out that if they charged all politicians with the same charges of rape and sex abuse that they've charged Assange, parliaments, Congress, the Senate would all be virtually empty.

AL: That's a very sad state of affairs.

HC: Every time I went to Washington to lobby I was propositioned by various congressmen. But as Henry Kissinger said, "Power is the ultimate aphrodisiac." The other thing I'd like to point out is the complicity of the *New York Times*, for instance, in arranging the Iraq invasion by publishing articles by Judith Miller. Five front-page articles saying that there was absolute evidence that those aluminum tubes were for processing uranium and that Iraq had weapons of mass destruction. The *New York Times* has kind of apologized, but it in fact helped to organize the invasion of Iraq. Is the media totally complicit now, or compliant with, government? They embedded the journalists with the troops going to Iraq, and their stories were censored by the Pentagon. So just from that perspective, Julian Assange is doing a very noble thing.

AL: I'd add to that point: The embedding process, of journalists actually having gone in battle tanks, is very effective from the government's perspective, but it's also an embedded mind-set. Some journalists love being close to power, they love being close to important people and getting important information. That is the problem. There's little transparency. Journalists are taken on many free trips. There's no acknowledgment of how that works. I should point out that Judith Miller's had a remarkable transformation. She now has a new career working for Fox News.

HC: Julian Assange has opened up the whole book so we can look at the way governments use our tax dollars, work behind closed doors, set up wars, work with corporations and the like in ways we really don't understand.

AL: That's why the Australian government, the American government, and most governments apart from Venezuela and a handful of others are so irate and trying to find a way to silence WikiLeaks. A few days after Cablegate was released, the Australian government and the prime minister came out and said very publicly that Julian Assange was doing illegal things and should be prosecuted. For what crimes? The prime minister couldn't name anything, and she still can't, because no laws have been broken. I think one of the things that you see in the United States as well about this kind of coverage is, it's framed in a very post-9/11 way. Any kind of revelations of how the United States works or how Australia works is helping our enemies. It's helping terrorists essentially get us from the inside; it's helping Assange. He's been accused in the United States of being on the side of the terrorists.

We shouldn't forget the rhetoric that's been directed at Assange in the United States has been quite extraordinary. Not just from fringe players. We're talking about major politicians, potential future presidents of America, talking openly about assassination; senior Fox News correspondents talking about launching strikes on Assange. This is the level of rhetoric. What's astounding is that there's no payback for that. You can say that kind of thing openly and no one blinks an eye. Simply, it's supposedly okay in a post-9/11 world to talk openly about assassinating people you don't like. Therefore, Assange rightfully fears for his life; he's [at the time of this writing] under house arrest in Britain. And hopefully will be released.

But one of the things that I as a journalist see is that it shows what the independent press could do. What I mean briefly is that, although they're working with the corporate press now, he has shown it's possible to release information, embarrass governments, yet not insulate yourself from criticism. The independent press has a major role to play in every country. It could learn a great deal from a site like WikiLeaks to get information that's important. Not necessarily always major political acts—it may be smaller—but there's no doubt that Assange has shown a model of how this can be done. He's been a trailblazer. And governments are trying to silence him, not realizing that you really can't put the genie back in the bottle.

I've found this in my *Blogging Revolution* book; many governments around the world, including the United States', don't realize that the Internet is not like a newspaper. You can shut down a website; you can put someone in jail and try and silence them. But we saw with WikiLeaks that when there were serious attempts, massive pressures to silence that website within about two hours there were a thousand mirror sites around the world put up by sympathetic supporters. Unless you shut down the entire Internet, which won't happen, WikiLeaks and what it stands for cannot be killed.

That is the real fear that many journalists and politicians have. WikiLeaks could disappear tomorrow, Assange could be put in jail for years, God forbid, but ultimately, other people have seen how it's done. The importance, or the danger, is that some people have criticized the release in the last few weeks, speculating that the result will be governments becoming more secretive, that governments are going to be less open. And in the short term, that's possible. Who knows? But at the same time, people have also seen how important it is to release this information. Daniel Ellsberg, the famous Pentagon Papers leaker, said for years before this recent controversy, almost begging in a way, for American soldiers, intelligence offices, someone in the U.S. government to leak information about 9/11, about the Iraq War, about the Afghan War to show Americans and the world what exactly went wrong, what happened, the lies, etc. And then a U.S. soldier or intelligence officer, allegedly Bradley Manning, released this information, and Assange released it to the world. There haven't been that many people, and there's been an absence of bravery.

Now at the same time, Manning is facing a lifetime in jail. The guy's in his early twenties; he's facing fifty-plus years in jail. That's of course an attempt to say to other people who might be considering it, If you release information, we're going to put you in jail for the rest of your life. But the hope is that people see Manning is a hero. We suspect there are many Americans in the establishment who feel the same way but haven't quite gotten to the point of getting it out there. I would encourage anyone who thinks about doing that, obviously there's a high price to pay, no one can underestimate that, but you can argue that Bradley Manning is actually doing the most patriotic thing imaginable.

HC: He'll go down in history as an instrumental figure. There are probably thousands who know how to hack and get into systems. They may have to go back to diplomatic pouches and send material by mail rather than by the Internet, to keep it secret.

I wonder where it's going to lead democracy, governments, the way they operate, and how they integrate with the corporations of the world.

AL: It's ironic in the extreme. Many people talk about issues of Web freedom, and there is growing pressure, not just in places like China and Iran, where you'd expect Internet censorship, but also in the West, in the United States and Australia and elsewhere to censor the Internet.

HC: Can it be censored, really?

AL: People say that to the extent that a lot of information's not available, yes, you can. If you have a massive infrastructure, which is what China has—with the assistance, I might add, of Microsoft and Cisco, which are Western companies—you can censor the Internet. China has something called a fifty-cent army, which is literally thousands of Chinese people whose job—and they get paid fifty cents per go—is to go onto online sites and put pro-government comments on sites. That's not in itself censorship, but it's controlling the conversation. One of the big issues in America is the issue of net neutrality.

HC: What does it mean?

AL: There's a design by many corporations to have a two-tier Internet system. You can pay up and get a very fast Internet with good access. If you can't, you get a slow Internet, and much slower access. The corporations are saying, Well, why couldn't we revive the infrastructure and put this money into the Internet? Why shouldn't we be able to charge more for users who can afford it? The opponents in the States say that a two-tier Internet is the opposite of what the Internet should be. It should be open to all, there should be access to all, there should be no choice between those who can afford it and those who cannot. That's not so much censorship as an attempt to impose some kind of very clear class systems on the Web. There's no doubt, though, that in the last few years—and again, 9/11 has been central to this—many prominent U.S. senators, and you see this in other countries too, talk about the idea of censoring information on the Web that endorses terrorism. For example, Hamas or Hezbollah, major movements in the Middle East. Some people love them, some people hate them, but the truth is that they have massive support in the Middle East, they're both elected—which we shouldn't forget, in Palestine and Lebanon— but in many Western countries they're regarded as terrorist organizations. In America and in Australia there's been an urge to say that citizens should not be able to access the websites of those groups, because we shouldn't have a right to access terrorist information. The problem with this is, on one hand, self-evident: these organizations are not terrorist organizations, which is a debate one can have some other time, but organizations and institutions that speak for many people. Shouldn't we have the right to see what they're saying? The problem from post-9/11 American foreign policy is that Islam is only seen in two ways: there's good Islam and there's bad Islam, there's good Muslims and there's bad Muslims. The U.S. view of Islam has been so narrow, so blinded by ideology, saying only one view of Islam is acceptable, one that's pro–United States, that they're excluding many Muslims around the world who may be interested in engaging with America. There are moves to censor websites of any Muslim organization that sees itself as Islamist—

that doesn't defend any terrible behavior that's gone on in the Arab world.

HC: But can they be censored?

AL: The answer is yes.

HC: How?

AL: You can, like in China, make certain websites inaccessible. I should say you can censor it, but there are always ways around it. We shouldn't underestimate that one of the reasons for censorship is to make people more fearful of going to those sites.

HC: What fear could be aroused by having a censored site?

AL: Monitoring access.

HC: What would happen if you monitored a censored site?

AL: For example, in Iran and China: if you are going to an Internet café—and many individuals can't afford their own computers so they go to massive Internet cafes—the computers themselves are monitored, the centers are monitored, people can see what you're looking at. I'm not suggesting that in China or Iran people aren't looking at so-called covert websites—they do all the time. There's no doubt that, for example, in Iran in the last year and a half there's been a massive crackdown on the dissent that existed in Iran. Although it's there, it's massively reduced. People are scared by the massive show of force by the regime against any dissidents. This is not to suggest there's not dissent. I follow it. There are bloggers and writers who still, mostly anonymously now, write in this kind of way.

Initially there were two ways to see the Internet. The so-called free world, America, Australia, and Europe, and the so-called repressive world, China, Iran, and other countries. And although that's generally true, increasingly many Western governments, and they've acknowledged this, look at a place like China and Iran and say, Maybe there's some good ideas over there. The kind of coalitions that are

forming to defend WikiLeaks in some ways ignore the left-right political divide, but in Australia, for example, in the United States and
in England, there are some from the left, from the libertarian right,
some from the center, the Web community, the free speech community, etc. Not particularly clearly left and right. Which I think
is a good thing. Wikileaks has come to represent far more than just
one man or website; it's an idea and true believers in free speech see
the importance of that.

HC: It's very interesting. We're talking about the extraordinary
power of the corporations, the Pentagon, and the military-industrial
complex. If you look at their leadership, they want to maintain their
position of superiority, especially as the rich are getting richer now
in America, they'll maintain that at any cost. Hackers now pose a
threat to the corporations and the powers that be who actually run
the world through globalization and the WTO. I think we need to
understand the very profound abnormalities that could occur in a
society and be ready to fight them. This is two sides coming together in an unholy throw down. Would you agree with that?

AL: Assange has claimed that he has documents about one of the
major U.S. banks, we think Bank of America but don't know for
sure, that could bring down the bank. Certainly he has incriminat-
ing documents about a major U.S. bank.

   You see how corporations have reacted to WikiLeaks. We
shouldn't forget that MasterCard, Visa, PayPal, and Amazon, all
major U.S. corporations, essentially buckled to U.S. government
pressure to exclude WikiLeaks and have imposed a banking block-
ade on the group. Assange said that it's clear those organizations
have toed the U.S. foreign policy. There are now growing calls to
boycott those organizations to make them aware of how they behave. When Google in 2006 made a clear decision to go into China
and censor its search engine, there was a massive backlash. Now,
the company still exists, but in the end there was a very bad stench

that emanated from Google about its behavior. Essentially it colluded with the Chinese regime. And it's tried to not make it as bad as before. There is a realization that public opinion does matter, and many corporations simply act as if the public doesn't exist. In other words, people are always going to access Amazon, because it's the biggest bookstore in the world, but one doesn't have to use Amazon, one doesn't have to use PayPal. I think there was a realization for many citizens that those corporations buckled without any evidence. Amazon or PayPal received a call saying WikiLeaks is doing something terrible, you guys really shouldn't be supporting them or hosting them. They're petrified of getting into a fight with the U.S. government. People notice that. There has been a growing online campaign to target those companies. We're now in the middle of a very strange development, kind of like a cyberwar. It's getting a bit of press, but many hackers around the world who are pro-WikiLeaks are saying, Well, if you guys as a corporation are going to behave that way and shut down the right to free speech, and shut down WikiLeaks, we're going to close down your website. The Anonymous group is behind some of this. Many hackers would say, Our aim is not to destroy Amazon; our aim is civil disobedience. Your website's inaccessible for one day, or you can't access Visa for a day—*The Guardian* ran an editorial on this that didn't condemn it. Essentially one side does one thing and one side does something back. That can escalate, potentially quite dangerously. That's what's happening now. The lead story in *The Independent* in London was that the British government was worried that depending on what happened to Julian Assange in his court case, hackers may well target the British government websites in retaliation. There's an ability to do so by those on the Web, as opposed to what's happened in the past, when the Chinese government or proxies of the Chinese government attempted to get information from the defense department website or from the Pentagon, or bring them down for a short period of time. Now you have a situation where activists or hackers are interested in showing corporations up. What people think about that kind of behavior is an interesting question. I think there's something to be said for that; you could argue that it shows that these corporations can be reached by average citizens. How people feel about websites being hacked into is a different debate, but the argument about whether this is civil disobedience is something worth considering.

HC: The power of the Internet is extraordinary. Almost all people now in Western nations, and others except the developing nations, have access to the Internet. Which leads into something that worries the hell out of me. We know that both Russia and America have thousands of hydrogen bombs and missiles on hair-trigger alert that give Putin or Obama a three-minute decision time to release them by decision, by accident, or by computer design. My question is, Can the Chinese hackers, or some irresponsible kids, get into the Pentagon early-warning system? Or the Russian early-warning system? Because all of these weapons are under computer control.

AL: I don't know. There is no doubt that the WikiLeaks cable dump in the last few weeks has shown that the Chinese government, or certainly proxies of the Chinese government, have quite deep access to very top secret U.S. government areas. Not, as far as we know, to nuclear codes.*

HC: We know that America's made a weapon called Stuxnet that they injected into the computer systems of uranium enrichment facilities. So, to use an Australian expression, you can bugger up anything.

AL: That computer worm allegedly came from Israel. Apparently it was an incredibly effective virus from their perspective. It has supposedly affected the Iranian uranium nuclear program. You could

---

* This interview was conducted soon after Cablegate was released in late 2010.

argue that it's better doing that than bombing Iran. Many people fear the idea of a military strike on Iran for Iran's alleged nuclear arms capability, which has never been proven. I wouldn't have much faith that the Obama administration would stop Israel. WikiLeaks, in fact, has shown that there has been serious pressure on Israel from the United States, and from the Arab countries, to bomb Iran. No one's talking about an invasion, just a good old bombing run. People who argue that have a hope that this will bring the Iranian people to rise up against the regime. The opposite is obvious to many of us. When I was there a few years ago, many Iranians who hated the government with a passion said the day the United States bombs our country, Israel, America, or anyone else, we'll rally around the government.

You mentioned before how the *New York Times* was essentially a mouthpiece for the Iraq War. In many ways the *New York Times* learned no lesson whatsoever, because much of its reporting about Iran, and its so-called nuclear capability, is no different. It is generally filled with anonymous sourcing from U.S. government officials talking about the growing Iranian threat. It's the same journalists, David Sanger and others. But there's no accountability. It's as if either the press has permanent amnesia, which is possible, or more pernicious than that—they see their role as generally mirroring U.S. foreign policy.

I read the *New York Times* every day, because it basically gives me good insight into how the U.S. government thinks. Finally, on the nuclear question, we've seen the [then] Australian foreign minister, Kevin Rudd, who hardly believes in human rights in practice, say that Israel has got nuclear weapons and should have to be inspected by the IAEA. Now Israel's not very pleased.

HC: Rudd is the only one, since Golda Meir and Nixon formed an agreement to neither confirm nor deny Israel's nuclear arsenal, ever to come out and say it has one, and that there should be inspectors there. Physicians for Social Responsibility did a study and estimated that if Israel dropped three small nuclear weapons on the two uranium facilities in Iran, the fallout would be such that it could kill up to a million people by acute radiation illness and cancer all the way over to Pakistan. We mustn't forget that we're playing with absolute fire. ∼

JOHN CHURCH

John Church is the world's leading expert on sea-level rise. Church is an Australian oceanographer with the Center for Australian Weather and Climate Research and the Antarctic Climate & Ecosystems Cooperative Research Center. His expertise lies in the role of the ocean in climate, particularly anthropogenic climate change. He was the co-convening lead author for the chapter on sea level in the International Panel on Climate Change Third Assessment Report. John Church was awarded the 2006 Roger Revelle Prize, which recognizes leaders whose outstanding contributions advance or promote research in the ocean, climate, and earth sciences.

———

HELEN CALDICOTT: I've read a published report that says that the Arctic has less ice this summer than ever before.

JOHN CHURCH: I haven't seen that report, but I have seen the area covered by sea ice, and for this time of year I think it's the lowest in the records.

HC: Why don't you explain what the albedo effect is?

JC: The albedo of the Earth is a measure of how much of the solar radiation is actually reflected by the Earth. So as the Earth is warmed by solar radiation, some of that is reflected by clouds and the remainder is absorbed, principally by the land surface, by the ocean surface, and some into the atmosphere as well. Then the Earth warms and radiates more energy.

HC: Specifically applying that to the Arctic and the Antarctic ice, obviously it's very white, and it reflects the heat of the sun back into the atmosphere, but what happens when the ice melts and there's no whiteness, only the black of the sea?

JC: The ice covers the land and the ocean, and snow cover is one of the mechanisms by which solar radiation is reflected. If you reduce the sea ice cover, or even change the reflectivity of the snow or sea ice, then you can actually reduce the amount of solar radiation reflected back to space. That's an additional amount of energy the Earth absorbs, and therefore it warms the Earth further. This is one of the positive feedbacks in climate change.

HC: When you say "positive feedbacks," it means that global warming is increased, because black water absorbs heat, while the white ice reflects the heat back into the atmosphere, right?

JC: That's right. The oceans reflect some of the solar energy, but the majority is absorbed, whereas the sea ice, particularly when it has snow cover on it, reflects most of the solar energy.

HC: I suppose that's true too for the mountains and the glaciers. I was fascinated to read the other day that in Argentina, people are so worried about the glacial melt and global warming, they're actually whitewashing the mountains. They're painting the black rock of the mountains white.

JC: I hadn't seen that.

HC: That seems a little naive and limited compared to what we're dealing with. I was fascinated by how scientists worked out that the ocean level is rising and that the seas are getting warmer. But going back to when the carbon dioxide levels were higher in the atmosphere: can you outline the progression of global warming from the ice ages through to where we are now?

JC: If we go back to about 130,000 years before the present, that's the time of the last interglacial, sometimes called the Eemian. At that time the Earth was slightly warmer than today, sea levels probably more than 6 meters [about 20 feet] higher than our current sea levels. The Earth was warmer, at temperatures that we might expect to get to late this century.

HC: What were the factors causing it to be warmer 130,000 years ago?

JC: I think primarily changes in solar radiation compared to today.

HC: How does solar radiation change, then? What happens in the Sun that causes the Earth to heat up? Is it solar flares?

JC: No, it's not primarily changes in the solar radiation but changes in the solar radiation received at the Earth, associated with changes in the Earth's orbit. So the orbit is tilted as it rotates around the Sun, and that tilt varies; the orbit is eccentric, and the eccentricity varies. All these factors combine to change the amount of solar radiation received at the Earth.

HC: What are the factors that alter the eccentricity of the Earth's orbit?

JC: These are natural factors associated with the long-term evolution of the Earth's orbit. We have no control over them.

HC: What does the interglacial period refer to?

JC: From about 130,000 up to about 20,000 years ago, the Earth gradually cooled, and sea levels fell as major ice sheets formed, particularly on North America and northern Europe. It fell to more

than 120 meters [131 yards] below present-day sea levels. That was
the Ice Age. Then the ice sheets started to melt and slide into the
ocean as the planet warmed, and from about 20,000 years ago to
about 7,000 years ago, sea levels rose rapidly by about a meter [three
feet] a century for several millennia. About 7,000 years ago, sea
levels started to stabilize, they rose less rapidly for a few thousand
years, and then, over the last couple of thousand years, the sea level
rises—up until about 1,800 A.D.—have been very small.

HC: Modern human beings have been around for how long?

JC: About 200,000 years.

HC: So climate change through the ages has had a huge impact on
human populations, and of course on animals as well. From the last
ice age, what caused the Earth to heat up again?

JC: For the last million years these ice age cycles have been paced by
solar radiation associated with the Earth's orbit. But that solar force
on its own is not strong enough to explain the observed changes in
climate.

HC: That's happening now?

JC: Changes in greenhouse gases in the atmosphere, principally carbon dioxide and methane, reinforced the warming that came from
changes in the solar radiation received from the Earth and led to
the Ice Age.

HC: There were no humans pumping carbon dioxide or other
greenhouse gases into the atmosphere at that time, so what caused
the carbon dioxide concentrations to increase those many thousands of years ago?

JC: This is again outside my area, and not fully understood, but it's
thought to be associated with changes in temperature, changes in
ice cover, in ocean circulation, and in the vegetation of the Earth.
Warm oceans can't carry as much carbon dioxide, and some of this

was released into the atmosphere, increasing the atmospheric green-house gases as the Earth warmed.

HC: Let's come up to the beginning of the last century. The concentration of carbon dioxide in the atmosphere was 280 ppm [parts per million]. Can you tell us what has happened since the beginning of the Industrial Revolution? That is, since anthropogenic, or man-made, changes began affecting the atmosphere.

JC: Carbon dioxide concentrations in the atmosphere have increased since the start of the Industrial Revolution. They're now about 390 ppm, compared to 280 ppm during most of the Holocene period. That compares to concentrations of 180 ppm during the Ice Age. It's now increasing at about 2 ppm per year, with the largest contribution coming from the burning of fossil fuels. But clearing of forests also contributes.

HC: And also plowing of the soil?

JC: There are many factors associated with the air and sea exchange of carbon dioxide; the terrestrial region is particularly important but less well understood. This exchange is with the trees and forests, etc., but also with the soil, and of course with the ocean. The annual exchange between the ocean and the atmosphere, and the atmosphere and the land, is very large. The ocean is about 90 gigatons of carbon dioxide per year, but that's a seasonal exchange. The oceans take up that amount of carbon dioxide and then release it again later, on a seasonal cycle.

HC: They release it during the winter?

JC: It depends where you are.

HC: What about the other very scary global warming gas, methane, now starting to be released in large quantities from the warming oceans, and also from the heat and permafrost that is now melting, particularly in the northern hemisphere?

JC: Methane is a greenhouse gas as well, and it is being released by the burning of fossil fuels, leakage from pipelines, etc. There are large amounts of peat and carbon, and large amounts of methane locked up in peat, especially in Europe and northern Asia, that potentially could be released. There are examples of that release occurring.

HC: As Arctic ice melts and the permafrost melts, in the northern hemisphere particularly, there are going to be huge increases in methane. Methane is twenty times more potent as a global warmer than carbon dioxide.

JC: Methane is a more potent greenhouse gas than carbon dioxide. It also has a shorter lifetime.

HC: Why is the sea level changing right now, and what is causing the rise?

JC: In the last thousand years the rate of rise was very small, only a few tenths of a millimeter per year, at most. The average rate of the rise during the end of the twentieth century was 1.7 millimeters per year; since 1993 the rate of rise has been over 3 millimeters per year, which has been confirmed both from satellite measurement and from our coastal sea-level measurements. There are really three major contributing reasons for the sea-level rise in the twentieth century. First, as the oceans warm they expand.

HC: Because water expands when it's heated?

JC: Yes. As with a thermometer, you heat the liquid and the liquid expands and rises. So the oceans are the Earth's thermometer. The oceans absorb huge amounts of heat. That's one of the two largest contributions to sea-level rise, particularly during the last fifty years. Second, there are glaciers and ice caps throughout the world, small glaciers, in places like Patagonia, Alaska, and the Himalayas. They contain about 60 centimeters of sea-level equivalent, if they all melted. There's widespread observations of melting glaciers and ice caps. Estimating their contributions to the sea level is difficult, but it's probably, along with ocean expansion, one of the two most important contributions to sea-level rise. Then there's the ice sheets. There's the Antarctic ice sheet, south of Australia, and the Greenland ice sheet, which contains enough water to raise the sea level by about seven meters [23 feet] if it were to completely melt. At the moment the Greenland ice sheet is a balance between snowfall, ice melting, and ice discharge. The snowfall compacts to form ice, and gradually that ice flows off into the ocean, discharging as icebergs. The surface of Greenland also melts, particularly during summer. At the moment the balance for the snowfall on the Atlantic is about 50 percent from iceberg discharge and 50 percent from ice melting. Since we now have satellite observations of Greenland we can see that the area of melt on the Greenland ice sheet has been increasing, and the volume of melt entering the ocean, and the flow of ice into the ocean, has also been increasing.

There's lots of ice melting on Greenland, and you can see it melting off as rivers, flowing down, forming holes in the ice sheet, and making its way down to the ice sheet, then flowing off into the ocean. There are examples where we can actually see a lake that has formed on the surface of the ice sheet suddenly broken through and drained very rapidly. Whether it made its way to the base is unclear. It's thought that this process is important, but it only contributes a relatively minor amount to the increased flow of the ice sheets.

But what is perhaps more concerning is that warm ocean water can penetrate below the ice shelves and melt them at their base, and they can melt the ice shelves at the grounding line. That's the point where the ice starts to float into the ocean. When they melt the ice shelves, they can release the buttressing that stops some of the ice flowing, and the ice can flow more rapidly into the ocean. This is a little bit like having a bottle lying on its side and taking out the cork, which allows water to flow more rapidly. If you destabilize the ice shelves, you let the ice sheets or the upper glaciers from the ice sheets flow more rapidly. That's thought to be the important process. There are observations of this occurring. There's starting to be models that seem to explain the observations, better than the process of surface melt and the surface melt making its way to the base of the glacier. But we don't have complete models that allow us to do proper projections of this process for both the Greenland and the Antarctic ice sheets at this stage.

All of these things have been contributing to the sea level.

HC: How thick is the ice sheet in Greenland?

JC: I think it's 3 kilometers [2 miles] at its thickest point.

HC: The West Antarctic Ice Sheet, which is at the south pole, is pretty big, isn't it? What exactly is happening there?

JC: The Antarctic ice sheet is much bigger than the Greenland ice sheet. It's divided into two, the West Antarctic Ice Sheet, which contains about 3 meters [10 feet] of sea level equivalent that could contribute to sea-level rise relatively rapidly. The East Antarctic Ice Sheet is bigger and relatively more stable. The same pressures occurring in some regions of the Greenland ice sheet are also occurring in the west Antarctic ice sheet. The critical point to recognize is that the ice is so thick for much of the west Antarctic ice sheet that it's resting on land, which is below current-day sea level. The process I described, of warm water penetrating under the ice sheet, is occurring in the west Antarctic ice sheet, particularly in the region of the Thwaites and the Pine Island Glaciers. We're seeing a loss of mass from these regions, and a more rapid flow of glaciers into the ocean. The base of parts of this ice sheet slopes downward as you go away from the ocean, rather than sloping up. When warm water penetrates underneath and starts melting the ice sheet at its base, the grounding line, these situations can become unstable. Either the melting progresses until it meets a new rise, which stabilizes it, or this melting process continues until some other mechanism to stop it is reached.

HC: I don't quite understand the significance of the fact that the ground underneath the west Antarctic ice sheet slopes down and not up below sea level. What is the dynamic of the warmer sea melting the sea at ground level, where the ice and rock merge?

JC: Warm ocean water that's dense has more salt in it. When sea ice forms, it rejects the salt.

HC: It's freshwater.

JC: The sea ice is fresh but the ocean water is dense, so it can penetrate beneath the ice shelves, melt part of the ice shelves, and so become fresher and lighter, and then it flows out underneath the base of the ice shelf, and more ocean water penetrates underneath. This process is an unstable situation in which the warm ocean water can continue to flow in, can continue to melt the ice sheet at its base, freeing it and allowing it to slide more rapidly.

HC: So then if you add up a 3-meter [10 feet] sea rise from the melt of the west Antarctic ice sheet and 7 meters [23 feet] from the Greenland ice sheet, you have a 10-meter [33 feet] sea-level rise?

JC: That's a potential scenario in the longer term. We're not talking about that amount of rise for the twenty-first century. There will be significant contributions from the warming of the ocean and from continued melting of the glaciers and ice caps around the world. There'll be continued changes in the surface mass balance, the amount of snowfall and the melting on the Greenland ice sheet. The projections from the last report were a rise in the sea level of 18 to 59 centimeters [7 to 23 inches] by 2100. What this did not include was the dynamic response we've been talking about; they didn't know how to estimate this additional component. But it's important to recognize that this is essentially a one-sided uncertainty. You can increase the amount of sea-level rise, but you can't substantially decrease it. There is a simple scaling argument that says perhaps an extra 10 or 20 centimeters [4 or 8 inches] by 2100, but we can't really be sure. That would make a range of about 18 to 80 centimeters [7 to 32 inches] by 2100. But we don't really understand these ice sheets very well, so it could be more.

HC: What's the worst-case scenario?

JC: We look back through the Earth's history to see if this has happened before, to help estimate how quickly things could change. Temperatures 130,000 years ago, in the last interglacial, were similar to what we might expect at the end of this century. Sea levels were higher, and coming into those high sea levels, rates of sea-level rise were very likely greater than 6 meters [20 feet] per millennia, so that's about 60 centimeters [24 inches] in a century if it continues at the average rate. There was very likely less than 9 meters [30 feet] per millennia, that's 90 centimeters [35 inches] in a century. That's consistent with the upper end of the IPCC projections, perhaps a little bit higher. Recently there's been a number of simple models developed that try to estimate sea levels by scaling them to global average temperatures. People did this as they recognized that this was a critically important issue, but we didn't know how to model the ice sheets as yet. And these models have come up with somewhat larger amounts, over a meter [3 feet] per century.

Personally I'm very cautious of such models. They're based on very simple ideas, and they're tuned to conditions in the twentieth century that probably won't be the major contributors in the twenty-first. However, rates of a meter [3 feet] per century may be possible in the future, and perhaps larger rates. It's also important to recognize that sea-level rise will not stop in 2100. Sea-level rise from ocean expansion will continue for centuries, probably millennia, even after greenhouse gas concentrations have stabilized. The ice sheets will continue to respond for millennia also.

What could happen? One of the important scenarios is the surface melting of the Greenland ice sheet. There's a temperature at which surface melting alone exceeds snowfall in Antarctica. This leads to an ongoing decay of the Greenland ice sheet, no matter what happens to the glacier flow. This threshold is thought to be between 2 degrees and 4 degrees Celsius [3.6 degrees and 7.2 degrees Fahrenheit], above preindustrial temperatures. We're already about 0.7 degrees [1.3 degrees], on the way to 2 degrees [3.6 degrees]. We're committed to at least another 0.6 degrees Celsius [1.1 degrees Fahrenheit], even if we stabilize concentrations at today's level, probably somewhat more. So we're well on the way to approaching this threshold, and crossing it late this century. That's very significant.

HC: What about storms, and how these climatic catastrophes are aggravated or can aggravate sea-level rise? How would people who are living at sea level or just above be affected?

JC: First, our society is essentially a coastal society. Many people around the world live near the coast. Many of our major cities are based right on the coast. This coastal society has developed over the last thousand-plus years, during a period of very stable sea levels. In some regions sea level relative to the land has been falling, because the land has been rising. This is associated with changes in the ice sheets and in the surface load of the Earth, so the shape of the Earth changes slightly. This has allowed us as a society to develop right up to the coastline and enjoy the ocean. Over the last century and a half or two centuries, in many areas where the sea level might have been falling very slightly, it's now rising, and rising more rapidly. Places like the east coast of America, where the sea level was already rising as a result of sinking land in that region, the rate of the rise has now increased. Our coastal society is impacted by extreme events, particularly storms associated with tropical cyclones or hurricanes. A good example is Hurricane Katrina and its impact on New Orleans. Changes in the sea level change the frequency at which a coastal flooding event of a given magnitude occurs; i.e., increases in the frequency of exceedance of a particular threshold, for which sea level has some impact on coastal cities or coastal developments. There are many locations where the frequency of exceeding these thresholds has increased markedly during the twentieth century. If you look at the east and west coasts of Australia, for example: Sydney and Fremantle, for which we have the two longest sea level records in Australia, extreme coastal flooding events occurred three times more frequently during the last half of the twentieth century than during the first half of the twentieth century. I'm not saying that the frequency of storms will increase. That's a separate issue. Just sea level alone causes coastal flooding events to increase in frequency, and that's a very robust finding, and it's a finding you can project into the future. So by 2100, for places like Sydney, the current coastal flooding event that happens once in one hundred years is likely to be happening several times per year.

HC: As the sea level rises, an ordinary storm that wouldn't have caused coastal flooding previously will now cause coastal flooding? What about areas like Bangladesh, where 200 million people or more live at sea level on a delta of a river?

JC: Many of the most densely populated areas around the world are deltaic regions like Bangladesh. So rising sea levels are impacting these regions. But, in addition, many of these deltaic regions are sinking. The sediments themselves compact, and if you extract water from the sediments, they compact more rapidly, and this is happening in many regions, Bangladesh included. Bangkok is another such place. This falling of the land can be quite significant, and in some regions, it can be larger than the rate of the sea-level rise. But it's in addition to the rate of the sea level's rise.

Let's just consider the one meter [39 inches] above current high-tide sea levels around the world. About 140 million people live in this area. There's about a trillion dollars of GDP generated in this first meter of sea level, so there is a lot at risk here. There are a number of responses we can have to this. We can retreat from and abandon parts of the coastline. This is already occurring in parts of the world. In parts of the UK, they have a plan for retreat because it's too expensive to protect all the areas of the coastline. Second, we can accommodate a rising sea level by building coastal infrastructure higher, for example having sports fields in low-lying areas so it's not so important if they're occasionally or repeatedly flooded. And third, in some cases we can protect valuable coastlines. Again, we're already doing that. We have the Thames Barrage protecting about 100 billion pounds [158 billion dollars] of assets in the city of London from storm surges. The Thames Barrage has been closed more frequently in recent years. A couple of years ago a storm surge came within a couple of centimeters of overtopping it, and they are actively planning what extensions they need to make in order to raise the protection level for the city of London. Rotterdam has a similar storm surge protection barrier.

HC: There's now robust debate going on in Australia about immigration here, and refugees. I say to the government, "You ain't seen nothin' yet," because it's been predicted for a long time, but it's now about to occur, that millions of ecological refugees will be fleeing because of rising sea levels. And they'll be coming to the shores of Australia, because Australia's virtually a huge empty content. I find it fascinating that although it's self-evident to me and you and many others like the climate change workers, it's not being addressed at all by the politicians.

JC: I feel that environmental refugees will be a major issue during the twenty-first century. The difficulty is that rising sea levels, like many other types of climate change, will be felt first through extreme coastal flooding events. New Orleans is a good example, although it wasn't primarily a result of rising sea levels; it was a combination of sinking land, sea-level rise, and an extreme event, which impacted society. That will continue during the twenty-first century and have more significant impacts on many more people around the world. There will be people fleeing from these situations that will occur first through acute situations. For example the cyclone that hit Myanmar a couple of years ago where over one hundred thousand people died in a storm surge. That's the type of thing that will continue throughout the twenty-first century. It's not whether they will occur but when and where they will occur and how we as a society are going to respond to and try to anticipate these events.

HC: We as scientists need to be warning governments about these potential catastrophes and the refugees. I think governments, particularly ours in Australia but many others as well, for example in the United States, are fairly unaware of what this actually means to societies such as ours.

JC: We haven't fully appreciated the urgency of the situation. The threshold for the melting of the Greenland ice sheet is rapidly approaching. What would that mean for the world in terms of meters of sea-level rise? If we don't take urgent and very significant action, then we will cross that threshold. ❧

RHETT BUTLER

R hett Butler is founder of Mongabay.com, an environmental science news website with a focus on tropical forests. He is co-founder of *Tropical Conservation Science*, an academic journal that aims to provide opportunities for scientists in developing countries to publish their research in their native languages. Rhett has a background in economics and has traveled widely in Africa, the Asia Pacific, and Latin America. His writing has appeared in *Yale Environment 360*, the *Jakarta Post*, *Conservation Letters*, and *Trends in Evolution and Ecology*.

———

HELEN CALDICOTT: Let's talk about how you first got involved with this whole issue of tropical forest conservation.

RHETT BUTLER: When I was a child I was fortunate enough to have opportunities to travel. My mother was a travel agent specializing in exotic travel, and my father had a lot of airline miles. So I had some unique opportunities to see the world. My family was always interested in wildlife, so we'd often end up in rain forests. Sometimes after returning home I would learn that a couple of places I had been were destroyed or greatly changed. That impacted me personally.

Then, around 1996 there was a particular incident in Borneo, where an area of forest was logged, and I thought about the animals and what happened to them. I decided to write a book about tropical rain forests that would appeal to the general public.

HC: What was the book called?

RB: *A Place Out of Time*. Actually, it wasn't published, so that's part of the story. The publisher didn't have enough funds to publish the kind of book that I was hoping for, with pictures. Kind of defeated the purpose to just have a textbook. Instead I decided to think about it for a while, and so after a few months, I decided to put it online for free for everyone to see, since that was really the objective. That was the origin of the website.

HC: And why is it called Mongabay?

RB: "Mongabay" is derived from an island off of Madagascar. The island is actually spelled differently and pronounced differently, but I wanted something totally unique, and I wanted to be able to track people as they referred to the site.

HC: Describe Madagascar. Tell us who runs the island, what nationalities live there, what its history is, and tell us about its ecology.

RB: Madagascar is that big island off the coast of southeast Africa, just north of South Africa. The island's about the size of California. Madagascar's been isolated for a long time, which means that a lot of the species are unique. It's considered an ecological wonder and has an incredible wealth of biodiversity.

The first people who colonized Madagascar came from Southeast Asia. They sailed across the Indian Ocean, and Africans came later. So it's a real mix of cultures. That, of course, in addition to lemurs and chameleons and all sorts of wildlife, as well as unique plant species. Today Madagascar is an independent country; it used to be a colony of France. The economy is highly dependent on ecotourism, so there's a vested interest in preserving these wild places and the wildlife.

HC: How many species of flora and fauna are there on the island?

RB: I'm not sure if anyone knows the answer to that question. A few years ago, 150,000 of the island's 200,000 species were endemic, meaning they were found nowhere else. I think that might include plants.

HC: Tell us about some of the amazing species you've seen.

RB: Madagascar is most famous for its lemurs, a type of primate that's somewhat like a monkey. Lemurs are only found in Madagascar, and there are nearly one hundred types. But they've radiated into all different sorts of habitats and behaviors, so you have a diversity of lemurs. You have one that's called Indri that's about the size of a large house cat, colored like a panda bear, and sort of humanlike in body form. It's also the largest lemur, famous for its song. It sings kind of like a humpback whale.

Then you have lemurs called sifakas, which are also black and white, and they're well-known for dancing. It's kind of like a sashay in ballet. But at the same time they make sounds like someone cursing, so it's kind of like a cursing ballet dancer. You have the famous ring-tailed lemur, which is popular in zoos. Then you have tiny mouse lemurs, which are among the smallest primates in the world. So there's a huge diversity.

Then you have the reptiles, chameleons that come in all different colors and are capable of rapid color change. Brightly colored day geckos and other cryptic artists of camouflage. It's really an amazing place.

HC: Has there been any logging or destruction of the forest in Madagascar?

RB: Madagascar is famous for its large-scale destruction of forests, mostly due to subsistence activities. It's a very poor country, but there's been a heavy impact on the forest cover. Right now less than 10 percent of the forest cover remains.

HC: That means most species and animals would not be there?

RB: That's what's remarkable. You have this incredible biodiversity despite large-scale forest loss. It makes it all the more important to conserve what's left. Unfortunately, since the political troubles in Madagascar—there was a coup—a lot of the governing structure has kind of evaporated. National parks aren't necessarily being manned, and people aren't watching out for the wildlife. In the northeast of the country, the most biodiverse part of the island, there's been large-scale poaching of wildlife, and logging. There were revelations that there's been a commercial bushmeat market for lemurs. Thousands of lemurs are being taken out of forests and sold to commercial markets in towns and cities. A lot of the aid that would have been coming in to support conservation is no longer coming in. Foreign governments have suspended support to the government in light of the coup.

HC: Is there nothing the international community can do?

RB: Resuming support for conservation activities would make a big difference. There was a lot of media attention, so the government ended up sending in police to crack down on the illegal logging. That's had a big impact. The areas seeing logging and poaching are areas where there is no police presence.

HC: Since the coup, the government isn't interested in protecting the forests?

RB: With Madagascar being a very poor country, in many areas people can't feed themselves. So there are a lot of issues that make demands on the country's resources. That's one reason why aid is important. In general, Madagascar's had a good record in terms of conservation management. These are relatively new problems.

HC: Who's doing the logging?

RB: It's criminal gangs that are often heavily armed and backed by local traders who are working with international companies. There's a big Chinese presence and a lot of the timber—rosewood ebonies and valuable hardwoods—are being shipped straight to China. The real problem is this foreign demand. As far as I know, lemurs aren't being exported.

HC: In Indonesia, Papua New Guinea, and Borneo, there's been illegal logging, particularly under the reign of Suharto, that wicked dictator who the CIA supported for years. Would you talk about what happened in Indonesia and Borneo during the Suharto years?

RB: Suharto basically divvied up the country to his offspring. These very powerful forestry companies were run by his relatives. The destruction was quite severe and really impacted the country's ecology. If you look at satellite pictures of Borneo, what once was majestic forest is now heavily degraded landscapes, often oil palm and forestry plantations that were concessions to friends and relatives.

HC: And to whom was the timber sold at that time?

RB: The timber went all over. A lot of it ended up in the United States, as well as in Europe. It's processed in China, and then it goes to the United States.

HC: On your website it said that there's an effort to stop illegal logging in Papua New Guinea.

RB: Papua New Guinea is heavily dependent on forestry. There's this new idea that could provide alternative livelihoods for people, instead of logging, that is known as REDD—reducing emissions from deforestation and degradation. It means that developing countries will be paid for keeping their forests standing.

HC: And how does that work?

RB: The money will come from industrialized countries that are trying to offset some of their emissions. This means that a power-producing company in the United States or Australia, maybe one that runs off of coal, could essentially cancel out their emissions on paper by funding activities that reduce emissions somewhere else. So if a company's pumping out X number of tons of carbon dioxide a year, they could continue, but they'd have to pay for protecting a certain area of forest that would basically sequester that same amount of carbon dioxide.

HC: That seems inane to me, because the forests have been there forever, except we're destroying them. One cancels out the other. I don't get this carbon credit thing.

RB: This is a big issue. This is not a new issue, in terms of the forest-carbon mechanism; it's been highly contentious. They're going to countries where deforestation is actively occurring. They can generate credits by reducing deforestation. So a place like Indonesia, which is losing 2 to 3 million hectares [5 to 7 million acres] a year, if they reduce this to zero, they're going to get credit and funding for reducing those emissions. So the emissions reductions are real. But a lot of environmentalists have issues with the idea that rich countries can get off by paying for cheap emissions reductions in other countries.

HC: And they can keep pumping out their carbon dioxide with equanimity.

RB: Yes. But in the United States for example, which obviously is no leader in this area, the Waxman-Markey bill* called for a 17 percent reduction in U.S. greenhouse emissions by 2020. If you factor in avoiding deforestation, or REDD, that reduction could actually increase to a 27 percent reduction. The reductions from forest conservation would be additional, so that would be another 10 percent. Companies would have to cut emissions. It's not a perfect offset. But again, there are definitely arguments that condemn the whole offsetting concept.

---

* This bill was also known as the American Clean Energy and Security Act of 2009 (ACES). The bill was approved by the House of Representatives but died in the Senate.

HC: One of your papers says exactly what tropical forests are worth in terms of global warming. Tropical forests store roughly 25 percent of the planet's terrestrial carbon, more than 300 billion tons. When forests are cut—their vegetation burned and timber converted in to wood products—much of this carbon is released in the atmosphere as carbon dioxide. The clearing of 50,000 square miles of forests annually accounts for roughly 20 percent of global emissions from human activities—a share larger than all the world's planes, ships, cars, and trucks combined.*

You go on:

> [R]educing deforestation is no simple effort. Forests are being destroyed as a consequence of global economic forces—demand for timber, pulpwood, beef, soybeans, and palm oil—as well as subsistence farming.

I'd like now to go to the Amazon, because there's a lot of interesting stuff happening there, and it includes many countries: Peru, Brazil, Venezuela, Bolivia, French Guyana, Ecuador. What percentage of the remaining tropical forest is the Amazon combined?

RB: It's more than half of the world's tropical forest.

HC: It controls a lot of the climate in that part of the world, and in North and South America as well.

RB: The Amazon plays a major role in global climate. Scientists have actually linked deforestation in the Amazon with rainfall in parts of Central America and North America. One could argue that, if you're cutting down that forest, it could affect ranching in Texas.

I've been to the Amazon many times. The last time was four months ago.

---

* Rhett A. Butler, "Are We on the Brink of Saving Rainforests?" Mongabay .com, August 14, 2009, http://news.mongabay.com/2009/0722-redd.html.

HC: I went to the Amazon years ago, 1989, so I could see it before it went. I hired a dugout canoe in Venezuela and went down with my nineteen-year-old son. We went down the Orinoco River, for days and days, and it was extraordinary. The perfume in the area was something like I'd never smelled before; the forest was so dense on either side of the river; it was impenetrable. At night, wild screams of all sorts of animals echoed through the forest. We set off at dawn each morning; we were in the prow of the ship on those hammocks. The sky was rosy pink, and every afternoon huge cumulus clouds would gather overhead, and there'd be a wild rainstorm. Then it would settle down. Then the Orinoco River joined the Amazon, and the river divided into the black part and the white part, about a mile wide at this point. We were dropped off at a certain little town. We had to walk a long way through a road being made to cut into the jungle. We were almost knee-deep in mud for about a mile, being bitten by everything that you can imagine, and then we saw areas that had been deforested. There's this humus underneath the forest on the floor, like a sort of feather pillow.

What is the forest being used for, and the land?

RB: The seventies and eighties deforestation in the Amazon was driven by big government projects, essentially colonization. In Brazil there was a big push to redistribute the land, or at least give more of the land to the urban population that had no land. The government embarked on some big projects to build roads and essentially give out free land, colonists paying to go out there. There was also a national security element. Brazil was a bit afraid that if the Amazon wasn't used, the United States would come in and take it over, or other countries would. Back then most of the deforestation was driven by poverty and government-sponsored land redistribution. But that's all changed. In the late eighties, nineties, and up until now, more deforestation is driven by enterprise activities. Cattle ranching actually accounts for 80 percent of deforestation in the

Brazilian Amazon. It's not so much direct logging, but loggers will go in and take out the valuable hardwoods; the rest will be scrap. They'll use bulldozers and chains to pull down the rest of the trees. Then they burn the land and eventually plant the grass seed, and the cattle come in. Forest offers really low productivity in terms of cattle.

HC: Are these Brazilian ranchers or U.S. ranchers doing it?

RB: These are mostly Brazilian ranchers. Right now you can't export fresh beef from Brazil to the United States; it's not allowed.

Getting back to why the land is being converted for cattle production: A lot of this is about land speculation. In order to establish a claim on land, you put cattle on it. Eventually you could sell that land at an increase. In Brazil, the forested land has very little value. You plant it with grass seed, it might increase by five to ten times. So this is being driven by ranchers, but also by wealthy landowners. That's not to say Brazil doesn't produce a lot of beef. Brazil is still the number one exporter of beef in the world. It has twice the number of cattle that the United States has. The Amazon alone contains 80 million head of cattle. These cattle are being slaughtered for beef or leather. The beef is being shipped to Russia, Europe, Venezuela. The leather is going to China and turned into products that are sold in the United States and Europe.

HC: Nike shoes.

RB: Exactly. This is a nice transition to a kind of positive development. Environmentalists have long known cattle ranching is the number-one cause of deforestation. But they haven't been very effective at getting that message out or making effective change. So the forests keep falling, and in Brazil the cattle industry got more powerful. Then Greenpeace linked major brands directly to illegal deforestation in the Amazon. We're talking, Nike, Toyota, Adidas, Timberland, products that were sold in major supermarkets,

Walmart. This report had an immediate, incredible impact. Within days the World Bank withdrew a $90 million loan to Brazil.

HC: That's amazing.

RB: The federal prosecutor's office in Brazil launched a federal lawsuit against one of Brazil's largest cattle processors. Marfrig, the world's fourth-largest beef trader, announced it would introduce a moratorium against cattle from deforested areas. Walmart and some of Brazil's other large chains announced moratoriums. They said they would suspend contracts with suppliers found to be involved with illegal deforestation. Then we had Nike, Adidas, and Timberland announce that they were going to implement new policies to ensure that their products weren't coming from deforested areas. This is incredible. Now you have politicians and major buyers of cattle products demanding some sort of system to ensure accountability. There'd be supply chain tracking to ensure that consumers don't have to worry about products that were produced through deforestation.

HC: That's stunning. This shows that there are ways we can get around corporate entities that are helping to destroy parts of the world. The Amazon is also used for gold mining, right?

RB: Right. Gold mining and logging are still the issue. Gold mining doesn't affect as large an area, but it causes extensive pollution and damage to rivers.

HC: Dreadful. Let's move on to the indigenous populations, those wonderful Indian tribes who've lived in the Amazon forever. I see that although the government says these are indigenous areas of the forest, the indigenous people don't own them. What is happening to their culture and the way they live?

RB: It depends on the country, in terms of ownership. In Brazil indigenous groups actually control a significant portion of the Amazon. But they don't actually own the land. So, if oil is found on their land, they don't have the rights to it necessarily, or even gold.

HC: It's their land; they have to have it to live. It's total exploitation of indigenous people.

RB: What's happening in Peru right now is especially distressing. About 70 percent of the Peruvian Amazon has been allocated for oil and gas exploration. The government is passing decrees to make it easier for foreign oil companies to move in and exploit their deposits. That's a direct consequence of U.S. foreign policy. They're passing these decrees in order to get a free trade pact with the United States. There are certain requirements for foreign investments.

HC: The United States can go in and do what it likes?

RB: The United States can go in and exploit these resources. Some of these claims conflict with indigenous groups. So the indigenous groups are rightfully quite angry, and there was a major uprising in which thirty thousand indigenous people and people in the Amazon—hundreds of tribes across Peru—blocked roads and restricted access to these areas that are going to be developed for oil and cows. We have this standoff, and then the Peruvian government decided to call in the police. There was bloodshed. Almost three dozen, possibly more, were killed.

HC: Tribal people.

RB: Well, actually a bunch of police were killed also. It had been nonviolent for a while. Then there was escalation; it's unclear as to exactly what happened, but the protesters were fired upon, and two hundred were injured. More than ten were killed. Then two dozen Peruvian police were killed as well. It's a very ugly event, and Peru took a step back to reduce the conflict and said it was going to revoke those laws. But they weren't laws, they were actually decrees; a couple of weeks ago the energy minister came out and said that Peru is going to go ahead with the auctions and is expected to raise $1.5 billion in each of the next two years selling off more Amazon land.

HC: You can see these tribal people are going to be destroyed.

RB: The situation is a little better in Brazil; they have more established land rights. We're seeing indigenous groups as champions of conservation. People are looking at them as the solution to reducing deforestation. A couple of tribes are now getting in with this low-carbon market concept, in which they would receive payments for conserving, for keeping their land forested. They've done a great job keeping the trees standing, and it's now time to recognize them for that, and to help them derive financial support to create a sustainable livelihood.

There's an initiative now by the Brazilian government to raise $20 billion over the next ten years to conserve the Amazon. The stated goal is to reduce emissions by 70 percent. There are a lot of details that still need to be worked out, and there's conflict over the proposal. What's interesting is that Brazil plans to raise that from foreign donors.

HC: The Amazon is a global treasure and is contributing to climatic conditions in that area of the world. If it goes, global warming is going to be so aggravated! And all the trees being burned would mean that billions of tons of carbon dioxide would be released, right?

RB: The Amazon stores over 100 billion tons of carbon, which is something like a dozen years of global emissions. It would affect rainfall and directly impact farmers in places like southern Brazil and Argentina, which is the major breadbasket for South America. So one of the ways that they're looking to fund Amazon conservation is to put a value on that rainfall: how much is agriculture worth in southern South America? Looking at hydroelectric dams, 80 percent of Brazil's electricity is generated from hydropower, so if rainfall were diminished from deforestation, what would be the cost to Brazil in terms of power?

HC: As the forest dries out as a result of ongoing logging, then you get forest fires. There was a dreadful fire in the Amazon in 2005, right?

RB: That was a really bad year for the Amazon. There was massive drought and these gigantic rivers were nothing but puddles. Communities were stranded, and there was that catastrophic forest fire that raged across a vast area.

HC: Have the rivers recovered?

RB: The rivers have now recovered. There was a period of about two years where there was this extremely severe drought, a lot of forest died and became susceptible to fire. There was a huge pulse of emissions in 2005 from the Amazon.

HC: Let's talk about soybeans.

RB: Soy is actually an interesting case, because the soy industry responded. The Greenpeace report in 2005 and 2006 basically said that a lot of deforestation in parts of the Amazon could be attributed to soy. Not just direct deforestation, but road building for soy was also driving other types of deforestation. So Greenpeace releases this report, linking McDonald's to soy, and it was a bit indirect. The chicken feed that was being used to feed the chickens that go into Chicken McNuggets was coming from Amazon deforestation. The Brazilian soy industry responded by establishing a moratorium, so that's been quite effective in reducing deforestation.

HC: Aren't the soybeans also sent off to Europe to feed animals?

RB: A lot of that soy was sent to Europe for animal feed, including the chickens in Chicken McNuggets. This is part of a bigger issue here. As I mentioned before, deforestation, and actually a number of forms of environmental degradation, were primarily driven by poverty twenty or thirty years ago. But now that it's shifted toward corporate-driven deforestation, it's created new opportunities for conservation, or at least for activism. Instead of targeting poor families who are just trying to put food on the table, you can now target these multinational corporations that are sensitive to their images. That's why things like the soy moratorium and the Greenpeace report on cattle ranching were so effective.

HC: Let's move on to palm oil plantations. I've been to Malaysia, and coming in from the airport, all you see are these palms everywhere. What's it used for?

RB: About 80 percent of palm oil goes into food production, processed foods or packaged foods. Cadbury in New Zealand was using palm oil instead of cocoa butter in their chocolate. After a lot of complaints they agreed to switch back to cocoa butter. Palm oil is also used in producing biodiesel. As palm oil prices fall, it becomes more viable for biodiesel. That's potentially a huge market, with so much switching to more biofuel consumption. China is expected to dramatically increase their biofuel consumption and car ownership.

HC: Does palm oil have cholesterol in it, saturated fat?

RB: Palm oil doesn't have trans fat; it has other types of fat. In the United States there's been a big push to ban trans fat. So an unexpected consequence of that is that you have palm oil ending up in more foods.

HC: How much deforestation has occurred in the tropical countries to produce palm oil?

RB: There's been more than 10 million hectares [25 million acres] of oil palm established across South Asia over the past twenty-five years. It's ongoing and it's one of the primary drivers of deforestation in Indonesia today. One of the big issues with oil palm is that it destroys habitats for species.

HC: Like the orangutan, which is endangered. What's your feeling about what's going to happen to these tropical rain forests?

RB: I'm somewhat optimistic. This idea of compensating countries for preserving the forests is incredibly important. Until now forests really haven't had that much value, as living entities. The best way to capitalize on the value of a forest was to chop it down for wood or to burn it for cattle pasture or oil palm. If you can place a value on living forests, and value is derived from forests on an ongoing basis, you set up an understanding. It's going to make conservation profitable.

HC: In Australia we've got temperate forests. Our deciduous trees store more carbon per ton than the rain forest timber, yet we've got a forestry department chopping trees down. There's been no way to get through to the state government. Do you have any ideas?

RB: The forestry sector in Australia is intent on logging your forests. If you look at the amount of carbon stored in forests, the all-time champion of the world is actually the eucalyptus forest in Victoria. In terms of solutions, a company in Tasmania announced the first forest-carbon deal there. They're going to pay landowners who have the right to cut down the forests on their land—not necessarily an environmental right, but it's their legal right. Instead of being paid from cutting down trees, they're going to be paid for the carbon conserved in those forests in order to save the forest.

HC: Where's that money coming from?

RB: That money's coming from the carbon market. This whole offset issue . . .

HC: I have to say as an Australian watching these huge logging trucks, it's like watching trucks full of dead human beings, because the tree's a living thing and houses so many other species. The magnificent parrots, birds, and koalas.

RB: That's the other reason I'm somewhat optimistic, besides the whole idea of payment for ecoservices. Right now the most tangible assets in forests is carbon. But the next thing is going to be water, and they're trying to figure out what biodiversity's worth. It's pretty complex, but there are really smart people working on these issues.

If you could figure out some way to hit corporations where it counts and attack that part of the equation, then you could get some changes that are practical.

HC: I have always said trees are the lungs of the Earth; they imbibe carbon dioxide and turn it into wood and exhale oxygen, which we breathe, whereas our lungs inhale oxygen and exhale carbon dioxide. So they're incredibly precious things. ∿

MARTIN SHEEN

Martin Sheen is best known for his performances in the films *Badlands* and *Apocalypse Now*, and in the television series *The West Wing*, for which he won a Golden Globe and two Screen Actors Guild awards. In addition to film and television, Sheen is known for his robust support of liberal political causes, such as opposition to United States military actions. He credits the Marianists at the University of Dayton as a major influence on his public activism. Martin Sheen has resisted calls to run for office, saying that there's no way he could be the president, because there can't be a pacifist in the White House.

———

HELEN CALDICOTT: I first met you at Los Alamos's labs on one of numerous protests. The police had set up an artificial line beyond which one must not move. You went to the line with other people, knelt down, and said the Hail Mary, got up, walked across the line, and they handcuffed you to take you to jail. But then you said you couldn't go to jail because you'd already committed to be president in *The West Wing* series. [*Laughter.*]

MARTIN SHEEN: Your recollection of the occasion at Los Alamos is very close. Amy Goodman was there reporting. And my dear friend and peacemaker Father John Dear was arrested with us, and one of the daughters of Philip Berrigan. You got everything right except the prayer. It was an Our Father. We always say the Our Father when we cross the line, and usually they arrest us before we get to "Forgive us our trespasses."

HC: And do you think it helps to say the Our Father when you're doing an action?

MS: It certainly helps me. Politicians generally are meant to serve a certain constituency, so they're not always free to vote with their conscience or act from their heart. I don't really have the kind of faith [in politics] that I have in grassroots movements, which are born of the people and really make the change. There are very few great things that have ever been accomplished by politicians in the beginning. It's usually brought to their attention by people like yourself, who agitate and educate people to what's going on, and then hopefully you can get people in positions of responsibility to do something about it. But in my own country in the sixties, the civil rights movement was not the breve of politicians. There was no one in public life who initiated the civil rights legislation or anything to do with civil rights; it was Reverend King and the nonviolent movement for civil rights. It's the same for unionism—the unions started from the workers, the people who suffered the most at the hands of abusive employers.

HC: That's really how a decent society has grown up with a minimum wage and rights for workers. Otherwise it was a virtually feudalistic system in the 1800s, until the unions got together.

MS: The unions form the middle class. The wealthy people never understood the importance of unionism, and how important it is for the majority of the people to be educated, and to have a stake in the future. They have to have a wage and good working conditions so that their children can benefit from their labor and carry on the society.

HC: You probably move among very wealthy people, living where you live. Do you talk to them about this?

MS: I'm so involved in the issues myself, and you don't see a lot of wealthy people on picket lines or in protest movements. They have a lot more at stake. The path that I have chosen does not attract a lot of wealthy people, because sometimes the path I go is challenging and costly.

I'm asked at times to debate these right-wing Tea Party people in my country. I refuse to debate with them, because they make a living doing what they're doing, and what I do is costly. So I don't like to feed into their channel.

HC: What are your main activities these days?

MS: We're supporting the union movement in the state of Wisconsin, and in my home state of Ohio, where they have blocked what had been fought for over the last fifty years—bargaining. It seems now to be a national movement to go after the unions, the union pensions and their right to collective bargaining. It's a big mistake, and it's backfired in Wisconsin, and it's starting to turn around in Ohio.

HC: What do we do about the Koch brothers?

MS: They are the biggest polluters, because they are the coal industry. These guys got a lock on it even in Congress—the people that they have sent to Congress, and the people who are on the committees that would have a say in EPA regulations and regulations of pollutants. Coal is the biggest polluter on the planet.

HC: I know, except for nuclear power.

MS: Nuclear power is the deadliest. It'll kill you quicker than coal. Future generations are going to be affected by it in the same kind of deadly way.

HC: All of our nuclear activities have brought global warming and random compulsory genetic engineering upon us for the rest of time. I quote Einstein, who said, "The unleashed power of the atom has changed everything save our modes of thinking, and we thus drift toward unparalleled catastrophes." The profundity of that statement has really never been taken onboard. I think it's up to the women now, 53 percent of the population, to harness the passion that a lioness has to protect her cubs. We've got to arouse the women to take over. We need a revolution now of Gandhian proportions.

MS: I agree. Dostoyevsky said the world will be saved by beauty. He meant women.

HC: We had a revolution in the eighties. I got together 23,000 doctors. Within five years 80 percent of Americans rose up and said we need to get rid of nuclear weapons. You've got to have access to the media, and it's damn hard now, isn't it?

MS: Yes, it is. But there are many new venues, with cable TV and satellite radio. The message is much more urgent these days. Look at Japan and this catastrophe. Do you know what's extraordinary? It's already off not just the front pages, but off the back pages. And the civilian catastrophic emergency's still going on. I don't even think the people in Japan are as well informed as they need to be about what's going on.

HC: There's a big cover-up, globally, by the nuclear industry in Japan.

MS: Isn't this the twenty-fifth anniversary of Chernobyl? This very day?

HC: Yes. I just taped a CNN International debate with three people from the corporate world. Do you know, they were talking about profits in the market? We're discussing Chernobyl, and I said, "Are we going to kill the Earth for money?"

I'm going to ask you a fairly serious question now. I want you to give your assessment of President Obama.

MS: The fact that he's there is a testament to our willingness to change as a nation, as a culture. I have a lot of reservations, which I find hard to talk about publicly, because I do support him and give thanks and praise to God every day that he's there, and that he hopefully will be there for another term. There are many issues that I'm uncomfortable with. The immigration issue—what a disastrous policy the federal government has on immigration currently, and the debate seems to have been stifled. During the campaign, he was very forthright about acknowledging the problem and promising to fix it. There's been very little movement.

Again, he's working with a Congress and a very conservative media that stifles much of his weight, and on so many of his initiatives he finds himself in these trench fights, over health care, for example, which took up almost a year of his administration with constant battles over implementation. There's such a profit margin in the health care system, hospitals and the whole medical profession, not the least of which goes to the pharmaceutical companies. Energy has been spent trying to get incremental changes through in a very hard-nosed Congress. Much of his health care legislation was tarnished in the right-wing media to such an extent that it made it impossible to understand what really was at stake. He was trying to foster a health care that was affordable to all Americans, and that's just one issue. For me it's health care, immigration, and of course the nuclear issue and big oil. We're told that we need to drill and become less dependent on foreign oil.

What I keep saying to people who complain about him is that we have to accept that he's not *them*. Through eight years Mr. Bush and that group pretty much had their sway, since 9/11, in every area, and made a mess of it. We're still trying to clean up. So he's not them. We're learning how difficult it is, even in that most powerful of positions, to make the slightest incremental change and lead a whole culture in a new direction. And nuclearism is part of that. But he can't even get the treaty on nuclear weapons reduction that he did with Russia confirmed.

HC: I thought it was ratified, except Senator Jon Kyle didn't vote for it.

MS: The whole thing about allowing for inspections is still a very touchy issue here, a very nationalistic concern. It is for the Russians too. We're one of seven nuclear nations, and if you look at Asia, India or Pakistan alone, these are two nuclear-armed nations that are constantly at each other's throat, and they live on the same border. We supply an awful lot of revenue and aid to both of those countries. If I was to have my wish granted for that region, I would tell both countries that until they disarm completely, I would have no trade with them. I would sanction both of them.

HC: Of the 25,000 or so nuclear weapons in the world, Russia and America own 97 percent of them. They're the real rogue states, holding the world at ransom when we could have a global nuclear war and the end of all life on the planet.

MS: Paranoia about our own security is bandied about.

HC: Security's got nothing to do with it. You're insecure when the Russians are targeting you with thousands of hydrogen bombs. There are forty-eight bombs targeted on New York and about sixty on Washington.

MS: Somebody ought to tell them it wouldn't take that many. Why don't you get rid of at least thirty-nine?

HC: What stimulated you in the first place to become so deeply involved in social issues?

MS: I'm a practicing Catholic. I returned to the church, after a long absence, in 1981. I'd gone through some deeply transforming personal things, and I came out the other end realizing that I needed to get involved in a spirituality, so I rejoined the Catholic church. But I didn't come back to the faith of my childhood, where I lived mostly in fear and dread. I came back to the radical action church of liberation theology. In the United States I became close to the Berrigan brothers, both Dan and Philip Berrigan, and they began to lead me in the way of radical action. Radical meaning root. So it is a road of social justice. The Old Testament calls for us to do justice, to love greatly, and to walk humbly. I have come to all of the social justice issues, including nuclearism, on the level of spirituality. I don't get involved in protests or any of the actions with the belief that I can change anyone's mind or make the weapons disappear. I do it basically for myself, because I can't truly be honest with myself if I don't speak up. And do it nonviolently, with a sense of self-effacement. My mission has been to stand there when I'm asked to participate in a social justice issue—whether it's nuclearism, homelessness, immigration, or any issue—to speak truth to power, to do it nonviolently, and to do it joyfully as well.

HC: From a basis of spirituality, how do you define that in relationship to the world and your place in it?

MS: Our nation began a terrible road to self-destruction after the war, when it began to arm, starting with atom bombs, moving to thermonuclear and a whole massive conglomeration of weapons and weapons-delivery systems that lasted all the way up unto the Reagan era. They still are in place today. It's mind-boggling, the amount of weapons, the amount of money, the energy that is spent, the risk to our health, and the risk to destroying the planet. We have reduced them in large measure over the years. Recently President Obama concluded a nuclear weapons reduction treaty with the Russians, which has not yet been fully ratified by the Congress. Still we have enough stockpiled nuclear weapons and delivery systems to destroy the world dozens and dozens of times. And we're just one nuclear nation of seven in the world.

HC: With the press of a button. But how do you define *your* spirituality? And how is it applied to the world?

MS: On this one issue alone I feel that we have developed a new religion, called nuclearism. We worship these weapons; we count on them for our safety, for our defense. And they are false gods. They are a reflection of evil, they rob the poor, they endanger the world, and they foreclose the future. So they have to be called what they are. And they have to be expelled from our culture. That's a long arduous journey, and not one that will happen in my lifetime, and maybe not in my children's lifetime, but it has to begin somewhere. We have to put a name on these things. These are false gods; these are an invitation to total darkness.

HC: Doesn't it say in the Old Testament, thou shalt not worship false gods?

MS: That's the whole point.

HC: So America's got two false gods: money and nuclear weapons. The ultimate violence is hydrogen explosions and blowing up the planet.

MS: There's a popular phrase that is used still to this day: bomb 'em into the Stone Age, when we're talking about our enemies. But we're called to love our enemies, and we still call ourselves a Christian nation. It is a reflection of our paranoia, and our moral bankruptcy. It goes hand in hand with the bankruptcy that these weapons have caused us. Reagan brought the Soviet Union to its knees in the arms race. That was a major reason why the Soviet Union collapsed, and even Gorbachev confessed that they couldn't keep up with the United States.

I want to make one point that I understand very few people are aware of, particularly in the United States. I was in England in April of 1986. During that time in April, Chernobyl occurred. I recall that it was discovered on the first day of the week. I believe it was the Swedes; they thought it was them. They said, Oh my God, we've had a meltdown, and they checked, and it was in Chernobyl. It belonged to the Soviets, in the Ukraine. They immediately alerted the Soviets, and they said yes, it happened either Friday night or Saturday morning. Now as soon as the news got out to the world, and that was on Monday morning, the cloud had already made its way over Western Europe. President Reagan was in Japan at the time at a conference. And when the news was announced that Chernobyl had happened, he condemned the Soviets for knowing about it and not saying anything.

In fact, the United States knew about it the instant it happened, via spy satellites. They thought initially that it was an aboveground test, which would have been against the nonproliferation agreement, and so they thought, Wait a minute. It's happening in a civilian area in the middle of a city. It proved to be a power meltdown at a nuclear plant. Now we [Americans] knew forty-eight hours before the world supposedly knew about it. The Soviets supposedly knew forty-eight hours before, and they were in a great hurry to try and fix it and cover it up. There's no doubt about that. But what about the American responsibility to alert the world? Reagan kept it quiet; he let the Soviets stew in it. His crime was in equal measure to the Soviet's crime of keeping it quiet until the destruction had already made its way across Western Europe and other parts of the world.

That's part of the nationalism and the paranoia that controls governments when they're dealing with these meltdowns and out-of-control nuclearism. I have a fear the same thing is happening with Japan. It's nowhere in our national press. We're getting absolutely nothing on what's happening in Fukushima, so we know there's no announcement that they've solved the problem, but we're very wary of what's going on. It is bringing to mind the awful situation that we went through with Chernobyl, and the lack of information surrounding it.

HC: You said we won't abolish nuclear weapons in your lifetime, or maybe your children's. Reagan and Gorbachev met in Reykjavik in

1987, and over a weekend they almost made an agreement between the two countries to abolish nuclear weapons.

MS: Reagan wanted to get rid of all of them.

HC: And Gorbachev did too, absolutely. They got stuck on Reagan's notion of Star Wars. So there is a precedent. We can agree to abolish nuclear weapons. When Clinton was president we handed him a mandate on a silver platter: 80 percent of Americans wanted to get rid of nuclear weapons. He could have flown over to meet Boris Yeltsin and said, Okay, Boris, here's a treaty. We're going to abolish nuclear weapons bilaterally, and we're 97 percent of all of them in the world, within five years. But Clinton was intimidated by the Pentagon, and he didn't have any moral fiber. His legacy was that the weapons remain on hair-trigger alert in Russia and America.

I met with Reagan in the White House—I don't know if you know this. I met his daughter Patty in the Playboy mansion, of all places. Hugh Hefner was excerpting a book called *With Enough Shovels*, about FEMA, and how, if there's a nuclear attack, you get out your trusty shovel and dig a hole six feet long and three feet deep and get in the hole.

MS: I remember that! And you'll be fine, right?

HC: And put two doors on top of it, and dirt. It's the dirt that does it. I gave the talk, and this tall, willowy, dark-haired girl came up, and she said, I think you're the only person on Earth who can change my father's mind. Would you meet him? I said I don't want Meese, Baker, or Deaver there. I'll see him alone or not at all. So she rang me and said, We've got an appointment at the end of his working day. She said 4:00 P.M. That left me a bit bewildered!

MS: [*Laughs loudly.*]

HC: We got into the Secret Service cars, into the southern portico, and into the downstairs library, in which there wasn't a book. He came and didn't know where to sit. I shook his hand and said, "Hello, Mr. President," and showed him where to sit. We embarked on an hour-and-a-quarter-long conversation. I had more time alone with him than any other person in his eight years of presidency. He knew nothing. I'd just finished my book on missile envy, and I was pouring out facts and figures. Everything he said, I'd stop him and correct him. When he'd get anxious he'd get a red flush on his cheeks, and I held his hand to reassure him. So half the time I held his hand and quickly established a doctor-patient relationship with him.

MS: Oh God, I love you! What an extraordinary story.

HC: I established his IQ to be about a one hundred, which is about average. I came out saying that I thought he had impending Alzheimer's. So my diagnosis was correct.

You wanted to ask what motivates me.

MS: Yes! You mentioned that you don't have a specific religious affiliation. So tell me about yourself. What motivates you to speak truth to power and to stand against nuclearism?

HC: I grew up with agnostic parents. As a little girl I used to dress myself up and go to the Sunday schools of various religions, looking for God, but I often found cruelty, so that didn't work. I've always been fascinated by physiology: if you drink water, where does the urine come from? What makes a snail tick? When I entered medicine, I just absolutely loved it. That is my religion, the life process. I've always been terrified of death, because I had a near-death experience when I was eighteen months old.

MS: And you remember it?

HC: I was left in a cold home for two weeks when my mother, who was very pregnant, and my father went on a holiday. I got a middle-ear infection. I remember being placed on a barouche, held down with two big arms covered with black hair and this ghastly mask on my face, breathing this awful stuff. I thought I was dying. Ever since then I've been terrified of death. I thought that if I did medicine I could have more control over death.

But my religion. I took the Hippocratic oath at seventeen; that's like becoming a nun. I'm totally devoted to medicine. I worship the sanctity of life. I live in a little fishing village in New South Wales, and the stars are unbelievable. I looked up, and I thought, I'm part of that. And suddenly my fear of death went away. I was part of that before I was conceived, and I'm part of the whole constellation when I die. I felt really good about that. So what motivates me is the truth. In medicine you're not scared of telling a patient the truth. I'm not courageous; I just speak truth, that's all. People in politics are scientifically and medically illiterate. How dare they be? I'm sick of it. I am here to save lives. I'm a conservative—for conserving life on the planet. Therefore, I'm never scared. I've had eight death threats, and some were pretty serious. But you know, what's my life compared to all the life in the whole universe? I'm prepared to die for that. As Martin Luther King said—I'm paraphrasing it—if you don't have something worth dying for, you're not really living.

MS: Yes, he did say that. Also, we've learned from the Gospel that Jesus tells us that God is worshiped in the truth.

HC: We're all sons and daughters of God. I think he said that too. Jesus, I think he was the greatest psychiatrist who ever lived. Talking in parables causes people to remember his preaching down the ages.

MS: And it cost him something. Sometimes what we believe causes us to do things that, because of our beliefs, are risky. Yet if our beliefs have any value at all, they have to lead somewhere that has to cost us something, or else we're left to question their value. ∽

ARJUN MAKHIJANI

Arjun Makhijani is the president of the Institute for Energy and Environmental Research in Tacoma Park, Maryland. A recognized authority on energy issues, Dr. Makhijani was the principal author of the first study of the energy-efficiency potential of the U.S. economy. He is the author of "Carbon-Free and Nuclear-Free: A Roadmap for U.S. Energy Policy." In 2007 he was elected a fellow of the American Physical Society. He has been published in the *Bulletin of the Atomic Scientists*, *The Progressive*, and the *Washington Post*, among other publications. Dr. Makhijani has served as a consultant on energy issues to the Lawrence Berkeley National Laboratory and to several agencies of the United Nations.

———

HELEN CALDICOTT: Tell us about your basic training in physics.

ARJUN MAKHIJANI: I did my undergraduate studies in India in electrical engineering, so that was power, electricity, consumption, production, transmission, and distribution: upper atmospheric, ionospheric physics. My doctorate is in plasma physics applied to nuclear fusion.

HC: What is plasma physics?

AM: The plasmas that physicists deal with are ionized gases. For fusion as high as in the interior of the Sun, for example, the temperatures are so high that the electrons that circle the nucleus of the atom get stripped off; you get free electrons negatively charged and free positive ions positively charged—a gas at a high temperature that consists of charged particles. In addition to gases like air, moving as neutral particles mechanically bumping into each other, you have electrical forces, and they dominate.

HC: What do they do?

AM: In fusion you try to make the gas very, very hot, like the interior of the Sun or hotter. That is because for fusion to occur the nuclei of atoms, which are positively charged, have to bump into each other frequently enough. To do that they must overcome electrical repulsive forces—like charge repel each other. That is why high particle energies—that is, high temperatures—are needed. But at such high temperatures, the plasma can't touch the walls of any container; if it does, it will cool down in short order, so you try to contain this hot, electrically charged gas in a magnetic field. Such arrangements are typically unstable and very difficult, so containment of plasmas for any length of time is extremely difficult. We've produced nuclear fusion in the form of thermonuclear bombs, also called hydrogen bombs. Of course, in a bomb, containment of the energy is not the objective.

HC: The hydrogen bomb. To quote Einstein: "The significant problems we face today cannot be solved by the same level of thinking that created them." Fusion and all this high-tech stuff fascinates a lot of men at the level at which Einstein was talking, whereas you, Arjun, created this wonderful document called "Carbon-Free and Nuclear-Free." Please explain to us what that document is. What did you find when you did the research?

AM: It was inspired by you and S. David Freeman and a conference that you had in 2006. David Freeman made this speech saying that we should really go to renewable energy 100 percent. I didn't think it was economically feasible.

David Freeman is the father of energy policy in the United States. He was worrying about oil imports when he worked in the White House in the 1960s. Then he started the Energy Policy Project of the Ford Foundation. I worked for him off and on in the 1970s. He was chairman of the Tennessee Valley Authority and has run public utilities much of his professional life. He is a pragmatic visionary, an inspiring person. Not just because he is a visionary, but because he can change his mind about things when he sees the reality, unlike a lot of people who occupy positions of authority and power. I began to look at economic feasibility. We know you have a lot of solar cells and attach batteries to them, and then, between the direct sunshine and the battery-stored electricity, you can generate electricity for twenty-four hours. But that's very expensive. My reaction was that it may not be economically practical. But when I looked at the reality as it was developing, I found that there is a technological revolution going on. For example, there are thirty-odd thousand houses that have been built in the last few years in Germany according to what are called passive building standards. This requires knowing where south is and insulating the house properly. So you put the windows in south facing in the northern hemisphere; you pick up the heat in the summer, and then you have an awning and shade the windows in the summer, reducing air-conditioning requirements. This eliminates 70 percent of the energy footprint of a house compared to an ordinary new house. The rest of the 30 percent is going to be very simple to supply with renewable energy. Hanover House in New Hampshire doesn't have air conditioning, but it is a well-built house. Leaving aside the custom features, it costs about $140 per square foot in 2010 dollars to build; for reference, the cheapest house you can build is probably $70 a square foot, and custom houses would be $500 a square foot, or more, if you really want a fancy house. So a $140-per-square-foot house is a pretty modestly priced house. This one is well insulated and has efficient appliances, south-facing windows, and a large solar water heater. Nothing high-tech. And a 1,200-gallon tank buried underground to store the hot water. In Hanover House almost all of the heating and hot water comes from circulating the hot water under the floor, in radiant heating. The annual net electricity use is only five thousand kilowatt-hours of electricity for everything—appliances, supplementary heating, supplemental hot water. That's only 15 percent of the energy footprint of a typical house in the United States.

HC: Why aren't architects designing these houses? Why not have laws written so that every house in the United States is a passive solar house?

AM: I have a lot of hope. I don't have a lot of hope in Washington, D.C. Everybody can see that Washington is broken. Fact-based and science-based discussion in Washington has become very difficult on many issues; climate has been among the more difficult of these issues. Even though Alan Greenspan said the war in Iraq is largely about oil, and we spent directly about a trillion dollars over there—3 trillion, in total, according to Joseph Stiglitz, if the broader indirect impacts are included.

There are two reasons I have hope. One, California has a 33 percent renewable portfolio standard; they want to generate 33 percent of their electricity from renewables—solar and wind—by 2020. That's only eight years from now. California is part of the western grid in the United States, and more than half the people in the western grid live in California. California is going to transform the western grid if they stick with it. California is a huge part of the American economy. If it were a country it would be the seventh or eighth largest in the world. Germany of course is even bigger than California. California is 40 million people, and Germany has about 80 million and also has a very advanced economy. Germany was already headed toward a mainly renewable nonnuclear electricity system, but after the Fukushima disaster, they've explicitly decided to get rid of nuclear on a fast timetable, by the year 2022. We don't argue whether they will achieve it or not. If they miss it by a year or two it doesn't matter. They are doing a very good thing. The direction is critical; so is the determination.

HC: A pioneering thing!

AM: A very good thing in setting an ambitious timetable, because they are going to transform their technological structure. One of their big energy companies is already a leader in offshore wind turbines. By setting an ambitious timetable they are going to have an immense lead in offshore wind technology, in how to do smart grids. They have a pretty good shot at succeeding, and they'll become a bigger export powerhouse than they already are.

HC: So what are the dynamics in Washington that prevent pragmatic, sensible solutions to the energy debate?

AM: You've got the nuclear lobby and the fossil fuel lobbies, and they are well financed. Everybody saw that we had a disaster last year in the Gulf of Mexico, but there are also a lot of jobs tied up in the fossil fuel industry. It's the economy of coastal Louisiana, which was suffering. There was a lot of pressure. Of course, oil companies ride that popular pressure and stoke it up. Everybody knows that campaign contributions make a lot of difference, and the smart-grid business, by comparison to the oil business—it's a fraction of 1 percent.

HC: Describe the smart grid.

AM: Let me tell you what the dumb grid is. We have a grid that works reasonably well in the United States. When you flip the switch, the lights come on, and overall the bills are pretty reasonable compared to the quality of the supply we're getting. But the reason it's a dumb grid is that there is very little communication between consumers and producers, only through the flip of a switch. You flip it on, it comes on; you flip it off, it goes off.

HC: And no one knows where their electricity is generated. I asked people all over the States; they have no idea.

AM: It's part of the malaise of living in cities. We think food grows in the grocery store and electricity comes out of the outlet. It's a part of why we're not really in touch with how we're affecting the planet. But the total amount of information between the consumer and producer of electricity in the whole United States can be fit on a $10 or $15 flash drive. That's it. What would a smart grid do? Your frost-free refrigerator has a defrost cycle. It only comes on once in a while, when a thin layer of ice might frost, might build up, and there is a little heater in there, and the heater comes on. Of course, the heater uses electricity. Now do you care, or do you know when the heater comes on to defrost your refrigerator? I don't, and I'm an energy guy. If your refrigerator was a smart refrigerator, and the grid was a smart grid, with wind and solar, when there was plenty of wind and solar energy the defrost cycle would work, and when there wasn't enough, the defrost cycle would get delayed. Nobody would know the difference. Your dishwasher could be connected in a similar way. A smart dishwasher would come on when there was plenty of renewable energy. If you wanted to wash your dishes immediately, you could override it, but you would pay more. These are a few examples. If we went to electrical transportation; you could use the vehicle batteries as reserve power for the grid. You sign up with a business and say, okay, I've got an electric car, a dishwasher, a clothes washer, and an air conditioner. If you want to increase the temperature in my house by one degree and sell that capacity to the utility, I'll agree to do it provided you give me $10 a month, for example. This kind of system would actually be much cheaper, much more efficient, require fewer resources, and be very amenable with the solar on your rooftop and a local storage battery at the utility substation, as well as wind and solar energy. Of course, there will have to be security and privacy protections.

This smart grid is being developed. It will be developed in California, Germany, and elsewhere. The Institute of Electronic and Electrical Engineers is developing standards. If you are going to have this kind of communication, you need communications protocols; otherwise everybody will make their own type of machine. It's like going to the hardware store and having nonstandard screws; it would not work. So we're in the beginning stages of this, but I'm convinced this is going to happen, despite Washington—and even Washington is paying some attention.

HC: Someone said to me that a lightbulb loses so much energy as heat, you only get about 18 percent of the energy as light from the bulb. Compared to what was generated originally in a reactor or electricity-generating station, how much energy is lost along the way?

AM: We think we are high-tech, but we're not. You're being a technological optimist with your numbers. When you burn the coal or fission the uranium atom, you get a certain amount of heat. Two thirds of that heat is wasted at the power plant, in the condenser water. Only one unit out of three of burning coal or fissioning uranium comes out as electricity. You put that electricity in your old-fashioned incandescent bulb, about 3 percent or 4 percent of that electricity comes out as visible light, and 96 or 97 percent is heat. So based on the electricity, your efficiency is about 3 or 4 percent. The modern compact fluorescents that have become symbols of efficiency are only about 10 or 12 percent efficient in terms of the electricity. In terms of the fuel, the incandescent bulb is about 1 percent efficient. It's pathetic that we have not invested in the science. That is changing. I think it started changing in 1973, when people finally realized the lifeline of the West runs through the Persian Gulf, and that wasn't a very good thing. That's why I saw Dave Freeman as a visionary and a really extraordinary person, because he was worrying about that in the 1960s. Actually, President Truman's Materials Policy Commission, a strategic national security commission, also known as the Paley Commission, estimated in 1952 that the United States would have an oil-related security problem in about twenty years.

HC: You have a solar collector on your roof. Let's translate the solar electricity you generate on your house to your lightbulb. What's the efficiency of that compared to 1 percent or 2 percent from a distant power station?

AM: The solar cell is only about 12 to 15 percent efficient in terms of the sunlight that shines on it. But you don't pay anything for sunlight. You pay for the solar panels. It's the same lightbulb, just a different source of electricity. Except you don't have the waste heat of the power plant.

HC: You don't have the transmission waste.

AM: Yes, you save that 8 to 10 percent on transmission and distribution. However, I don't generate electricity from my solar panels for twenty-four hours a day; I only generate electricity on my roof when the sun is shining, depending on the day. And certainly by the seasons. So I put surplus energy into the grid when it's very sunny in May, when I'm not consuming a lot of electricity, and then I get electricity back from the grid at night or in the summer when I use air-conditioning. So even my solar energy use creates some distribution losses, which are most of the losses on the grid because they use low-voltage wires. This is a problem currently with the way we are doing solar energy. Everybody wants the subsidies to do solar, but nobody really wants to pay for the distribution system that's necessary.

HC: I don't understand. You sell it back to the grid, and then when you need it, you take it from the grid, when the sun isn't shining. What do people need to pay for?

AM: You've got to pay for the wires, because my solar collector needs the utility's wires for the utility to be able to take it from me and buy it from me and sell it to somebody else.

HC: So do you pay for the wires?

AM: If I don't pay for the wires, of course the utility will go bust eventually [*laughs*]. Currently there is no charge for me to put electricity into the grid, even though it uses the utility's wires. On the other hand, I give the utility energy at peak times during parts of the year and have arranged for my air-conditioning to be cut off for part of the time on the hottest days, so I am actually giving the utility quite a benefit. It's a pretty complex calculation. But we must attend to it carefully as solar energy grows.

HC: It boils down to economic arguments, instead of moral, altruistic, philosophical arguments, for why we're going to spend some money to save the earth.

AM: The central technical message is that we can pay more per kilowatt-hour for electricity, but if we make our homes more efficient, our total bills will not go up. You pay a bit more for having more efficient home insulation and better windows, you consume less energy, and you're just as comfortable. Except the money you spend isn't going toward buying coal or nuclear. It's going toward buying wind and solar energy. These are somewhat more expensive than coal and gas, though not more expensive than new nuclear, and the money is going toward buying efficient buildings and appliances.

HC: As a plasma physicist, please tell us in a brief, precise way your summary of what's happening at Fukushima and Fort Calhoun.

AM: They are very different stories. Fort Calhoun fortunately is in a safe shutdown mode; they have electricity and their cooling systems are operating. Let's step back and figure out why emergency cooling is needed for a nuclear reactor. A nuclear reactor's just a pressure cooker with a heat source on the inside. Normally when you have a pressure cooker you turn off the gas, you turn off the heat source; it'll cool down slowly. In the case of a nuclear reactor, with the heat source on the inside, when you're generating electricity by splitting the uranium and plutonium atoms that build up inside the fuel, you get these radioactive fission products. Even when you turn off the reactor, the radioactive products that have built up from the chain reaction during the operation are still there. They generate heat and you can't turn them off. They will just decay at their natural decay rate. Some radionuclides decay in seconds; some in hours; some in days, years, tens of years, centuries, tens of thousands of years. So a certain amount of heat is generated just from the fission product even after you've turned off the reactor; it's a fire you can't turn off. So you've got to keep these fuel rods cool, and you keep them cool by circulating water, which carries away the heat.

If you don't do that you eventually get a meltdown, which is what happened at Fukushima. The power lines were swept away by the tsunami or downed by the earthquakes, or both, then the emergency generators came on and failed very soon because of the tsunami. A battery lasted for four hours, and then was gone too. The water stopped circulating in the reactor, and then it started boiling. When the water starts boiling, and the fuel rods become uncovered and come into contact with the steam, a chemical reaction happens between the fuel rod material, the zirconium, and the steam. The zirconium becomes zirconium oxide from the oxygen in the steam water, and then free liberated hydrogen is released. Now you've got pressure building up from the steam inside, and the inside of the reactor is becoming hotter and hotter, because this chemical reaction is liberating more heat. If you don't vent the pressure, you're going to get an explosion, as you would with a pressure cooker that has heat underneath and no release valve. You have to have a release valve.

What happened at Fukushima is that the hydrogen got into the reactor building and exploded, and blew off the top of the reactor building in Unit 1. In Unit 2, there apparently was a hydrogen explosion in the cooling system, a part of the emergency suppression pool around the reactor. In reactor 3 there also was a hydrogen explosion that blew off a good bit of the buildings. And there was a hydrogen explosion in Unit 4 even though there was no fuel in the reactor—it was all in the spent fuel pool. The source of the hydrogen that blew up a good part of the secondary containment of Unit 4 still needs to be clearly understood.

HC: Very hot, used fuel.

AM: You've got multiple sources of problems in these reactors, and not just in the reactors. You've got the used fuel that's stored in the reactor building near the top of the reactor off to one side. One of the horrible things that has happened from these explosions, which is going to create a very big, long-term problem, is that the explosions severely damaged the cranes that are used to handle and move the spent radioactive fuel rods; now there is no functioning equipment to handle this spent fuel or the highly radioactive melted fuel in the reactors. It's a real mess. You've got a highly radioactive site and highly radioactive water leaking into the ocean. Surroundings with very difficult hot spots. Quite a lot of the area around the plant is going to be uninhabitable. How much is hard to say at present. It will depend partly on how radioactive it is, partly on the level of radiation people are willing to tolerate or subject their children to, and partly how much cleanup they do. It's going to be very difficult to decommission the nuclear plant site, because the handling equipment has been so severely damaged, and these spent-fuel rods near the top of the building are so radioactive that approaching them is lethal. So rebuilding any structure and handling equipment— it's going to be very, very hard. This is a tragedy, an accident of a type that had never been imagined. There are seven major sources of radioactivity with damaged secondary containment buildings. Radioactivity emissions continued months after the start of the accident.

HC: There still could be some major accidents in the future if there is a very large aftershock and Building 4 collapses, or the melted fuel reacts with the concrete floor and there is a hydrogen or steam explosion.

AM: The risks are there, and there are other reactors along the same coast that this earthquake has rearranged. It is my understanding that it may have rearranged the seismic risks for the area, making bigger earthquakes somewhat more probable. And I think Japan cannot tolerate another accident like this. They need to act with more alacrity than Germany, in my opinion.

HC: What, to shut down all their reactors?

AM: They need to go to a different electricity system. I believe that. They can start by doing something really sensible that will save them money. They should shut down that sodium-cooled reactor that has operated for one hour in the last sixteen years.

HC: At Monju. Describe that one.

AM: There is a special reactor that many physicists love, because in theory it can make more fuel than it consumes. It is cooled by liquid sodium. Liquid sodium burns on contact with air and explodes on contact with water, and if you have a leak, and you get sodium oxide powder all over the place, it's very hard to clean up. It's not like taking a mop to water. It is powder that contaminates everything. The reactor at Monju had such a fire; it took them fifteen years to get it to restart for testing, and then equipment fell into the reactor.

HC: It was 3.3 tons of equipment.

AM: They should save money by shutting that reactor down.

They should shut down their reprocessing plant, which isn't

producing anything, at Rokkasho. That's where they should start. They should reevaluate their energy strategy. Shut these two useless things that are money sinkholes, and sure they'll have to import some more liquid natural gas; they've already got the facilities. They can become leaders in renewable. Just imagine, we've already got California, and we've got Germany. If Japan were added to that it would be three highly technological societies—I'm thinking out loud, getting excited—going carbon-free, nuclear-free, in the next twenty-five years. I think the economic force of that would transform global energy.

HC: What are the obstacles for Japan to proceed on such a path right now?

AM: Big institutions with vested interests don't seem to want to change, even when disaster is not only staring them in the face, it has already happened. But they are beginning to think about phasing out nuclear in Japan.

HC: And Washington?

AM: Yes. The problem is staring us in the face. We've got a fiscal problem, we've got a climate problem, and to some extent, we've had these disasters that no single flood or tornado or series of tornadoes can be linked to—I don't call it climate change. I don't call it global warming. I call it severe climate disruption. Now we're having hundred-year floods every five years. You know, you have to be able to see the handwriting on the wall. The head of Tokyo Electric did not go to the power plant site for one month. These are types of denial.

HC: Psychic numbing.

AM: The nuclear establishment is trying to regroup. They are going to need their reactors for some time, just like Germany. We have 104 in the United States. We can't switch them all off overnight. But we ought to think like Germany and switch off some of the ones with greater vulnerabilities in places where we have surplus capacity. We should complement this with emergency implementation of efficiency and by producing more renewable electricity.

HC: Don't the blinking lights on home electronics—televisions, DVD players, computers—consume over 6 percent of the energy used in America?

AM: Yes. I think there is a cultural aspect to this.

HC: Of entitlement.

AM: Some organizations and institutions are beginning to attend to it. Twenty-five years ago, where I live in Montgomery County, Maryland, we were debating recycling. Many in the county said, Americans—we'll never learn how to separate newspaper from cans and plastic in a big way. We tried to prevent the county from building a huge incinerator, because I thought, if people recycle, you won't have the trash to put in it. I think the children were actually the motivating force. The young people caught on to recycling, and they actually forced us old fogeys to be better. And the trash scene today in Montgomery County is drastically different than it was twenty-five years ago. The main waste from my house that goes into the garbage dump is kitty litter.

My wife composts, and we have a pretty big compost pile improving the soil in her vegetable garden.

HC: Over and over people say, What about thorium? India's moving into thorium. Can you outline why thorium nuclear reactors are so impractical and dangerous?

AM: So long as you have nuclear fission you are going to have radioactivity and long-lived radionuclides and fissile materials. A thorium reactor is just a boiler. Everything else you have to have—the generator, the transmission, the distribution—that's 80 percent of the investment. And now you've got a more expensive boiler, because nuclear fission inherently means fission products, radioactivity, and control problems. The Indians have known for a long time that they have huge thorium resources, but you cannot sustain a chain reaction with thorium 232, which is not a fissile material. It's physically impossible. We have a small thorium reactor here in Oak Ridge, which operated for a few years in the sixties. What did it need? Enriched uranium.

HC: Uranium 235.

AM: Or plutonium, to start the thing. It was a small, seven-megawatt thermal reactor that never generated a kilowatt-hour of electricity. The cost estimates for maintaining and monitoring the site to the year 2050 and decommissioning the reactor and dealing with it all exceeds $400 million. Yet there is no clear answer. You've got all this molten salt sitting in these cells. There isn't a good solution to the problem. When you have thorium 232 in a reactor, you generate uranium 232 in the reactor. It has highly radioactive decay products. This kind of reactor is carbon-moderated. Fukushima now rivals Chernobyl in many ways, but Chernobyl was a graphite-moderated reactor, like this particular one at Oak Ridge that is a graphite-moderated reactor. You have uranium 233 separation capabilities, so people say the United States isn't going to be proliferation-prone because it won't use the U233 with U232 in it. But the United States already has plenty of surplus nuclear weapons materials and is highly unlikely to use such a reactor for making weapons materials. But what about other countries? So long as you're making uranium 233, the proliferation potential is there. It may be more difficult to make weapons when you separate out U233, because it is contaminated with U232, but you think that a terrorist group that wants nuclear weapons would care that much? I don't think so.

This is a complex problem, and I am still researching it. I will write about it when I am done. But my review so far reveals that each reactor, including the liquid fuel thorium reactor, has its own pluses and minuses. Why make fissile materials and long-lived radionuclides here on Earth just to boil water when we have a thermonuclear reactor that is safely 93 million miles away and we have the technology to make electricity from it and even to store the energy now? There is a power plant in Spain with molten salt storage, similar to the molten salt in the liquid fuel thorium reactor but without the radioactivity and the fissile materials. It can generate electricity twenty-four hours a day.

There is no easy exit when we are dealing with radioactive materials in large amounts. And of course there is no exit from the nuclear proliferation problem. You can't get rid of it, though it is more or less difficult to proliferate with different designs, depending on a variety of factors. A very important factor is time. All new reactor designs will take time to build, to develop, to test, and to prove out. A new waste-management and disposal design different from light water reactors would need to be developed for liquid fuel; the difficulties with the reactor at Oak Ridge indicate that it will take a long time to figure that out, possibly a couple of decades. Even the sodium cooled reactor, on which $100 billion has been spent worldwide, has an estimated commercialization date now of about 2050. It will likely be too late to effectively forestall the worst aspects of climate disruption.

If we want to do something about severe climate disruption and get rid of fossil fuels, which I believe we must do in nearly 100 percent in the Western countries, and to a large extent in the developing countries, as long before 2050 as possible. The foundation should be energy efficiency. It is here, it is practical, it is economical, and it is available now. Couple that with renewable energy—mainly wind and solar energy—and we can solve the problem in twenty-five or thirty years. I am actually now more optimistic about the timetable than when I finished "Carbon-Free and Nuclear-Free" in 2007. But we need the political muscle, the vision, and the courage to get it done.

HC: How can we stop people from leaving their lights on all night?

AM: It requires a cultural change, and I can't say I have a good fix on that. I did the first energy-efficiency calculations for the U.S. economy way back in 1971, and I brought up this issue of lighting the daylight. One of the buildings in Berkeley had a beautiful skylight and dozens and dozens of bulbs that were lighting up the daylight. When I pointed this out, they said, You're attacking the American way of life. How can it be a part of a way of life to light up the daylight? President Nixon liked to make the White House really cold in the summer so he could have a fire and be comfortable. It's that kind of idea. It's a different place than logic, far away from environmental protection and leaving the Earth in at least as good shape as we found it.

HC: That's why we as scientists, you and I, have to appeal to the midbrain and the emotions. Otherwise people are not going to change. ～

LILY TOMLIN

Lily Tomlin, one of America's most beloved actresses and comedians, is also a writer and producer. She has won Tony, Emmy, Grammy, and Peabody awards and been nominated for an Academy Award. Renowned for her versatility, Tomlin's interest in theater and performing arts began at Wayne State University. She began doing stand-up comedy in nightclubs in Detroit and New York City. Her first television appearance was on *The Garry Moore Show* in 1966. She's created many well-known characters in her forty-year career, including the telephone operator Ernestine and the sandbox philosopher five-year-old Edith Ann, both of whom became famous on *Rowan & Martin's Laugh-In*. Her films include Robert Altman's *Nashville* and the comedies *Big Business*, *The Incredible Shrinking Woman*, and *All of Me*. Lily Tomlin has also enjoyed success in television, with roles in the popular sitcoms *Murphy Brown* and *Will & Grace*. She starred on the dramatic series *Damages* and on *The West Wing* in the role of the presidential secretary Deborah Fiderer.

HELEN CALDICOTT: I loved *The West Wing*. Sometimes when I've finished watching an episode I think, This is real! We're not really dealing with the fantasy of George Bush. This is really the president.

LILY TOMLIN: Indeed. Some of us would have a suspension of disbelief, as though we were in the White House and that Jed Bartlett *was* the president, which was one ray of hope in our lives at the time. So often they were ahead of the curve. They would talk about issues, and they would suddenly come right into sync with what was going on in life, in government, in the media.

HC: I got to brief the writers of *The West Wing* about nuclear war and nuclear power. They did several episodes on nuclear power, a meltdown, and one on the threat of nuclear war.

LT: They did lots of research and brought in experts to flesh stuff out and give them the lowdown.

HC: As a very well-informed and intelligent American citizen: how are you feeling about the state of your country now?

LT: I'm terribly distressed. With the economy and housing. . . . It was bad enough with the war and our reputation, the destruction that we were initiating way across the world. Now all of this is starting to collapse in on the average person. It's pretty distressing, because the people in charge really don't seem to care. Everything has been done, it seems, to line their pockets. The fact that they would trade human beings for money. . . .

HC: It takes us back to the Iraq War, and although they would say it's not about oil and capitalism, obviously it has been.

LT: It's beyond that. There's no way you can talk about it in any kind of simple human terms, because there's so much suffering and destruction behind it. And so much inequity, exploitation of people and resources in the country, and of our own people. To think that somebody can make the decision to send young people into combat and danger and not think first, Is this the absolute final resort? It harks back to when Bush did that silly, awful thing right after the war had started, and he's saying, There must be some weapons of mass destruction in there somewhere, at one of those big politicians' dinners. With that smirk on his face.

I used to be stunned by the first Iraq War. I'd read about flyers having to inure themselves to the fact of what they're really doing—bombing sites and killing humans. I would read about how they would high-five each other if they had made a good strike. The high-fiving used to fill me with a sickening feeling, the idea that it's like a sport. I'll forgive that because they're people put into that position.

HC: One of the books I want to write is going to be called *Why Men Kill*. I'm going to dedicate it to Donald Rumsfeld. I found out that they show the men in service porno films before they take off on their bombing runs. There's some funny connection between sex and killing. Why do soldiers rape women when they conquer a territory? I know that the United Nations has passed a resolution against rape.

LT: I want to believe in the humanity of most men, and their basic goodness, just as part of our species. It harks back to Kissinger saying, "Power is the ultimate aphrodisiac." Whatever that sense of dominance is, why any one group wants to dominate another group is more than I can understand.

HC: It's so scary, Lily. Sometimes I wish I could bury my head in the sand like an ostrich. But I can't, because I sort of intuitively know what's going on, and I suppose you're the same?

LT: Well, you've known it for a long time. You've led a lot of people to that realization. I'm in a situation where I'm not faced with it in a literal way in life. Yes, I'm aware, but it's very hard to enjoy your freedom and your comforts when so many people are in need and are hurt just for the dollar. It's all collapsing around us. I'm amazed that anyone would even admit that they voted for Bush, but they do. I was with somebody not too long ago, and I didn't know her very well, but I came to know her and like her very much as a person. She said, "I think President Bush has done an okay job." I took her head in my hands and my heart ripped for her even wanting to convince herself that that's true. I said, "No, no, he did not do an okay job." I kissed her on the cheek; that's all I could do.

HC: We're having a big celebration in Sydney for World Earth Day when the pope is here. There are 150,000 pilgrims from all over the world. The pope flies in this huge airplane with his red shoes and all the pomp and circumstance. I can't help but keep thinking of what Jesus said: "It's more difficult for a rich man to enter the kingdom of heaven than the camel to pass through the eye of a needle." Many rich Americans call themselves Christians.

LT: I'm not going to single out the Christians entirely, because most religious people think that they're the blessed ones. Certain preachers have spun it, because you're going to get a bigger congregation if you preach that you should have material things, a big house, plenty of cars, fine clothes, because you're blessed. You're one of God's chosen people. Everybody else is going to go to hell and you're going to go to heaven. If you focus on it, it's profoundly upsetting. You've always amazed me, because your knowledge is so deep and so broad, and you reveal so much that people haven't known. Somehow you've kept your loving, lively persona in the world and give that kind of vibe off. I'd probably have to take to my bed if I knew as much as you do.

HC: [*laughs*] Lily, why don't we talk about how we first met?

LT: My recollection is that you were doing Earth Day here in L.A., or one of the antinuke concerts. I was doing Trudy, the street person—this is thirty some years ago. Carter had just gone into a nuclear plant where there had been a leak, wearing those yellow plastic booties.

HC: It was Three Mile Island, that's right! And he took his wife in there too.

LT: Trudy was running around in some yellow plastic booties and telling everybody that they could protect themselves from radiation with these yellow plastic booties; she kind of satirized the whole thing. I heard you speak, and I was knocked out. Then Sally Field and I both would join you on television, or try to be present when you were speaking, so the messages could draw a larger audience.

HC: The first time was with Phil Donahue. We had a whole hour. Sally was in the makeup room with her hair all in curlers and getting her makeup done. You were pacing the corridor with reams of paper, learning all the numbers of weapons and all the technology, so by the time I came on, you'd covered the whole subject. There was nothing for me to talk about!

Do you remember when we went to Mexico to the jai alai games? We came back and the television in the limo was playing Nancy Reagan talking about the little gun that she kept under her pillow when Ronnie was away.

LT: Patty Davis wrote a book about mothers, but the chapter she wrote about her own mother is really wrenching. It was very moving, about Nancy and how they were somewhat estranged, even though they've come closer together. People who've been involved in many things that you might have a very negative view of, and then anything human about them. . . . You don't know why you can't reach that human part of someone like Dick Cheney; you think maybe there isn't one.

I used to do a line after the election in 2004. I'd say, "Gosh, Vice President Cheney has been more morose than usual." And I'd say, "But Lynne Cheney said that's what turned her on in the first place."

HC: I'll never forget, after that election: there was the vice president and Lynne, and George and Laura, on the stage. George had the twins, and Cheney had his daughter, who is gay, with her partner. The whole election was run by Karl Rove, against gays, and here standing up there was this metaphor for what they ran the election against. Cheney's daughter is gay and I think she was already pregnant.

LT: I'm not sure she was pregnant yet, but she did become pregnant later.

HC: I'm sure he loves his grandbaby, but how do you get people to understand?

I remember when I went to see General Bennie L. Davies, the head of the Strategic Air Command in Omaha, Nebraska. His whole office—everywhere you looked was covered with models of missiles. And he talked about the Soviets and how wicked they were for about twenty minutes. I couldn't crack this façade: an "if necessary, we've got to have nuclear war and kill them all" type of thing.

LT: I'm surprised he saw you. That's a testament to you and your reputation to have an audience with someone like that.

HC: I was in the media a lot at that time. But I said to him, "Have you got grandchildren?" And he sort of stumbled a bit, and then said, "Yes," and I said, "Well, how old are they?" and he said, "Two and ten months." Suddenly his face just cracked, and I got into his soul in a way. I said, "What about their future?" and he conceded then. It's like Carter at Camp David with Sadat and Begin. He couldn't get them together until he finally got them to show photographs of their grandchildren. And then the three of them could talk.

LT: I've become a little more accepting of people's human frailties, but still, someone like Karl Rove or Rumsfeld. The idea that they would send somebody into a phony war is unbelievable. They have to think they're so right. I can only think that they are so cold, and somehow even their own grandchildren—like you said, that guy's face breaks—what is cut off in them that allows them to have a worldview like that? That one particular way of life is so superior to another that you have to destroy the other way of life, or you destroy life just to make money. I know I'm rambling, but I don't know where that lack of empathy comes from. You can't believe that there's just business and art and some divide in there. The person who's inclined to be more of an artist is more empathetic, a push-over, too soft, and the other people have to be so hard, so cut off. I don't believe it.

I sat next to a guy in Texas who is extremely rich, I've seen him in *Forbes* many times. A friend got me into this event because I was doing some research on a Texas project. And of course he said to me, You're from Hollywood and you're just brainwashed. I said, Well, why don't you educate me? Maybe I could learn something here tonight. I guess I really engaged him. As the evening went on he bragged to me that he was the architect or one of the architects of the Swift Boat campaign against Kerry. Later in the evening I said, Are you confessing or telling me that's something you're proud of? At the end of the evening I said, Don't you think we should try to make the world just a little better for a few more people? And he said quickly and emphatically, No. He said, Let the free market go, and it'll take care of everything. I said, Well, of course, it's doing a good job right now [*sarcastically*].

HC: On their deathbeds these people see the fragility of life and how precious it is. Why is it that some people can know that, like you, all the way along, and others seem totally blocked? I think it's part of the societal dynamic, particularly in the United States.

LT: We still are so puritanical and provincial in so many ways; we don't really deal with death. It's like Mel Gibson, when he had that outburst about how he just had to believe that he was going to go to heaven some day. Maybe it was to see his mother again, I don't know. Some people are so narcissistic that I don't think they can imagine themselves ending. Politicians have to be somewhat nar-cissistic. If I step on a snail outside, I usually am somewhat over-wrought. Accidental killing is an awful thing, and purposeful killing is really hard to live with unless you're a murderer or you're so cut off that life means nothing to you. I understand what you're saying about people having some sort of revelation at the end, but it's not soon enough, is it?

HC: When I give speeches I give fact after fact. Once I have their attention, I go to where they really live and try and engender their emotions. I find that most people underneath their cold exterior really love to smell the roses and the orange blossoms.

LT: I totally agree. That's why I said I believe in the humanity of *most* men and women. But where do these few ruthless people come from that don't care about the destruction of other people? I used to do another line when Bush had so much approval in the country, which was so hard to understand. Ernestine the telephone operator was talking to Bush, and she'd say something like "The Iraqi people haven't shown you enough appreciation. Hallmark hasn't made a card yet saying 'Thank you for destroying our country.'" There was so much you could do at that time.

I was playing Flint, Michigan, where Michael Moore is from. Of course, I'm sure that city is split severely—the people who adore him adore him, and the people who don't, really don't. I had a question come up to the stage: who would you rather have for president, George W. Bush or the Marquis de Sade? I read the question cold, and of course I started laughing. The audience got into a big uproar about the Iraq War, and people yelling, My child is over there fighting this war and you hate America. They really equate that kind of dissent with a lack of patriotism and a lack of caring.

HC: I thought that after 9/11 America turned into one big tribe, projecting the anger out onto others.

LT: I was probably really naive at the time, but I don't think President Bush made that speech until about three weeks after the 9/11 attack. I kept thinking—I'm ever hopeful—that it's going to be so ironic that this fellow is going to be the one who does something differently. He's not going to retaliate. He's going to do something magnificent. It's like in *The Search for Signs of Intelligent Life in the Universe*, Jane Wagner's play: Trudy the street person at the end of the play is talking about why humans get goose bumps; why do we get them collectively? We listen to a piece of music and we get a lump in our throat. We have these feelings that can sweep through us and unify us. After she's talked about humans having this experience, then she says, about her space chimps who've been traveling here to find intelligent life in the universe, "and someday maybe we'll do something so magnificent everybody in the universe will get goose bumps."

And I have this hopeful idea that this is possible. Here we had the world in our corner, and we had a moment to show that there's another way to deal with things. And I really thought this was possible. I don't know how I could have been such a schmuck at that time. Then you know what else happened. During 9/11, the plane that went down in Pennsylvania—when the passengers realized what was happening they tried to turn the plane around. After we attacked I felt like that plane had been a metaphor for this country. If we had known, we would never have allowed this to proceed.

HC: It seems from *The Lancet*, a British medical journal, that over a million civilians now have been killed in Iraq. The place has just been decimated. Everything that was set up for civil society: hospitals are destroyed; the sewage system doesn't work; people are being electrocuted because they're putting the electrical cables on the wrong way. Huge amounts of money have been ripped off by Halliburton and Cheney's people.

Tell me what you think of Obama. He has had the courage to say that he wouldn't bomb Iran; he'd go and talk to them.

LT: I though at last that somebody has said something that has a glimmer of something different. Of course he had to modify that.

Maybe you run on one particular sensibility during the pre-election, and in the general you run for the center. I still have every hope that Obama's going to make a difference. The system is so entrenched; do you think it is possible? Is it that we're somehow going to take a different tack after 9/11?

HC: We really need a strong leader, like Roosevelt. If he hadn't died he was going to nationalize medicine in America, so that you would have had free medical care. What are we going to do?

LT: We have to hang in there. Something good might happen. I don't want to divide Americans between the positive and the negative or the liberal and the conservative. I have a Chinese doctor who would say that 5 percent of the world is very, very bad and 5 percent is very, very good, and it's the 5 percent who are bad and the 5 percent who are good who have to fight each other. The people don't have the luxury of time and information; they have a daily life to live. Most people want to smell the roses—my mother used to say I stop and smell the garlic; I tried the roses and it didn't work. [*Laughter.*]

HC: But they're facing reality now. You could say this might be a good thing, especially in America, which is leading the world either toward survival or destruction. Maybe this crisis that's occurring now with the economy . . .

LT: How else could Obama have surfaced? He's part of—hopefully—this evolution of awareness. But it's like a cat or a dog knowing the earthquake's coming.

HC: I think underneath he's a highly intelligent, extremely wise person. I mean, the speech he gave on racism—some of the speeches have been so profound. This is him; this is the man.

LT: In no way do I think Obama's perfect, and I certainly don't expect him to be. That's one of the fallacies that people have, because that's what the media does. They look for every little crack and drive a big wedge in between. He seems to be different from what we usually endure.

HC: Lily, you once told me how you grew up in Detroit, and how you developed your acting, how you'd go to different people's apartments and do your stand-up routines. Tell us about that.

LT: It was an old apartment house, where you're exposed to a lot of different people. It was a very racially mixed neighborhood, and predominantly black, so I had a lot of black friends I went to school with, and I went to their houses. And the old apartment house I lived in had every economic class and level of education. There were very radical people; very conservative and apolitical ones. Older people lived there who were on pensions and couldn't afford to leave, even though they probably wanted to move away. My mother and dad were working-class Southerners who came up to Detroit so my dad could work in the auto factories. I was madly in love with the people in these apartments. Everyone was so different. And I'd be propagandized by one person in an apartment with communist and very radical literature, then I'd spend my evenings with Mrs. Rupert, who was a botanist and ultraconservative, reactionary, really. And then all the Southerners in the building, and the kids I went to school with—I was just immersed in this multidiverse culture.

What I had the experience of seeing was how alike everybody was, and how they all could be really base or how they could be really high. They all made me smile or laugh, and they all made me weep a bit.

HC: Didn't you do stand-up routines?

LT: Oh God, yeah. I'd put on shows. I might as well have been like P.T. Barnum or something. And if a new kid moved in the building, I would immediately try to cast him. These two kids from Georgia moved in, Tommy and Billy Barnes, and they both had red curly hair and freckles. I was influenced by radio and television, and as soon as I saw them, these two kids with red curly hair, I said Howdy-Doody and Arthur Godfrey. So I was able to make up material for them to do, and to try to play those parts. Then I could play satellite parts, like Holly Lokey or Princess Summerfall Winterspring. And they would leave in the middle of the show half the time, or they wouldn't show up for rehearsal, so I started working alone. I started doing it myself.

HC: Didn't you do it with your brother too?

LT: I did it with my brother, and he did the *same* thing. And my brother is naturally funny. I just sort of invent things to do that are funny. At the end of high school and college, I used to work in the coffeehouses in Detroit. I'd been influenced by Ruth Draper, and I adored the monologue form. I also liked to do sketches with other people. I'd get something for my brother and I to do together, and he would just leave in the middle of the show. He'd say, This is so embarrassing—I guess he meant the material—and he'd walk off. By now I was really quite serious about doing it, so I started doing it by myself.

HC: You started really young. This is has been your whole raison d'être, your love really, hasn't it?

LT: I have done it always, but I didn't know that people made a living doing it. I had a teacher in grade school who used to read old dialect poems to us on Friday before we'd go home. I'm sure they're considered politically incorrect now in the school system, because they were very phonetically written. They were German, Yiddish, black, Italian. But they would be like a radio show. We didn't get a TV until I was ten, and I loved radio so much. Also, I had already been politicized, just from the neighborhood I lived in. I went to school with kids who lived in what to me would have been mansions, and I also went to school with kids who were pretty poor. But our neighborhood was just the way it was. I was exposed to a lot of different classes.

The biggest misconception I had for a long time, until I was about twelve or thirteen, is that if people were intelligent they would do the right thing. Did you think that?

HC: Yeah—that morality would obviously be practiced. Then you look at Kissinger.

LT: You know what else irks me? They'll call Karl Rove a mastermind, and they'll call Osama bin Laden a mastermind. It's such a bad use of language. They should be called what they are: demons.

HC: I don't know how they've gotten away with this for so long. After people's awareness turned so consciously, and people began to back away from the war, none of those commentators who fostered the war and supported Bush, and I mean on both sides of the aisle, ever stood up and said, "We were wrong, we should apologize to the American people for misleading them." Let alone the Iraqi people.

LT: They should have, and stepped down from their jobs. Instead they went on as if they'd never said anything positive about Bush or the war.

HC: Judith Miller had five front-page articles in the *New York Times* that actually instigated the war.

LT: Oh, I know. That Cheney would plant it and then go on and quote it. The manipulation is just unconscionable. And the fact that we're not taking any action—it would exonerate us in the eyes of so many in this world if we did.

HC: It's called humility, to say you're sorry.

LT: Humility. That's something that most politicians don't have.

HC: You give us joy and hope, and anyone who can make us laugh like you do, gives us more energy to go on and do what we have to do.

LT: I get that from the audience, I really do. One of the things I loved about *The Search* when I was doing it in New York: I'd go outside after a show, back in the eighties, and there would be a yuppie couple dressed to the teeth, gorgeous, you know, and there'd be three middle-aged women from middle America, dressed very homely, and there'd be two or three goth kids out there all punked out with black lipstick and white makeup, and they would all be standing there in a little clump together, where they wouldn't normally be together at all. And from Jane's words, the play would validate their humanity and make that collective experience in the audience at the end of the play. There was this outpouring of affection. I felt so lucky to have that experience every night.

The object of the play was to give the audience goose bumps, and I was a part of the audience too, and I almost always had goose bumps at the end of the night.

HC: What are you doing now?

LT: I do a lot of concerts. I did a series on HBO; that's how I happened to be in Texas when I sat at that dinner table with that fella. It was about a very, very rich family in Texas, written by Linda Bloodworth, who did *Designing Women*. But the former head of HBO got fired. We shot six episodes, spent millions of dollars, and it's been shelved. I'm a part of this website Wowowow.com: Liz Smith and Leslie Stahl from *60 Minutes* and Mary Wells, a big ad person, and Joni Evans, and Peggy Noonan were part of the founding group. Now there's Candice Bergen and me and Whoopi and Marlo Thomas and Jane Wagner. We contribute now and then. Jane's been doing a lot of what she calls cartoons, like eco cartoons showing animals. Edith Ann also has a column.

HC: I think you need to do a show on everything we've just talked about. You're very profound in your thinking, and you could satirize Karl Rove or the guy you met in Texas.

LT: Hopefully they'll fade to memory soon.

HC: It's very important that these people be brought out.

LT: That's why the Congress should take action; they should have done something. To not even accuse them of stuff that's been done is unbelievable.

HC: I thought Pelosi would do that.

LT: Right away she took it off the table—impeachment—before they even won the election.

HC: We could talk for another hour.

LT: Yes, Helen. [*In voice of Edith Ann*] I would like to sometime. [*As Lily*] Edith, sit down. [*HC laughs.*] Edith used to say, "Helen, I have to go to two different schools. One to learn about baby Jesus and one to learn about smog." ∾

MICHAEL MADSEN

Michael Madsen is director of the documentary *Into Eternity*, a film about the vast amounts of radioactive waste created by nuclear power plants throughout the world and the constant challenge to find an adequate way to store it. A review in *The Guardian* said that it is "one of the most extraordinary factual films. . . . [It] does not merely ask tough questions about the implications of nuclear energy . . . but about how we, as a race, conceive our own future." Madsen has been a guest lecturer at the Royal Danish Academy of Fine Arts, the National Danish Film School, and the Danish School of Design. He also directed the award-winning *To Damascus*, a film on interpretation.

HELEN CALDICOTT: How did you conceive a film about nuclear waste? What initiated your interest in the whole thing?

MICHAEL MADSEN: It was the hundred-thousand-year aspect. Somebody in Finland is building a facility that has to last in a foolproof manner for one hundred thousand years. That caught my attention. I thought that, first of all, they'll have to be able to understand what one hundred thousand years is, which I think is very,

very difficult. And second, they'll have to have some scenarios for the future; that to me was really, really interesting. And I thought, This has got to be the first time in the history of mankind that we are building something like this that's not in any religious context, as would be the case with the cathedrals in the Middle Ages or the pyramids. So my basic question has been throughout making this film, What does such a facility tell us about our own time and what is its true significance? It's something beyond being a storage space for nuclear waste.

HC: What do you mean, it's something beyond being a storage facility for nuclear waste?

MM: Well, I have this suspicion that this is not just digging a hole in the ground and building a bunkerlike structure. This facility is built in a way so that it is able to operate without any human interference. Once it is completed, about 120 years from now, it will be sealed off, and then it will enter silent mode operations. The facility has to be independent of human surveillance and any power supply, because with any such interim facility today, where the waste is, there's these pools cooling the waste. The reason for this silent mode element is that, in this time span the scientists simply do not expect civilization as we know it today to last. That means that the knowledge about what nuclear energy is, and what radiation is, will simply vanish. And therefore it is considered possible that any kind of . . . you can say that it has to be independent of what we humans know in the future, because otherwise it would be too dangerous. It's more safe if it can operate by itself. The Onkalo facility in Finland is, as one critic said and wrote, possibly the last human structure on Earth, or the first post-human structure. In its very construction it has the notion that civilization as we know it today will not last, over this time span. Some of the scientists that I've been working with for this film have expressed less concern in terms of the danger, at least toward humans, because it is conceivable that mankind will not last for this long. In the Swedish legislation concerning high-level nuclear waste, the talk is about the "creatures," living creatures, and not just humans.

HC: Interesting. I think the EPA in America says it should be isolated from the environment for a million years, not one hundred thousand years.

MM: I'm using the figure of one hundred thousand years and into eternity because it is what the law in Finland states. This is the quarantine time. These two figures tell us that the experts do not agree. One independent nuclear waste scientist who I consulted, so I would have somebody to verify what I was being told by the participating experts in the film, told me that it should be at least a quarter of a million years. But one of the problems, and one of the unknowns in making specific dates, is that we don't have any experience with nuclear waste in such concentrations in such a repository. And what happens inside the waste is unknown, because nuclear waste does not only contain plutonium and uranium—almost every known element in the universe is created. What will happen inside the reactions in the waste is not fully clear. The basic problem is: Can we ask future generations to do maintenance? Second: Is that possible? That will require that knowledge can be carried on. And is this question about whether or not we should warn or inform the future? You can also put forward the argument that it's better not to inform the future. That is the preferred strategy in Finland, to hide it. And "Onkalo" means "hiding place." What we are actually fighting here is not a technological problem; we can make that kind of bunker. But an even bigger problem is human curiosity, and therefore something within our very nature. Even if we have stone tablets with information, it's still not clear if this will be understood one hundred thousand years from now.

HC: If you think back two thousand years ago, which we now think is antiquity, when Jesus lived, English hadn't even been developed. That's only two thousand years ago.

MM: Regarding language: the only thing we know is that it changes over time. That is why we'd have problems understanding a person from the Middle Ages. But if the real problem is human curiosity, if they find some kind of indication that something is buried, and you're not able to detect what it is because all knowledge about radiation is gone, then you might have someone who inadvertently opens it and brings out the materials.

HC: It reminds me a bit of the village in Brazil where a hospital sent a capsule of cesium 137 to the rubbish dump because they didn't need it anymore. A family found it, and discovered that it glowed blue in the dark. They used it to paint their faces, they ate it, and they put it under their beds and watched it at night. The whole family died. The whole village was contaminated because people had no idea what they were doing with it.

MM: Exactly. And this may happen then somebody gets an idea that this is actually dangerous, and then it can be used as a kind of dirty bomb. So there's military power in the waste.

HC: I think the Americans chose a million years because plutonium has a half life of 24,600 years. So to encompass the whole gradient of radioactive elements would put the number at a million.

MM: In Finland I received two kinds of answers within the same company. The communication manager said, "Michael, you have to understand that nuclear waste becomes less and less toxic because of the half life. So really, Michael, the problem is diminishing all the time, from day to day." Then the safety expert, the head of long-term safety, said, "I do not agree with this way of talking about these time spans with nuclear waste, because essentially, when we're talking about these time spans, it is forever. In the human timescale, it's forever." It is about one hundred thousand years since Homo sapiens left Africa for the first time, about three thousand generations.

HC: The Department of Energy in America has been employing

anthropologists to work out what sort of signs to put on their waste dumps. Skull and crossbones, or *The Scream* by Munch.

MM: The only thing that there has been some kind of consensus about is *The Scream*. Some universal symbol that any society would be able to understand, any culture, at any point in time. It's impossible to test, but you will still need the marker to survive for one hundred thousand years, or a million years. You need this marker to stay at the same point. In the United States, a concrete slab was placed at the first nuclear test blast. It's a cow field. The cows have been scratching their backs on this concrete slab for forty years, and it's moved ten meters [thirty-three feet] from this scratching.

HC: You wouldn't want any earthquakes either.

MM: There are three possibilities as far as communicating with the future. One is a marker with a universal symbol on it, the other is a kind of archive system, which is really what the Finnish state wants and has taken upon itself to perform, but that depends on whether one generation actually will pass on the information to the next.

HC: What do you mean, an archive system?

MM: The Finnish idea is to have a manned library for a hundred thousand years. People who constantly operate the information.

HC: That's like a fairy tale.

MM: In the film, the man responsible for this idea hesitates as to whether this will take place. The last idea is that, if we can create a kind of a myth that will by itself be retold because of the strength in the narrative, from generation to generation, then this could be another way of passing down information into eternity. I believe that the reason why one is going to such extremes to try to build something to last a hundred thousand years is that it is extremely dangerous, and that there are dangers beyond a few casualties.

HC: Like? Describe the dangers beyond a few casualties.

MM: There is an explanation about what radiation will do to living tissue, to living creatures. There's the instant effects, which we have now seen, what the workers at the Fukushima power plant have been exposed to. Burns that will never heal, and also mutations. The genetic code is not only damaged, but changed. What that would mean, nobody knows.

HC: And the birds. The barn swallows, the insects, and other animals are showing evidence now of mutation.

MM: That is the main threat. We have to understand that today, all the waste in the world is sitting next to the power plants in these pools, where it needs to be cooled for forty years, at least. If we imagine that these facilities will need to be turned into some kind of permanent solution, then there will be repositories all over the world. So it is not only a certain part of the Earth that may have a problem; it may be many different zones.

HC: It will be ubiquitous. Around the time I wrote *Nuclear Madness* in 1978, I thought, Imagine generations ahead, the children born deformed or with genetic disease, developing cancers at the age of six because they're exposed to radiation so much earlier. And that's a legacy that we leave to future generations. With the spread of nuclear power all over the world, I can't see people doing what the Finns have done.

MM: I am trying to stay out of this part of the discussion, because I'm trying to pass on those questions through my film to any individual in the audience. It is clear that something needs to be done because the nuclear waste exists. And even though you may be against the use of nuclear power, this will not in itself make the nuclear waste go away. So something needs to be done with the waste we already have. And as we have seen at the Fukushima power plant, the spent nuclear fuel, sitting next to the reactors, has made trouble, because the cooling of this waste went away along with the reactor cooling. This is the situation all over the world, at any site with a nuclear power plant. The problem of world wars or new states being formed, all this instability aboveground, is a real threat to such facilities. Therefore, having it buried may be a better solution than having it aboveground. But some scientists in the film told me that they find it very difficult to think that every nation in the world will be able to have such a facility, not only in the so-called third world, but also in a country like Japan, because of the earthquakes. In my opinion, this is the fact of what they have now in Fukushima: even if they can get total control of the situation, they can only cover it up. But what I think is important to understand in all of this discussion is that one hundred thousand years is perhaps beyond human comprehension. It is such a vast time span that we simply can't relate to it. We may have a similar problem in Japan. One reason why the authorities, as I understand it, have not been telling the full scope of the events could be because it is more or less unthinkable to evacuate more than thirty kilometers [nineteen miles], perhaps the whole Tokyo area. These things are bordering not only on what is physically possible, but it can be really difficult to understand how bad this really is. It's outside our human comprehension. And we, as humans tend to hope for the best.

But in these matters, as I say in this film, nuclear energy stands on the shoulders of all the scientific knowledge that we have about the universe. It is really the powers of the universe that we are harvesting. So much knowledge is sort of fused together in this technology, and in that sense it's the hallmark of human civilization. But the flip side is that the waste has a time span beyond what we can really understand. It's suddenly impossible to act responsibly.

HC: About the Onkalo project: would you describe what they are doing in Finland?

MM: In Finland they are trying to create the world's first permanent repository for nuclear waste, a bunkerlike facility 0.5 kilometers [547 yards] down underground in a system of tunnels.

HC: It's granite bedrock, but does it have cracks in the granite so water can seep through?

MM: It's the main floor for such a facility, because groundwater is what will flush out the nucleides. But any man-made structure is bound to crumble over time. So the Onkalo facility—as I said earlier, it means "hiding place"—is a delay mechanism. One hundred thousand years, at least, to render the waste harmless to its half-lifes. Just as you have several city walls around a medieval city, it's the same idea. If you breach one barrier, you still have another one. What I'm interested in in *Into Eternity* is really the question about communication, and therefore the question about human curiosity. Any time we have found something in the ground, a pyramid or a burial chamber, we have opened it because we wanted to see what's in there. Even if you know it's dangerous, you may still want to have a look.

HC: I wonder how much nuclear waste do the Finns actually have? They're about to open this huge nuclear power plant that was built by AREVA, a French company, but there have been terrible problems with the construction. And there's been intrigue. Would you talk about the new reactor AREVA has been constructing?

MM: The new reactor is only a few kilometers away from the Onkalo facility. They have had very big difficulties. If we were comparing reactors to the automobile industry, a nuclear reactor, first of all, is a luxury car. It's the greatest car ever built. The problem with the nuclear industry is that they have not been building cars since Chernobyl. There have been no new reactors. That means there is a lack of knowledge, because the engineers have gone on pension or they're dead. When you don't have the right components anymore, and you're wanting to build something even more complex, more safe, but you don't have the know-how anymore, then it's extremely difficult. This is one of the problems that has been faced in Finland. We were essentially unwanted at the Onkalo facility when making the film. The resistance that we encountered in the last part of the production perhaps came from the problems of the mother company building Onkalo, from problems which they encountered with the reactor. So they wanted as little public discussion about the facility as possible. To return to the amount of waste in Finland: the idea is that the capacity of the Onkalo facility is twelve thousand metric tons and that one hundred thousand years from now, it will hold all the waste in Finland. Now that another private operator has been granted a license to build another power plant in Finland, the waste production from this power plant is not calculated in relation to the Onkalo facility. What is so weird, in my opinion, about this is that the money financing the company building this facility, something like €3 billion [about $4 billion] is coming from a tax taken from the Finnish citizens ever since the nuclear energy production started. So this is paid for by every Finnish citizen, but now the know-how rests within the private company.

HC: What do you think about private companies building nuclear power plants?

MM: It is in my mind very clear that a private company can only have one goal in this world, and that is to earn money. That's the logic of private enterprise. Therefore, it is simply not reasonable to expect a private company to act beyond its own survival. This is what we see TEPCO do in Japan, and to believe that they should be acting on behalf of society is simply false. It's a false belief. I don't think you can actually blame a private company for acting in its own interest.

HC: But in the nuclear area, do you then not believe in capitalism?

MM: We have to have another system if we want to have control, for example, or transparency. Some say radiation does not know any borders. With Chernobyl, the nuclear cloud traveled all over Europe. So there is a problem for you to say that a private company's acting in its own interest in a spot on this Earth but the consequences may travel all over the world. And then you can ask, Is that reasonable? Is it even wise? That is the question to put forward. You cannot control where a war takes place. Let's imagine that the Second World War was happening today, with the reactors in large parts of Europe. We again encounter a scenario that is very difficult to comprehend because we would have to entertain the idea that a visit to Paris, Rome, Berlin would be impossible.

HC: Does it worry you that you live in Denmark, travel through Europe and Kazakhstan, and some of the food you're eating is almost certainly radioactive?

MM: If I was thinking about that it would be difficult to go to sleep.

HC: When I go to Europe I practice psychic numbing. But living in Australia, the southern hemisphere, we have nonradioactive food. Yet we sell uranium to the rest of the world, including to Japan.

MM: I'm sorry to tell you that ever since the first nuclear test explosion, the background radiation in the world has been higher, so you will also have radioactive background radiation at a higher level in Australia. Even worse, one of the foremost critics of the project said to me that to build a facility like Onkalo in Finland is crazy, because we know that there will be an ice age. The weight of the ice will depress the crust of the Earth seven hundred meters [765 yards] down and that will enhance the fault lines. The water flow will increase, and perhaps new fault lines will break into the depository. If we really want to act responsibly, in terms of building the depository, it has to be in Australia. Australia has the most stable bedrock in the world, and there will be no ice age.

HC: You don't know there won't be an ice age down here. We're heading into that situation, because the federal government has found a piece of aboriginal land (we're a very racist country) in the Northern Territory, and it's called Muckaty Station. It sits atop a tributary of the Great Artesian Basin, which is archaeological water that supplies water to a large part of the continent. A deal was done by our former prime minister, John Howard, with George W. Bush in the global nuclear energy partnership that we may receive some of America's radioactive waste. This bill is being pushed through parliament despite tremendous opposition by the indigenous people and many others. I can't say that we don't deserve it, having exported all this uranium all over the world like there's no tomorrow.

MM: Perhaps it's not a question about deserving it or not. If you entertained the idea that you didn't even export uranium, still, this is the only truly suitable place in the world. Is it not fair that in the spirit of global brotherhood—

HC: I see from a philosophical perspective why you would ask that rhetorical question, and looking at the aspect of nuclear waste down the ages, it's a reasonable question to ask.

MM: I think it is too. With every such facility the argument is that the bedrock has been stable for such-and-such a long time, and therefore it will be stable in the future. But it is not a scientific argument to say the past looked like that, that's what the future will look like. But that's what the whole thing rests upon in Finland, and in every such repository in the world, wherever they will be built. That's one of the paradoxes in trying to handle nuclear waste responsibly. We have nothing to compare with, and we have nothing to test it on, simply because the time span is so big—

HC: It's like the Fukushima accident. Five meltdowns occurring within a few days of each other, and hydrogen explosions left, right, and center, isn't in the textbooks and no one's ever thought about this before.

MM: I'm working on a new project that will take me to Kazakhstan, to the Baikonur Cosmodrome where Soviet and Russian militaries fired rockets into the sky; this is what our new project is about.

HC: So describe what's happening in Kazakhstan.

MM: It is simply that this is the world's biggest facility for launches into space. That's partly my interest for the new film I'm working on, which I cannot really talk that much about. But again, it is a project that is trying to look at things from a more philosophical angle. Sometimes, for me, documentary filmmaking is a possibility to investigate my own time and to journey into my own time.

HC: The director's note from you, I think it's absolutely profound:

> I am interested in the areas of documentary filmmaking where additional reality is created. By this I mean that I do not think reality constitutes a fixed entity, which accordingly can be documented or revealed in this or that respect. Instead, I suspect reality to be dependent on and susceptible to the nature of its interpretation. I am, in other words, interested in the potentials and requirements of how reality can be, and is, interpreted. The Onkalo Project of creating the world's first final nuclear waste facility, capable of lasting at least one hundred thousand years, transgresses both in construction and on a philosophical level, all of the previous human endeavors. It represents something new. And in a sense I suspect it to be emblematic of our time, and in a strange way out of time, a unique vantage point for any documentary.

Can you just enlarge on that? Out of time, emblematic of time?

MM: I can best explain perhaps by the way the narrative is created in *Into Eternity*. *Into Eternity* plays around with the narrative I see of addressing a future audience. An audience far, far away, in time, from today. And this address to the future has the idea that, when you watch the film, in a way, you are watching the film as if you were looking back on our time from fifty thousand years from now or one hundred thousand years from now. It gives you a perspective, so suddenly it's possible to look at our own time with another perspective, with other eyes. The problem of being contemporary is that you cannot see the forest for the trees, because you're in the midst of it. But in trying to create this perspective of looking back at our time, I hope that this narrative device, in a way, will enable us perhaps to get a glimpse of things that otherwise would be invisible to us. This kind of imaginary dialogue with the future is an attempt to try to put a new kind of gaze on something outside of our particular time. ❧

BOB
HERBERT

B ob Herbert joined the *New York Times* as an op-
ed columnist in June 1993, writing about politics,
urban affairs, and social trends in a twice-weekly column. His career began in 1970 as a reporter, then night
city editor at the *Star-Ledger* in Newark, New Jersey.
Herbert earned a BS in journalism from SUNY Empire
State College. He has taught journalism at Brooklyn
College and the notable Columbia University School of
Journalism. He won the Meyer Berger award for coverage
of New York City, the American Society of Newspaper
Editors award for distinguished newspaper writing, and
the David Nyhan Prize from the Shorenstein Center at
Harvard University for excellence in political reporting.
He is currently a distinguished senior fellow at Demos, a
multi-issue policy and advocacy organization that aims
to influence public debates and catalyze change.

―――

HC: I'm interviewing you on the fourteenth of January in 2009,
and by the time the program airs Obama will have been inaugurated
as the new president. How do you feel about that?

BH: I'm still a little stunned at the turn of events. It's incredible that he came politically out of nowhere. I remember going out to Chicago when he was running for the senate seat. I had gotten a tip from a friend of mine, a producer at ABC who was very savvy about politics. She said, "Bob, you need to go out to Illinois and take a look at this fella named Barack Obama. He's African American, he's running for U.S. Senate, and he's gonna win." I said to my friend, This sounds ludicrous to me, a black guy running for the Senate named Barack Obama. I've never heard of him. And she said, he's a new kind of politician. I went to Chicago, followed him around. And I did think that he stood for a new kind of politics, but it never occurred to me that he'd be elected president of the Unites States.

HC: It's a revolution.

BH: That remains to be seen. Obama is a very interesting and complex fellow. As I've been looking at him reasonably closely, I can see that he's above all a politician. He's very smart, very savvy, he has a sophisticated grasp of the issues, and I like most of his positions. But he is above all a politician. And the United States is in a very tough situation—dire economic straits and the wars going on in Iraq and Afghanistan. I would like to see someone who is progressive in their policies, not just their stated politics. If he's as progressive as I'd like, then you would see a revolution. My guess is that he'll fall short of that, but I can't imagine he'd be anything other than a welcome change from the Bush years.

HC: I also use that term "revolutionary" cautiously, but in terms of the black population in America and their terrible history, it's an outstanding thing for them, isn't it?

BH: It's been amazing. I was going all over the country covering the campaign, and he began to close in on the nomination. After he won the nomination it began to look like he had a good shot at winning the presidency—I can't tell you how many tears I saw when I would go into African American communities and interview people. At times they would just break down and cry. I remember one time here in New York, I was at home on the West Side and I had ordered in. A fellow came to deliver the meal. I'd seen him several times, so we knew each other, but he was a very quiet person; you'd give him a tip, he'd say thank you, and leave. This was the night that Obama secured the nomination. This delivery man is African American, probably mid- to late fifties. He came to the door, I paid him, gave him a tip, said thank you, and he said thank you, but he paused. He looked up at me and said, "Mr. Obama won, didn't he?" I said, Yes, he did. And there was another pause, and he said, For sure? And I said, Yeah, he won the nomination. And I must tell you, the biggest grin spread across his face. His face had always been impassive. Just the biggest grin, and he turned and walked down the hall. It's been that kind of thing.

HC: I think it's going to give self-esteem to the African Americans. This is going to elevate them into a new sphere of being, don't you?

BH: I absolutely agree. I see it more in casual conversations, where you get a different take on things. It's much more political when you're doing interviews. But in ordinary conversations with people you know, people you don't know. I've noticed that among blacks there is an almost palpable feeling of holding your head a little higher. A little more power, if you will, in a person's step. A feeling of, Yes, we've arrived. We've known all along that discrimination is wrong; there is no reason to look down on yourself because of the way some people treat you. Nevertheless, with the success of Obama there's this palpable pride and a sense of uplift. I think it's very real.

HC: I loved it when he arrived at his hotel in Washington to begin his preinauguration affairs and put his children in school, and these wonderful African American women from D.C., all dressed up in their best, and furs and everything, came to greet him. To be there, they said, was a historic occasion.

BH: I've watched this in the course of my lifetime—and I'm actually going to give George W. Bush a bit of credit here, believe it or not. I've always been a big believer in things becoming normal. You have to make things happen, and then over a period of time, people accept it as normal, and they don't much think about it anymore. That's one of the reasons why I thought as a youngster that integration was so important in the public schools. When I was a young kid there were no black reporters, no black anchors on the newscast. There were hardly any blacks who had television programs. Nat Cole had a show, and it was considered an extremely big deal, After a while you saw more and more blacks on television. and then you took it for granted that you would see blacks on television.

When I was at the *Star-Ledger* back in the early seventies, there were very few black elected officials in high public office. The first black person to become elected mayor of Newark, New Jersey, was Kenneth Gibson. That was a big deal. Enormous screaming headlines. But over the years, you've gotten more people into elective office—then came the Bush administration, which was so harmful. Nevertheless, he appointed black people to high positions in his cabinet—whether Condi Rice or Colin Powell in the position of secretary of state. After a while Americans got used to the idea that the secretary of state could be an African American. At some point it's no longer a big deal.

And now Obama has reset the final hurdle. You have an African American who's president of the United States. Even though it takes a long time, it's so important for this stuff to become normal. It gives me hope that we're still moving in the right direction.

HC: Do you know about Obama's background in politics in Illinois and how he worked with the black community there as a community organizer?

BH: That's one of the things that is interesting, because we know that Chicago politics can be treacherous. He remained aloof from the nuts and bolts of Chicago politics. He understood that if you got too close to this flame, you could get singed. Nevertheless, he needed alliances. He's always been very good at getting mentors, powerful figures who'd shepherd him along. He's also been lucky in terms of his opponents. In his Senate race there were a couple of people who were favored who self-destructed because of personal problems. The Republicans couldn't field a competitive candidate against Obama. But his political genius is that he knows how to take advantage of these opportunities.

One of the most amazing things about Obama, and I'm still admiringly baffled by this, is where he got the ability to mount this enormous national campaign for president, manage it so well, this astonishing fund-raising apparatus. He was up against Hillary Clinton, with all the resources the Clintons were able to draw upon, and he won. To me that's the most astonishing aspect of this Obama phenomenon, that he was able to pull that off. It was a staggering achievement.

HC: And then we need to look at his appointees, not least of which is Hillary Clinton herself. I always feel kind of uncomfortable watching Hillary, I'm not really sure if I trust her. Can you give us a feeling of who she is and what you think she can achieve in this extraordinarily dangerous world today?

BH: That is complicated. There were rumors that she was being considered for secretary of state. This was Obama the politician at work. It was a brilliant stroke in terms of being president, running an administration, having someone who is very smart, very talented, knowledgeable about foreign affairs, bringing that person into the cabinet in a position that has to work closely with the president. She's not there in the Senate hurling thunderbolts at the administration. It shores him up. There were women who felt that it was a woman's time to be president in the United States. Most of Hillary's supporters voted for Obama, but there was still a sense of disappointment. And secretary of state is the premier post in the cabinet. When you think about it, if she's not going to be president, the idea of a family where the husband was president of the United States and the wife was secretary of state, no historian is going to be able to ignore that. That's a pretty profound historic statement, which is the main reason why I think Hillary wanted it.

Obama really got his start on the national stage by being opposed to the Iraq War. He was saying, I'm not opposed to all wars, but I'm opposed to stupid wars. Hillary had been in favor of the war. Now that Obama's been elected president, he's moving slowly in terms of a withdrawal from Iraq. He's also talking about substantially beefing up our involvement in Afghanistan, which I'm opposed to. I was in favor of the United States going into Afghanistan after September 11, but that's seven years ago; he could be getting himself into a quagmire.

HC: The fact that Osama was there didn't necessarily tie it in with the terrorists who hit the World Trade towers, four of whom were from Saudi Arabia, and one was from Egypt.

BH: It was true that the Taliban had allowed Al Qaeda to have terrorist training grounds in Afghanistan. And the Taliban was an evil group itself. I did not have a problem with the United States going into Afghanistan in the aftermath of 9/11. But the goal then would be to rout the Taliban, destroy Al Qaeda if you could, and track down Osama bin Laden. To be diverted from that goal and conduct what I consider to be an insane war in Iraq was just ridiculous. To now come into Afghanistan and double the U.S. presence without a clearly stated mission, I don't see how this is a good move for the United States.

HC: Do you think Obama is placating the military, the Pentagon, by saying he'll persist in Afghanistan? In your article "The Afghan Quagmire" you quote Michael Gordon: "Afghanistan presents a unique set of problems: a rural-based insurgency, an enemy sanctuary in neighboring Pakistan, the chronic weakness of the Afghan government, a thriving narcotics trade, poorly developed infrastructure and forbidding terrain."

BH: I asked the question, What's the upside? If you're looking in a very selfish way at doubling our troop presence in Afghanistan. I do not find an answer to that. It's not an exact parallel, but it reminds me of when John F. Kennedy took over as president in January of 1961. In his short tenure as president we beefed up what they called "advisers" in Vietnam. We didn't learn our lesson from the French, who had been routed in Indochina. It looks like we haven't learned our lesson from the Soviet Union in Afghanistan. You send your troops into places where they have this unforgiving terrain. They're going to be vulnerable to guerrilla warfare, because that's the kind of warfare that will be conducted against them. We're not good at that; we're good at bombing and destroying with conventional forces. And our economy is in the tank! We can't pay for the forces we have in Iraq and Afghanistan right now.

HC: England was routed in Afghanistan, and so was the Soviet Union, when the United States fought the Soviet Union and helped to initiate the formation of the Taliban and Al Qaeda in Afghanistan, and armed them! The role the United States played in the emergence of the Taliban is not well told.

BH: Before the 9/11 attacks I was writing about the Taliban. One of the things that has always outraged me was the treatment of women in Afghanistan.

HC: Just one more question about Hillary. I'm worried about Iran. My brother was a diplomat in Iran. It's a very beautiful country, a country of poets; they're Persians. Ahmadinejad is a bit of a crazy guy. The head of the clergy there is really the president. They're enriching uranium because they say they want nuclear power, yet they're sitting on a huge reservoir of oil. Israel's got huge numbers of nuclear weapons, maybe the third-largest nuclear arsenal in the world. This has to be diplomatically finessed. Obama has talked about negotiating and talking to Iran, which is the way to go. Do you think Hillary has the capability, the diplomatic skills, after she said she would annihilate Iran in the election campaign?

BH: We have to look to Obama. This is going to require the most sophisticated, delicate, diplomatic approach one can imagine. Obama gave the signal that that's what he favors. We don't know what the administration line is going to be. Hillary will be influential in the development of our approach to Iran, but I don't think you can really go by what was said in the campaign. If Obama wants to move in a sophisticated, diplomatic way in his dealings with Iran—I'm not under the illusion that any of that would be easy. If Hillary got her marching orders, she would carry that out. I believe she's competent and smart enough to do it effectively. This move into Afghanistan is so worrisome. These presidents like to flex their military muscles. You're commander in chief of the most powerful military the world has ever known. I've seen one president after another do nonsensical stuff when it comes to war. I'm hoping that this Afghanistan thing is a bit of an aberration, and that when he looks at it he'll find out that it may not be the road to follow. And that we'll start thinking in terms of peace rather than endless, not just destructive, but self-destructive, wars.

HC: You've written about the debt in America. The United States has close to a trillion dollars a year, if all the black accounts in the intelligence areas are counted, and the war in Afghanistan, and the war in Iraq—you move into the debt that Bush has incurred and you're up to $10 trillion in foreign debt, the $700 billion that Paulsen has promised to the banks and the people who did the awful stuff in the economy, and another $600 billion or so that Obama has promised to ramp up the economy. You were pessimistic when you wrote your article "Where the Money Is." You've got up to 21 million people who are out of jobs nor do you have free health care. Will Obama have the guts to start looking after Americans and stand up and do the right thing?

BH: I grew up in New Jersey in a wonderful town called Montclair, about twelve miles outside of New York. Lovely place for kids to grow up, back in the 1950s. I have a sister who is four years younger. Our parents were not really strict. If my sister and I were misbehaving, we didn't get spankings, and my father didn't yell at us. My father would give us a look. He'd look at us, and we'd stop, and we'd stare back at him, and he'd say, "Have you lost your mind?" I look at the stuff that's going on, and I wonder if we haven't collectively lost our mind.

Quick example: Bush goes into Afghanistan and into Iraq after September 11, and at the same time he cuts taxes. He's cutting taxes in wartime, which is insane. Now Obama is going to beef up our presence in Afghanistan. And he's cutting taxes. He's giving middle-class tax cuts now. It seems like insanity, even if Obama is serious about trying to address the struggle of middle-class people who are losing jobs and have lost their 401Ks in the stock market crash and don't have health care. Then you go beyond that to working people, and poor people, who are forgotten; they're hardly ever even talked about in the United States anymore. If he's serious about address-ing the needs of these millions of people—we've got these deficits, we've got the $350 billion that we've given most of to the banks and the brokerage houses, he's asking for another $350 billion in the Troubled Asset Relief Program. Initially Treasury Secretary Paulsen planned to spend $700 billion to take these toxic securities off the hands of the banks and free up the banks to behave normally again, to free up the frozen credit market. That never even happened. He looked at what was going on in England and decided, We're not going to buy these troubled assets that nobody knows how to value anyway. We're going to funnel the money to the banks, essentially nationalizing them, to some extent. The program was badly con-ceived, there was very little oversight, and no one is really clear what happened to the first half of that money.

HC: That's $350 billion down the tubes?

BH: It's $350 billion, but we don't know if it's down the tubes. They did not use the money to free up the credit markets to any tremendous extent. The public is very upset about the way this money was spent, without oversight. Now Obama wants the other $350 billion to help people who are in danger of having their homes foreclosed, so the money wouldn't all be going to the banks. There's a fight over that money, whether Congress wants to allow the president to spend this other $350 billion. You've got $700 billion of these TARP funds. You've got the deficits that you were talking about. You've got the $800 billion stimulus plan that Obama has proposed that will probably be approved by the Congress. That's going to jack the deficits up enormously.

So what is going to happen is, a year or two from now you're going to get the more conservative elements in the Congress stepping up and saying, we cannot continue to spend all this money. Look at these mounting deficits. And they're going to be opposed to raising taxes, because they're always opposed to raising taxes. So what are they going to do? They're going to say, These things that you liberals are saying we need to help ordinary people, we can't afford it. We're not going to be able to have health care, we're not going to be able to improve the public schools, we're not going to be able to provide a reasonable safety net, even though we know that we're in terrible economic hard times. And they're just going to cut it off. I am positive that in another year, eighteen months or two years, that's what's going to happen. They're going to say we can't spend any more money.

HC: That's terrifying, when you think that 47 million people in America have no health insurance.

BH: The reason it's especially weird is because we have two forms of socialized medicine in America that work extremely well. One is Medicare, for older Americans. I love that story where there was a woman, a voter, who was talking to a Republican running for Congress. He was talking about socialism, too much big government, and she was saying, "You tell the government to keep its hands off my Medicare!" She loves Medicare and has no conception that this is a government program, or socialized medicine. That's one example. The other example is the military. You get medical coverage for everyone who is in the military, and it works extremely well. Health care provided by the government. The idea that you have these obscene profits being made by corporations and others in the health industry while at the same time you have 49 or 50 million Americans without any coverage at all is an absolute disgrace.

HC: Medicine is not an industry; it's a profession that serves the people.

BH: But the point is, it is an industry in the United States. That's the reason why you can't get health coverage to all Americans, because so many people are making so much money, and they're unwilling to relinquish it.

HC: Who's going to have the guts to take on this wicked industry?

BH: There are people in the United States right now who are forgoing their medicine to spend the money on food for their families. I'm talking about people with extremely serious illnesses.

You're talking about getting the insurance industry out of health care. That's not even the plan. When Obama and Hillary were running, the idea they gave is to compel people to buy insurance. That's how you get universal coverage.

HC: Hillary screwed it up when she was given the mandate with Bill's election to nationalize medicine. What did she do? She worked in the West Wing and brought in all the insurance companies.

BH: I don't know how this happened, but in this country we have made people who are poor, sick, or lose their jobs out to be villains, as though they had done something wrong. Why should the rest of the country take care of them? It's a sick approach to society.

HC: It should come out of the government. Instead of spending a trillion dollars on killing people.

BH: I don't think we're there. I don't expect that from Obama. I don't think that we're going to get socialized medicine in the United States anytime soon. So we're in trouble. We're in an emergency economic situation; going ahead it will be a case of putting up your arm and trying to fend off catastrophe.

HC: It feels a bit like the Roman Empire.

BH: It feels very much like the Roman Empire. As we were talking about Afghanistan, it's as though we do not learn our lessons from history. They're trying to keep the house of cards upright.

HC: If you look at the world's resources, this is a finite planet with finite resources. The truth is that we cannot keep growing and buying and selling stuff, because we're going to run out.

BH: One of the problems for the United States is that we never look past the day after tomorrow. What's happening today, maybe what's happening tomorrow, but certainly not a sustainable future.

HC: Obama has some very good environmentalists in his program.

BH: I'm worried that the economy tends to trump everything else. We don't know the direction this administration is going to take. Is he going to listen to the more progressive voices. Hilda Solis, for example, is the labor secretary; she's progressive when it comes to the rights of workers, stopping these attacks on union organizing. Is Obama going to have a more conservative approach coming from a Larry Summers, or Geithner, who had been the head of the New York Fed? It'll be interesting to see who he listens to. I hope he's not like Bill Clinton in this triangulation strategy—a step to the left, a step to the right, we'll slice it in half. I worry about that. He has appointed talented, smart people. That is a welcome change from the Bush administration, in which there was a bunch of ideologues and incompetents running the country.

HC: Bush shouldn't go off scot-free after making such a hell of a mess. If you were Obama, what would you do?

BH: I have mixed feelings. The country is in such a difficult situation right now, I don't think that it would be helpful to go after the Bush-Cheney crowd in terms of prosecutions unless there were some clear criminal instances that cried out for prosecutions. If you are starting to talk about war crimes, and torture, which is evil—I think if the Obama administration went after them on that stuff it would tear the country apart. We would not be able to address these very serious problems we have now. But the media, the public, and the various organizations, there should be an outcry over what this guy and his administration have done to the country and to other parts of the world. I think they have been profoundly destructive. There should be more outrage in the national conversation in the United States. ∼

FRANCES FOX PIVEN

Frances Fox Piven is distinguished professor of sociology and political science at the Graduate Center of the City University of New York. She is a former president of the American Sociological Association, has taught at numerous universities in the United States and Europe, and is the author of over a dozen books, including *Poor People's Movements: Why They Succeed, How They Fail*, with Richard A. Cloward; *Keeping Down the Black Vote: Race and the Demobilization of American*, with Lorraine Minnite and Margaret Groarke; and most recently *Who's Afraid of Frances Fox Piven?: The Essential Writings of the Professor Glenn Beck Loves to Hate*. Frances is the recipient of a number of academic and public awards for her work. She has said that her lifetime preoccupation has been with the uses of social science to promote democratic reform.

—∞—

HELEN CALDICOTT: I've always admired you and your work. You've been struggling against difficult odds. Suddenly you've become notorious because Glenn Beck has attacked you and keeps on attacking you. The focus of his attack is a paper that you wrote with your late husband, "The Weight of the Poor," about signing up poor people for welfare payments and saying that then the government would have to give them guaranteed income. Tell us about what Beck's saying and your analysis of him.

FRANCES FOX PIVEN: I'd love to. First let me explain that Glenn Beck focuses on an article that Richard and I wrote forty-five years ago. He has also focused on a short article I wrote more recently in *The Nation*. The in-between period, forty-five years, he says nothing about that, nothing about anything I have written in the interim. I'm sure he hasn't read much of that, but he probably hasn't read the things he does talk about, either. He focuses on this article from 1966 and another little article in 2011.

HC: And what did the articles say?

FFP: The first article was based on research that Richard and I had done that showed that the welfare system, the system of cash assistance for poor mothers and their children, was only reaching about one third of the people who were eligible. The way the system worked, it was very hard for poor mothers and children to get the benefits that they were entitled to. They were rebuffed or intimidated, or it was simply made too complicated. Mothers were humiliated by questions about their sexual behavior, or by intrusive investigations, sometimes in the middle of the night. There were a lot of features of this system that were designed to keep people from claiming the benefits to which they were entitled.

So we proposed that social workers, lawyers, and community organizers work with the poor themselves to claim these benefits, and then we extrapolated what we thought would be the political and financial consequences. We felt that this would raise costs at a time when there was a lot of racial conflict in the cities. And that under those circumstances, a Democratic national government would look for ways to cool things off, because the Democrats depended on urban support, both black and white. One way to keep things on an even keel would be to replace welfare with some kind of guaranteed income paid for by the federal government.

People talk about this as if it were a crazy idea, but in fact Richard Nixon proposed a guaranteed income just a couple of years later, to cope with the rising welfare rolls and rising welfare costs, some of which resulted from an emerging welfare rights movement with which we worked. Now, sensible, reasonable people might say this wasn't the right thing to do. You shouldn't get mothers and their children welfare assistance; you should get them jobs.

HC: How?

FFP: It's hard, but lots of people nevertheless would say that. However, that's not exactly the point—not now, not forty-five years later. The point is that Glenn Beck calls this a blueprint for an orchestrated crisis to bring down capitalism. He has a diagram in the shape of a tree that he draws on his chalkboard. At the trunk of the tree is Cloward and Piven, and then there are big branches that go off from the trunk to SDS, the Students for Democratic Society, to George Soros and the Open Society Institute, to the New York City fiscal crisis in 1976, to the recent financial meltdown, to the election of Barack Obama. All of this originates in this article, which laid out a plan to reform welfare.

Glenn Beck has been propounding this theory for almost two years now. Then, in the beginning of January, I wrote an article in *The Nation* that was mainly about the obstacles to organizing the unemployed in the United States—the problems that organizers have to overcome. Problems such as the fact that the unemployed are dispersed; they're no longer gathered together at one workplace. They're also ashamed of the fact that they don't have a job. And there isn't a natural local target for their action. But then I said, We have to try to overcome these obstacles, because we need a movement of the unemployed such as exists in other parts of the world. Because protest movements make a difference.

HC: Like Egypt!

FFP: It could be Egypt. Or it could be the protests that are sweeping through England—the UK Uncut protests. It could be Greece. But my endorsement of protests by the unemployed was treated by the right-wing blogs as a call for violent and bloody revolution. So they take words that are properly part of democratic discourse and treat them as a call for violent revolution. Glenn Beck's blog actually did frame some of my words with a burning American flag with my head in the middle of the flames.

HC: Oh my God!

FFP: The consequence was that, on their blogs, hundreds and hundreds of people posted curses and death threats against me. So I began to speak out about this on television and in the print media. Other academic and liberal organizations began to denounce Glenn Beck, Fox News, and the Murdoch empire for irresponsible programming that encouraged death threats. We all know that in the United States death threats have a certain traction. We are a culture with a lot of violence; lots of Americans like guns.

The upside of all this was that twenty-three academic associations released public statements that said I was very eminent, that I had made a major contribution to social science and social policy, especially to welfare policy and voting rights, and these sorts of attacks were unacceptable. Glenn Beck was trying to stifle democratic and academic discourse by intimidation and Fox News should take him off the air. About the same time, liberal organizations also rallied to support me. I think it was important not to ignore what Beck and his ilk were doing because this is how fascist movements start—they start with the spinning of paranoid fantasies. People are anxious. Big changes have overtaken your country, my country, other countries. Some of those changes have included deindustrialization and the financial collapse of the last few years. A lot of people are suffering economic hardship in the United States as a result of declining wages, joblessness, or cutbacks in public social programs. Although we know from survey data that the people who respond that they sympathize with the Tea Party policy positions are not the people who are experiencing the worst economic hardship.

HC: That's very interesting. What is the true rate of unemployment in America now? Do you think there are any resonances with post–World War I Germany?

FFP: The rate of real unemployment now is probably about 15 percent. Everybody makes their own calculations and guesses based on how many people are in part-time work, or are discouraged and have stopped looking for work. We know that the unemployment rate among African Americans is much, much higher. And it's horrific. There's a lot of homelessness. People are losing their homes. They've been suckered into mortgages that they cannot pay. Subprime mortgages with ballooning payments required as time goes on. A lot of people are in homes that are either being foreclosed or what we call underwater, meaning that they owe more on the house than the house is now worth, because of the drop in housing prices. These people probably should walk away from their houses and leave the bank with the deficit, whatever it is.

We also know that hunger is increasing. And that not only is official poverty increasing—and the official poverty line is set very low in the United States—but the numbers *below* that line are increasing. And the numbers that we call desperately poor, those that live in extreme poverty, are increasing even more rapidly. So there is a lot of hardship in the United States. But the Tea Party–style protests are not occurring among the most hard-hit parts of the population. The people in surveys who express sympathy for the Tea Party politics are older, they're almost all white, and they are not as likely to report economic hardship. Nevertheless, these people also experience anxiety about changes that have overtaken the country. They're anxious when their community changes because the only factory has closed, even though they were not factory workers. And they're anxious about changes that have taken place in our sexual and family mores, for example. They remember nostalgically a time when a man was a man and a woman was a woman and everybody got married before they had a baby, and got married in a church, and so forth. Changes of this sort generate a lot of anxiety.

Also, the United States is becoming a country of immigrants. Not only are we becoming a country with a very diverse population, but we have an African American president. We have a political etiquette in this country which requires that no one says that's the problem. Instead they say, "He's not really born in the United States" or "He's really a Muslim." But I think what actually drives some people berserk is that we have an African American president and, in states like Arizona, in no time at all, they'll have a majority minority population.

HC: Of Hispanics.

FFP: Yes.

HC: You've got a black first lady and two black children in the White House. In fact, this is a latent or cryptogenic racism that's going on.

FFP: Yes, I think so.

HC: Why doesn't anyone spell it out?

FFP: They would deny it. The right would certainly deny it. Glenn Beck at his peak had almost 3.5 million viewers. He had three hours a day on TV. Two hours on radio. He has a bestselling book, he has an Internet blog. This is a very important person if you want to understand the currents of popular politics in the United States and the extraordinary timidity of mainstream leaders.

HC: Why are they so scared? That's what I can't understand. I think Obama is a highly intelligent, moral, scrupulous man, but he's been enveloped by the powers that be, the corporations, the Pentagon, and the like. And yet he had the moral advantage of being elected by a large majority of people, and he could have really flown and been an inspirational leader. So what do you think has happened?

FFP: I think his nature is to be cautious. And he is a politician. And I don't say that as a criticism. He's a cautious man. He carefully calculates the obstacles he'll have to overcome, the pressures that he'll experience, the advantages he can gain. He's been operating in an environment with a lot of what we call heavy hitters in the United States. A lot of fat cats in politics, big money contributors. He got a lot of money from Wall Street.

HC: And from the nuclear industry. A quarter of a million dollars.

FFP: I didn't know that. I'm glad to know that.

And at the same time, there are no big movements to light a fire under him. I think there will be. There have been, until now, no movements from his base. His base has given him a free ride. If we want Obama to become a leader, a president that moves the United States in a direction that is more democratic, then he needs to be pressed from the bottom by his base. He needs to be pressed by protest movements.

HC: The trouble is social engineering. The trouble is television. When people watch television many hours a day, especially if they're unemployed and depressed at home with their children, and poor, the brain goes into an anaesthetized state and there's not enough time to analyze. What is being said also passes the neocortex into the midbrain, and they haven't got any outstanding leaders to say, let's rise up. They're also being preempted by Glenn Beck and my fellow countryman Rupert Murdoch.

FFP: There is certainly a lot of truth to what you're saying. But look at the examples that we have in the world today of people who do suddenly break through the kind of fog created by television and heavy-handed propaganda. Look at Egypt, look at the protests in England.

HC: Or Tunisia, where that lovely college student set himself on fire. He was selling vegetables and he couldn't stand the police crackdown any longer. That was a spark to a revolution in Tunisia, which has now spread to Egypt.

FFP: And to Bahrain, perhaps Libya. In the United States, I've been hearing more and more reports of protests. For example, fifteen thousand students turned out in Wisconsin for a rally to protest against the new Republican Tea Party governor there, Scott Walker, who made an announcement that he was determined to strip public sector workers of their right to collective bargaining. And in case they didn't like it, he was calling out the National Guard. Incredibly, over the weekend, fifteen thousand students organized to come to the state capital. They had chants, banners, posters, and picket signs. It was a wonderful demonstration, and it happened overnight.

HC: Blogging, Facebook, Twitter, social networking.

FFP: So you shouldn't be so sure that people can be anaesthetized for such a long time. I think we may see a series of protest movements in the United States. Maybe over foreclosures targeting the banks, maybe over student loans and the extorted repayments that the banks are asking.

HC: I thought they passed a law preventing that.

FFP: That's for new students. It doesn't cover the ones who are already indebted. Although I'm glad you follow U.S. politics closely.

HC: I read the *New York Times*, the *Washington Post*, and *The Guardian* every day.

Would you think that the movement could be led with these students? Often revolutions are led by students, the young ones that have no fear. And the Facebook social networking begun at Harvard so a guy interested in meeting more women now may help to mobilize the United States of America.

FFP: I think it could happen. I see some signs. Maybe we'll see a revival of the immigrant youth who had a kind of movement before they became intimidated by the horrendous anti-immigrant propaganda that began to come from the right, and the police crackdowns on immigrants pushed by the right. Maybe we'll see a movement against foreclosures, against exorbitant interest rates on student debt, a movement against increases in tuition, a movement against public sector cutbacks and—this is going to be ferocious—the new right-wing drive to destroy public sector unions. Private-sector unions have already been reduced and intimidated in the United States. The public-sector unions are the main base of unionism now, and the state fiscal crises, the shortfall in government revenues due to a crisis created by the banks, that shortfall has become the occasion for vicious campaigns against public sector workers, against their wages and pensions.

HC: And what about the Republican Congress wanting to foreclose any funding to NPR and PBS?

FFP: So that nobody will be able to understand anything that happens.

HC: I've just found an article in *Common Dreams* written by Joseph Huff-Hannon and Andy Bichlbaum about the Chamber of Commerce. They say you would think the CoC works on ordinary things and people's business, but they are a huge force in opposing health care reform, employee free choice, labor legislation, veterans' rights, banking regulations, and transparency. And they're working on dirty tricks that come straight out of COINTELPRO, the FBI's notorious 1960s program. It seems to me these people could be behind Glenn Beck. Who orchestrates his information? Where does he get this stuff about you? Who's mobilizing this stuff?

FFP: I've read about the chamber on the Internet too, on a blog by Brad Friedman. In the blog he argued that the chamber was using strategies developed by the FBI and the Defense Department. Very interesting and alarming. However, the chamber is acting sort of like a political party for business lobbyists. They are not exclusively a propaganda operation the way Glenn Beck is. Glenn Beck just has a mouth, and he has to know what to use the mouth for. He happens to have gotten the story about me and Richard, about our article as the plan for taking down capitalism, from a small group of people who moved from the left to the right around 1970.

HC: Who were those people? Would you like to name them?

FFP: Sure. David Horowitz, who had been an editor of *Ramparts* in the 1960s and moved to the right in the 1970s. He was involved in operations like Campus Watch, in which right-wing Zionists were calling on students to watch their professors in case they said anything against Israel, for example. Another one was Fred Siegel, a member of the Democratic Socialists of America who then moved later, in the 1980s, to the Manhattan Institute, a right-wing think tank and became an adviser to Rudolph Giuliani, who was the mayor of New York. Jim Sleeper, who had been on the board of *Dissent* Magazine, is another one. [*Sarcastically whispering.*] They posture as informants of a sort; they've been on the left, so they know what's *really* happening. They don't know a damn thing. And then they go over to the right and their stories sell very well. It makes them feel important.

HC: Why do they do it?

FFP: The weather is better, the pay is better. And also they're embittered, especially by the complex race issues inside the Democratic Party in the late 1960s, early 1970s. American social democrats argued that everything was going along so swimmingly, we had a majority Democratic Party, and then blacks rose up and made noisy demands, with the consequence that the white South left the Democratic Party. And all of this is often said to be the fault of outside agitators, like me, for example. This is very unreal.

HC: You trained at the University of Chicago. That's where Leo Strauss and his colleagues emanated from. They propounded free enterprise and capitalism for all the countries in the world.

FFP: Milton Friedman is the even more famous University of Chicago person, who actually did try to sell free markets everywhere in the world, including in Chile after Allende was killed and Pinochet, the military dictator, took power. The Friedman acolytes went down there to advise Pinochet on how to establish markets. The Leo Strauss acolytes were more philosophical than practical. Although they did have a very big influence on the neocons, who in turn became important contributors to the changing and growing American right and were very close allies of both Reagan and George W. Bush. I come from the University of Chicago, but the University of Chicago had many parts to it. I went there as a fifteen-year-old and I went to a college that had been designed by Robert Hutchins. Whatever else he was, he was certainly not a neocon or an extreme right-winger. When I finished college I entered an interdisciplinary program in social and economic planning that had been started by Rexford Tugwell, who had been part of the New Deal. So there are parts of the University of Chicago that also belonged on the broad left of American society. The universities in general in the United States are places where more social democratic and democratic ideas are, in a sense, protected. The great sweep of the country toward the right did not really take over the universities.

HC: I want you to give us your take on Rupert Murdoch.

FFP: I don't know that I have a distinctive take on Rupert Murdoch. He is a media megalomaniac, he has aggressively tried to take over as many media outlets as he could, he has an enormous fortune to back him up, and he has very conservative views. I don't know the details of his relations with other very aggressive right-wing businessmen, such as Richard Mellon Schaife, or the Koch brothers, who have been very important in the Tea Party. But we have a situation here in the United States where we have a right that is composed importantly of aggressive right-wing business and banking leaders. That clique is partnered with a planned effort to build a mass movement of extreme right-wing discontented people. That's what the Tea Party represents. We've seen this before in the world. It certainly occurred in Europe in the 1930s. It's very dangerous; it could succeed. I don't think it will, but it could.

HC: I'm not really sure where it's going. You talked about those fifteen thousand students at the University of Wisconsin, and Wisconsin has always been a very progressive state. There was a wonderful historian, Laswell, who said, When the powers that be lose the chains of iron, beware the chains of silver. And that is what I think is happening, that the very rich manipulate through propaganda and control society.

FFP: They're trying.

HC: I read an interesting article that talked about Madoff. It said that the real criminals in the whole scandal are the bankers who brought down American society through the global financial crisis, and indeed much of the world, who now are making huge profits again, and no one's brought them to heel.

FFP: Although there are some investigations going on, and I thought it was very interesting that Bernie Madoff, sitting in jail for God knows how long, is beginning to talk about the bankers with whom he worked. That's interesting. Somebody's gotta squeal.

HC: Although America may be declining economically, compared to China and India and other countries, still, militarily it's the most powerful nation on Earth. I can't separate that. Until we get rid of those nuclear weapons, life is very insecure on the planet.

FFP: Yes, it is. And it's also insecure because of climate change. The Right has been very adamant, and I think pretty successful, in arguing that climate change is a bunch of bologna spouted by half-baked scientists and that none of it is true.

HC: I don't believe in freedom of speech when it comes to science and medicine. If I lied about medicine I would be deregistered as a doctor, because I'd be killing my patients. These people are lying about science involving the future of the planet, and they're helping to kill the planet. I mean, there's no doubt about this from the scientific data. I've appealed to the powers that be in the United States about how these people should be censored, but there's no law. And they're free to lie however they want.

FFP: Here's the problem. Scientists don't know things with absolute certainty. Their opinions about climate change are in a sense hypotheses, the best guesses that we have.

HC: They're prognostications.

FFP: So we can't close off the possibility of their being challenged. We want them to be challenged. But I do think that the challenges should go forward in forums that are monitored by scientists, or monitored by philosophers, who at least understand the process of scientific investigation.

HC: It's like how every week in hospitals we have what's called grand rounds. We bring together all the doctors working in that hospital and we present a patient. We discuss the prognosis, the cause of the disease, and whether we did the right thing. Were our guesses accurate or not accurate? And that's how we learn—in credible forums. But when Glenn Beck gets on his high horse, or Rush Limbaugh, just spouting pure lies and propaganda in a paranoid fashion, it's terribly dangerous.

FFP: It's dangerous because the world is very complicated. Everything that people are called on to try to understand as democratic participants in our society is so hard to understand. It's hard even for academics to understand. So they become susceptible to the storytelling, which can be lunatic and paranoid stories. I don't think there's a simple solution to this, at least I can't think of one.

HC: Another thing that occurs to me, and I almost can't say it in a public forum but it's sticking out very clearly, the racism that we talked about in the Tea Party toward Obama is reminiscent of the racism that accrued in Germany.

FFP: By the way, Glenn Beck is also anti-Semitic.

HC: Is he? What does he say?

FFP: Well, he named the nine most dangerous people in the world, beginning with Sigmund Freud. I was one of them, which elevated my status. Eight of those nine people were Jews. His tirades against George Soros accused Soros, a Hungarian Jew who was fourteen at the time when the Germans occupied Hungary, of collaborating in the Holocaust. So he both pilloried a Jew, George Soros, and he pilloried him for collaborating in a campaign to exterminate Jews. I don't know what that is if not anti-Semitic.

HC: Have the American Jewish organizations risen up against Glenn Beck?

FFP: There's been some of that with regard to George Soros. But Glenn Beck would totally deny any anti-Semitism. And a lot of the Christian Right is ambiguous in that regard, because there is a segment of the Christian Right that is very pro-Zionist. They call themselves Zionist Christians, because they believe in the biblical prophecy that only when the Israelites occupy again the land of Israel, only then will the blessed rise up to heaven to be received I suppose by Jesus. And so they're very much in favor of defending the uncontested right of Israel to the historical land of Palestine, whatever the borders of that land. The irony is, according to the biblical prophecy as I understand it—and this is definitely not my field—the Jews who are in Palestine will not rise up with the Christians, because they, after all, have not been saved. They will go into limbo. So their job is to occupy the land and defend it so that the Christians can be saved.

HC: I think there are about 40 million evangelical Christians who believe in what you just said—in Revelations, the end times, and in rising up to meet Jesus. Many actually are praying for the nuclear holocaust to happen, because it means they'll all be saved.

FFP: I think that political developments in the United States over the last few years have been very depressing. On the one hand we've had a kind of financial meltdown that has affected not only our country but people across the globe. We have responded as a nation to that financial meltdown by taking taxpayer money and bailing out the banks and bailing out a number of large corporations as well. And we did this without imposing any strong conditions on these financial institutions or on these corporations. It's widely agreed that one of the reasons for the meltdown is that these operators in finance were running wild. They were unchecked in their maneuverings and dealings. One of the reasons they were unchecked is that they had used their political influence to push for the rollback of regulation.

HC: Now you've got to give us a very quick optimistic note.

FFP: Well, so far people have just been talking about the Tea Party movement. But I think that I see signs of protest emerging, not from the Tea partiers, who are not the people who have been hurt from all of this, but emerging from students and workers. I hear report after report, just in the last two weeks, of people gaining inspiration from the Egyptians who protested in Tahrir Square, gaining inspiration from the protesters in England and from their own compatriots, from other students, from other workers. I think that we may well see a several-pronged movement emerging against the banks for foreclosing on people and for squeezing students for the debts that they have incurred to go to school. A movement against the Republican state governments that are now targeting public sector workers and public services. A movement that would bring together, although on different tracks, but nevertheless would bring together students and working people, and maybe reverse the terrible path that has been taken by decision makers in the United States. ∿

DENIS HAYES

Denis Hayes, honorary chair of the now global Earth Day Network and author of numerous books and articles, is perhaps best known for having been national coordinator of the first Earth Day, when he was just twenty-five years old. He directed the National Renewable Energy Laboratory during the Carter administration and has been a visiting scholar at the Woodrow Wilson International Center for Scholars, a senior fellow at the World Watch Institute, an adjunct professor of engineering at Stanford University, a Silicon Valley lawyer, and president of the Bullitt Foundation. He has served on governing boards at Stanford University, the World Resources Institute, and the Federation of American Scientists.

HELEN CALDICOTT: How did you get into the environmental movement?

DENIS HAYES: By the age of nineteen I'd become enormously disenchanted with life. We were having enormous problems in the United States: in a war in Southeast Asia; great problems with civil rights; the nuclear shadow of the Cold War looming over us; chemical and biological warfare research marching mindlessly ahead. I was from a small paper-making community. I was upset about all of these things, but I was fairly impotent to do anything about them. That's when I went trekking around the world for three years, just trying to find some meaning and purpose. Before I left I'd taken a course in ecology and had mastered all the basic principles, but I'd done it mostly as an academic exercise. One day in what is now Namibia I trekked from a small town on the coast back to the main highway, and I went out over the hill on an incredibly clear, starlit, moon-filled night that you only get in the desert. Suddenly a whole bunch of things came together in my mind. The essence of it was that all life on earth, including monkeys, gorillas, orang-utans, and chimpanzees, is governed by certain basic principles of ecology. Humans, too, prior to the coal-based industrial revolution, had operated within an ecological context. With access to cheap, abundant energy, we began to break lots of little laws. Now the big laws—nature's laws—were starting to catch up with us. I wanted to figure out how to design and operate a modern state founded on ecological principles.

I didn't have a vocabulary for what I was thinking about at that point, but today you would find it in such disciplines as urban ecology, industrial ecology, and community ecology. I literally left the following morning knowing what I wanted to do with my life, went to Stanford, and got started on my career.

HC: You had an epiphany.

DH: You see this pattern repeatedly, in all the different basic faiths. Frustrated people go into the desert; get very hungry, hot, cold, and very lonely; and have epiphanies. In my own nonreligious way, but with a strong, latent environmental value system, I experienced the same sort of thing.

HC: What were the dynamics that brought about Earth Day in 1970?

DH: The origin of the whole thing was a series of speeches given by a senator, Gaylord Nelson from Wisconsin, calling for an environmental teach-in on the nation's campuses. I was a graduate student at Harvard, and it seemed to tie into my value system, all rooted back in Namibia. So, with all of the arrogance of youth, I flew down to Washington and got a meeting with Senator Nelson, who had decided to set up an organization and had asked Republican congressman Pete McCloskey from California to be his co-chair. The two of them were looking for someone to head it. It came out that I'd received my undergraduate degree at Stanford University. McCloskey was the congressman from the Stanford area and one of the founding board members was Paul Ehrlich, who also was at Stanford and had been one of my mentors. So I was connected to the inner sanctum, though I didn't know it before I arrived. I went back with a charter to organize Boston and meanwhile all those guys compared notes on me. Two days later I had a call from Washington—would you consider dropping out and coming down to organize the United States? In 1969, no one would turn down an offer like that!

HC: How did you do it?

DH: I brought in a bunch of people who'd cut their teeth in the antiwar, civil rights, and Chicano movements, and one person who had been active in the feminist movement. They applied organizational skills that they'd acquired elsewhere to the environment. One of the important things to remember about Earth Day: it was 1970, just coming out of the sixties, a unique period in American history during which a lot of people really knew how to put together events. So I hired these key regional organizers from across the country. They found a huge number of people doing very diverse things. Some were worried about protecting the local natural area, others were concerned by the terrible quality of the air or the water where they worked, some were worried about pesticides. Others were worried about the freeway cutting through their vibrant inner-city neighborhood. Each of them seemed to find a way to buy into this, so we had this sense that we actually could weave all of these diverse strands into a fabric of a new value system that actually might have some political impact.

But almost none of them were interested in the concept of a teach-in. The college students thought teach-ins were terribly passé. We'd already had teach-ins in 1964 and 1965. The people in the community wanted to lie down in front of the bulldozers, not have a public gab session. There was no way to control the spontaneous things that we wanted to stimulate in thousands of places across the country. Some of them were likely to be things that Nelson and Mc-Closkey would rather not be too closely involved with, because there were some very strong activists involved. The two of them remained co-chairs and raised most of the money for the campaign, but it was a very hands-off kind of operation. The "board" only met one time.

About the time it became clear that we had to dump the "Environmental Teach-In" name, a very creative advertising executive named Julian Koenig volunteered to help us for free. We explained what we were trying to do and how the teach-in nomenclature generated the wrong image. We had decided to take out an ad in the Sunday *New York Times*, and we asked him to "rebrand" us, though we would have been embarrassed to think of it in those terms. He proposed a whole series of layouts, including Earth Day: The Beginning; E-Day: The Beginning; Ecology Day: The Beginning; Environment Day: The Beginning; Green Day. He recommended Earth Day. When I pulled my whole staff together for pizza and beer, and we laid out all these mocked-up ads, it was clear that Earth Day was the one that resonated. And the event was reborn. When I took the event international in 1990, Earth Day turned out to be absolutely transparent as to what it means, in every language on the Earth.

HC: What was the budget for that first Earth Day? And what did you do?

DH: [*laughs*] The budget was everything we could raise, and that turned out to be about probably $150,000 to $160,000. Of course, remember that $150,000 in 1970 is worth more than $800,000 today. And most of our staff were part-time student volunteers. All of the full-time staff were paid a flat $4,500 a year, but most worked on it for a half year or less, so they were paid $2,000. My salary for the whole thing was under $3,000. The United Auto Workers contributed all of our printing and all of our postage for free. We stretched the money pretty far. Obviously there was no Internet and we couldn't even afford much in the way of telephones, though we did install a couple of toll-free lines. We sent people out across the country; they always stayed with somebody we were working with someplace—we didn't use hotels. In the end it was about building lists of key organizers in key places and then sending them materials by mail as the campaign developed. We had something called an addressograph machine [*laughs*]. You took these tin plates, and you'd type the name and address, one on each, and put this whole tray full of tin plates into a machine, and it would scoop one off at a time and address in ink all of the envelopes, as somebody turned the wheel. The guy who did that is now a United States senator [*laughs*].

HC: Who is it?

DH: Kent Conrad. The whole effort was terribly hands-on, incredibly grassroots, wildly underfunded, and spectacularly successful.

HC: How was it successful? What actually happened on Earth Day?

DH: Just about anything that you can imagine. The prime event was in New York City, where Mayor John Lindsay, a very progressive Republican, was very upset with President Nixon. Nixon had embarked upon his "Southern strategy," trying to steal the South for the Republican Party, which had been consistently Democratic ever since the Civil War. Remember, the Republicans had been the party of Lincoln and Teddy Roosevelt, and it still had many progressives in it in the late 1960s. Nixon's strategy was freezing out the progressives, including Lindsay, who saw this popular new environmental movement as something that might begin to shift that pendulum back. He was incredibly helpful. He shut down Fifth Avenue for the day, gave us the Great Lawn in Central Park. The crowd in New York City was more than a million people, probably the largest planned and organized event up to that time in American history. At that point, a million people was mind-boggling, especially on this issue that nobody had even understood six months earlier. New York was the home of three television networks—NBC, ABC, CBS—that dominated the airwaves. We had the *New York Times*, *Time*, *Newsweek*; it was the perfect anchor place for them to have all their correspondents from across the country feeding in stuff and putting it together to sort of show the impact. It's the first time we were able to pull together the Rachel Carson concerns with pesticides, the antiwar concerns with the use of carcinogenic defoliants in Southeast Asia, the nuclear fallout from atmospheric testing concerns along with worries about lead paint and rats in the ghetto and stopping freeways from destroying their neighborhood and local wetlands. And the big one—in much of the country then—was air pollution, which was getting worse each year.

We passed a clean air act a few months later—that put the environment on the map as a political force to be reckoned with. This was a piece of legislation strenuously opposed by the automobile industry, the steel industry, the coal industry, the gold industry, the oil industry, the electric utility industry. The CEOs of the automobile industry walked arm in arm to every member of the relevant committee of the Senate and said, If you pass this bill, it will turn America into a third world nation, and the Senate saw through their posturing and passed it unanimously. The House passed it on a voice vote. In the three years after Earth Day we also passed the Clean Water Act, the Safe Drinking Water Act, the Endangered

Species Act, Superfund to deal with toxics, Marine Mammal Protection Act, National Environmental Education Act, and a half dozen other bills. Stuff that came out those three years fundamentally changed the way that America does business. I've never seen anybody do this tally, but I would expect that if you consider the amount of money spent by government, by the private sector, and by individuals, those three years have probably sent $10 to $15 trillion into directions that they otherwise would not have flown, and made the world a much better place. It's literally the biggest social transformation in the United States since the New Deal.

HC: So you're a pioneer?

DH: I was part of a pioneering generation at the right place at the right time.

HC: After Earth Day in 1970, what eventuated after that?

DH: That all took place in Republican administrations, and part of it was people rebelling against antienvironmental policies. The secretary of interior and the secretary of commerce in the Nixon administration were both adamantly antienvironmental. When President Carter was elected a few years later, a bunch of us were brought inside the government, and there started to be this perception that everything was pretty well taken care of. And the enthusiasm in the grassroots fervor was channeled into very local events and away from the national scene for several years. In 1970 there was not much sophistication. People would read a study that says that breathing the air in L.A. is the equivalent of smoking two packs of cigarettes a day, and they realized that they wouldn't want their children smoking two packs a day. There was this huge emotional, visceral kind of response.

Forty years later, the movement has an immense sense of sophistication, but it has lost much of the raw emotion. We have PhDs in chemistry, biology, physics, and economics. We are swimming in environmental lawyers. The quality of research and analysis done is worlds better. But somehow, in the process, some of that grassroots intensity was lost. And in American politics, intensity is really important. The typical environmentalist is a college-educated relatively progressive person who, when looking at a political candidate, will wonder, Well, what does he think about the war in the Middle East? What about health care? About the environment? It's that huge balancing act. The people who are able to shift policy dramatically tend to be the single-issue zealots who want to be able to carry firearms into the local coffee shop, who are intense on abortion. And you don't see much of that in environmental politics.

HC: Harvey Wasserman's been working against nuclear power since Seabrook in the seventies. He said the climate bill is the ultimate challenge of the global grassroots green movement to transform into something that can save the planet. For the atomic power industry the bill would cap a decade-long $640 million–plus cleansing of its radioactive image. We'll have the Obama administration, Senators John Kerry, Joe Lieberman, and Lindsey Graham embracing substantial taxpayer subsidies for building new nuclear power plants and new offshore drilling and clean coal. The markers have been laid for a greenwashed business approach toward pretending to deal with global climate change and the life-threatening pollution in which our corporate power structure is drowning us. There's an unwillingness or inertia in the political climate.

DH: There is an alternative bill in the United States called the Cantwell-Collins bill, by two women senators, one from Washington and one from Maine, that is a much better piece of legislation. Unfortunately, it does not have much support among their colleagues. Democrats from states that are dominated by the coal industry, even ones who are usually progressive, will fight it because it will hurt the industry and cost jobs. The Richard Nixon Southern strategy was hugely effective in places like Texas and the Gulf Coast, and the Republican Party is basically controlled by big oil. Politicians trying to pass a carbon cap have compromised and compromised. Now they have a bill that would have a cap but would give away, in the first year, 85 percent of the permits for carbon. A bill that would not control mobile sources initially, just stationary sources. A bill that would create a huge derivatives market for trading carbon credits, with all the shenanigans that Wall Street can dream up. A bill that would allow rich subsidies for so-called clean coal and shale gas, as well as ridiculous subsidies for nuclear power that might prompt someone to actually build another reactor or two.

This is all scary, but inside the Beltway in Washington, D.C., the "revealed truth" is that you cannot pass a bill unless you can get coal state Democrats and pronuclear Republicans—enough to get sixty votes. What we need is not to change the legislation but to change the politics. Even though Cantwell-Collins had flaws—it tiptoes into the issue rather than cannonballing into the middle of the pool—at least it's got a structure that gets tougher over time: it has a real cap; it auctions all of the carbon permits; it put them very far upstream, wherever carbon enters the economy, not downstream on tailpipes and smokestacks. Interestingly, Cantwell-Collins takes 75 percent of the money that's obtained from the auctioning of these carbon permits and returns it to the people on a pro-rata basis. And since an upstream auction of those permits captures all the direct and indirect energy use, it's actually a progressive energy tax. If you capture both the direct and indirect energy use, rich people use proportionally more energy than poor people do. If all of that revenue is returned proportionally, it amounts to a transfer from rich to poor, as well as from guzzlers to the thrifty.

HC: It seems to me the way you organized way back was by education. I and my fellow physicians in 1978 started doing what we call the bombing run, illustrating the potentially devastating consequences of nuclear war within five years. Eighty percent of Americans opposed the concept of nuclear war and wanted the arms race to end. But it was only through a massive grassroots movements with the passion yours originally had in the seventies, and that we saw with a million people in Central Park in 1982 that, in fact, forced the politicians to take everything seriously. Without that incredible democratic action that we learned about in the sixties in America, the politicians are in the pocket of the corporations who are destroying the planet.

DH: Candidly, we caught them off guard. In the early seventies, companies had never been attacked on the basis of the pollution they were emitting—"the smell of prosperity"—and they had real difficulty figuring out how to respond. They were criticized not just by people out on the streets, but by their friends and colleagues at their own country clubs. What are you doing, putting that toxic waste under the water?

HC: [*Laughs.*]

DH: There is no way for the coal industry to lose the climate and to remain an economically viable industry, so it will spend whatever it takes to win. It will be as ruthless as any enterprise fighting for survival. The fossil fuel industry has spent a fortune—a literal fortune—on phony think tanks and slick advertising campaigns and comic books to tell lies to schoolchildren.

Although they can outspend us dramatically, the Internet may prove to be an enormous leveling device. We can use this in a way that pulls together the grassroots. Not unlike that first Earth Day, where we managed to get an incredible bang per buck.

HC: This is probably the only way we can arouse a massive grassroots movement of people whose future lies ahead of them. We're old now. I'm seventy-two, but it's their future.

DH: We have Earth Day TV, where we are streaming the movies available; a whole bunch of YouTube links; social-networking opportunities for people to get together around common causes. This is the wave of the future.

HC: You've got a tremendous paragraph on the most worrisome environmental problem, human population growth. It says:

> If everyone currently in the world aspires to consume at the same level as, say, the average Swede does the human population *already* exceeds the planet's carrying capacity. With humans counting, directly and indirectly, for 40 percent of the earth's net biological productivity, we are squeezing other species into extinction at a catastrophic rate. But because the population issue is inextricably linked to such political third rails as immigration, abortion, racism, religious objections to contraception, and Social Security, our politicians resolutely ignore it.*

DH: I was part of the delegation from the United States to the 1994 United Nations population conference in Cairo. The religious vehemence of the Catholics and Islamic leaders to addressing this issue was mind-numbing. In a democracy, if one group holds its percentage of the population steady while others grow, it is going to be in a minority status forever. Some of the pro-growth rhetoric sounds pretty much like breeding for political power. And, of course, all the mainstream economists just love population growth because it is inherent to their paradigm of *everything* growing forever. Amen.

Let me give you some interesting figures. The total biomass of all the higher animals, the vertebrates, is a little under two hundred megatons of carbon. Of that, forty megatons are human beings and another hundred megatons are our domesticated animals. Roughly five megatons are all the wild animals on the land—the lions and antelope, the grizzlies and the primates, the wolverines and the kangaroos. The remaining fifty megatons are aquatic vertebrates. Humans, by ourselves, weigh eight times as much as all wild animals, and we are growing while they are shrinking. There are more tigers

---

* National Resources Defence Council profile of Denis Hayes, www.nrdc.org/reference/profiles/prohayes.asp.

in zoos in the United States than in the wild around the world. Yet we have politicians trying to make it impossible for women to gain access to contraceptives!

HC: Now is a human life unit a human being?

DH: If I understand the question, yes, but the person's environmental impact is a function of his or her consumption. Is it a Chinese peasant or an American investment banker? If everybody in the world were content to live as a Chinese peasant does, we would not have too much difficulty supporting 8 or 9 billion people. But even Chinese peasants don't want to live like Chinese peasants anymore.

HC: Robert F. Kennedy said:

> [T]he gross national product includes air pollution and advertising for cigarettes, and ambulances to clear our highways of carnage. It counts special locks for our doors and jails for the people who break them. The gross national product includes the destruction of our redwoods and the death of Lake Superior. It grows with the production of napalm and missiles and nuclear warheads. . . .
>
> And if the gross national product includes all this, there is much that it does not comprehend. It does not allow for the health of our families, the quality of their education, or the joy of their play. It's indifferent to the decency of our factories and the safety of our streets alike. It does not include the beauty of our poetry or the strength of our marriages, the intelligence of our public debate or the integrity of our public officials. . . . The gross national product measures neither our wit nor our courage, neither our wisdom nor our learning, neither our compassion nor our devotion to country. It measures everything, in short, except that which makes life worthwhile; and it can tell us everything about America—except whether we are proud to be Americans.

DH: Many scholars think of history as the product of vast inexorable forces. But every now and then, there are individual people who really do make a difference. Robert Kennedy was something of a villain in his early years, but he evolved into a person of enormous compassion and integrity, not to mention charisma, and not just as a vehicle for a social movement but out of a certain integrity that he brought to things. Kennedy uttered those words two years before the first Earth Day—I quoted them in numerous speeches leading up to Earth Day. He was very smart and very prescient. Had he not been assassinated during the California primary, he would likely have won the Democratic nomination for president. He might well have then won the presidency itself from Nixon, and the whole world might have been a very different place. Alas, we have to work in the world that we have, not the world that might have been. ∾

PHIL RADFORD

P hil Radford is the executive director of Greenpeace USA, the world's largest environmental organization. For six years Phil was Greenpeace's USA environmental director, and during that time he created a $9 million grassroots program that greatly expanded Greenpeace USA's online grassroots student organizing and training, as well as street and door-to-door canvassing. Recent corporate targets of Greenpeace campaigns include Kimberly-Clark, a major tree cutter that makes Kleenex, and Exxon Mobil. Greenpeace is largely sustained by hundreds of thousands of small monthly donations, and it is uniquely positioned to mobilize consumers to help or hurt decision makers, depending on their position on the environment.

———— ∞ ————

HELEN CALDICOTT: The first thing we need to discuss is the spill in the Gulf of Mexico, BP [British Petroleum], and Halliburton. Number two is the Kerry-Lieberman-Graham so-called environment bill.

PHIL RADFORD: "So-called" is great.

HC: Let's talk about the oil spill.

PR: BP's oil spill. It's probably BP and Halliburton that are behind this. It's kind of a who's-who of the worst polluters and all that profit from oil, which causes global warming and leads to warmer oceans. It's a disaster. This spill is the Chernobyl of the fossil fuel industry. President Obama and other politicians have said that this is a fluke instead of something that we can never let happen again. If those politicians decided to be real leaders they'd say this is a sign, that this needs to be the sign that we need to get off of oil within ten to twenty years.

HC: That's not happening.

PR: It could happen if people like us and people around the world say, We need a ban on oil drilling, especially offshore oil drilling, and then Honda and Cisco Systems and big electric utilities agree that in countries like the United States 30 percent of our cars could be plug-in electrics or plug in hybrids by 2020, and 90 percent by 2030. Political will to do this will come from people who care.

HC: Give us your take on how to change a society.

PR: Young people care surprisingly more than their parents and tend to be more active. We find that if we go to a campus with a coal plant, and say, Let's shut down this coal plant, the students are so excited to protest, to lobby their administration, to clean up that coal plant and make sure their campus is 100 percent clean energy. I think young people are ready to push for a clean energy revolution.

HC: It's my generation that has produced this inordinate mess on the planet, and we've handed it to them as their legacy, which is a terrible thing to do. Please briefly outline the inequities of the Kerry-Lieberman-Graham bill. Kerry is a friend of mine, and I'm amazed that he's come out with this extraordinary climate change bill.

PR: Senator Kerry, for decades, has been a tremendous champion for the environment and working families. He's a hero on many fronts. He's worked incredibly hard to get his bill passed; unfortunately, he compromised too much. He listened too much to industry. Unfortunately, global warming's like a train, and our children are on the tracks. We need to decrease global warming pollution by 40 percent from 1990 levels by 2020.

What this bill aimed to do was cut this to 3 percent. Our kids are on the tracks and a train's coming; we nudged them a bit, but they were still in danger. It just doesn't cut it to move your kids a little bit. Unfortunately, it didn't do enough to address the possible catastrophes of global warming.

Senator Kerry's bill cut pollution a bit. I can't complain about that, except for the fact that if you only cut pollution a little bit, you're still talking about 30 percent to 60 percent of the world's species going extinct within a century. On top of that, it almost allowed a huge amount of offshore oil drilling right before this leak [the BP spill] happened. Now it reduced the incentives for offshore drilling, but it still gave states the option to allow more offshore oil drilling. That's their concession to the oil industry. The price on carbon dioxide from the coal industry, for their pollution, is very low. The only way to cut carbon pollution is to fine just a few plants. We know how much pollution comes out of coal and oil ultimately. You say, Okay, we're capping pollution from those sources. There's a small number where you can measure the pollution coming out, and we can cap it.

HC: What do you mean, cap it?

PR: You cap the total amount of pollution that can come out of all these places, and it declines over the years. If it's cheaper for one plant to develop a way to clean their plant than it is for another plant, they can trade their "permit to pollute" so it's cheaper overall to reduce pollution. Over time you would hope that it closes plants, because you can't stop global warming without limiting the burning of coal. The problem was that the cap was so weak, and the tax was so low on the price of carbon, that it wouldn't have resulted in cleaner industry. I think that capping and trading is a bit of a sham, and it's really tough to enforce. There are simple tools, like a straight tax that gives back to people to support clean energy.

HC: Looking at the Kerry-Lieberman-Graham bill: it was trading, it was marking, it was absolute nonsense. What we really need is a leader with guts and vision, a prophetic leader to say, No, this is the way it's going to go. And it's very simple.

PR: There was a great hope that President Obama would be such a leader, and he's been missing in action on this issue. The more world leaders say, We need more from you, and the more that American citizens say, President Obama, we had a dream of your clean energy vision, the more chance we have.

HC: Why do you think President Obama is missing in action on global warming? Many young American people are feeling disappointed but still hopeful.

PR: He's said that he's treating being president like being a manager, where you delegate things to your staff, as if Congress is his staff. He would let them do things and then help them at the end. The problem with that analogy is that he doesn't have authority over Congress. He has allowed Congress to run wild and make some crazy deals and completely ruin his agenda. He needs to get more involved and say, Here are my principles, here's what needs to happen, come up with a solution. We need to make sure clean energy takes over. He never really led on principles, and because of that he got that hodgepodge of a compromise with billions of dollars for nuclear energy and billions for burning coal, and incentives for oil drilling. The true victory would have been a principled victory. We didn't see him pushing that.

HC: It surprised me, because he was so profoundly positive when he ran for president. "It's a change, we can all have change." It feels like he's fallen back into the hands of the polluters and the big corporations. I know he took money from them to get elected. I agree he needs people to push him. How many young people have you recruited in the United States in your $9 million grassroots campaign in Greenpeace, and what have you got them doing?

PR: We've recruited a quarter of a million people to support us as members. About twenty thousand on call will do work with us on campaigns. Then there's a few thousand who really run our campaigns across the country.

HC: Let's talk about the notion of clean coal. Could you describe what that means?

PR: Ha! There's no such thing. Over a dozen miners just died in the United States in a coal mine. In the United States we've blown up over 150 mountains. We're so desperate to get the last of the coal that we'll blow the tops off of mountains, turn them into plateaus, and scrape out the last pieces of coal, destroying the rivers below, destroying communities. Seventy percent or so of women in the United States of childbearing age have so much mercury in their bodies that their babies are at risk of brain damage. That mercury comes from burning coal. When people say there's something called clean coal, ask those mothers of children who have birth defects; ask the kids who have asthma attacks from the pollution of coal plants. The coal industry has this theory that you can capture carbon dioxide produced from coal burning and somehow bury it underground. It's very impractical. Even if it turns out that it can work, you couldn't scale it up enough for it to be a good solution to global warming. It's basically a lie that the coal industry has used to convince senators and members of Congress that they shouldn't be regulated.

HC: Why are these senators, congressmen, and congresswomen so dumb? Just imagine trying to squash millions of tons of the gas carbon dioxide underneath the earth and thinking it won't leak out through cracks! This is not going to work.

PR: The ultimate problem is that corporations in the United States have far too much power. The coal industry, through campaign contributions, intimidation, spending hundreds of millions of dollars lobbying and on advertisements, and sometimes through bribery of local officials, has really built up too much power and control in the United States, so a lot of people are afraid of the power of the coal industry. That's why, in the United States, and in China and Australia, and in other countries, Greenpeace is working to shut coal plants—to reduce their impact.

HC: Coal is the most polluting of all the methods to generate electricity except nuclear, because the carbon is so concentrated. You pick it up and it just looks like solid carbon. It boggles my mind that the United States is run by corporations lobbying to influence legislation. Now the Supreme Court has granted corporations the same rights of free speech as an individual, in the *Citizens United* lawsuit. They can get in and spend as much money as they want orchestrating an election. Do you feel that that's the beginning of the end, that decision?

PR: It was a terrible decision by the Supreme Court, that a corporation is the same thing as a human being, and therefore deserves the same free speech rights as a human being and should have as much voice in elections as a regular voter. I think that there are real ways that we can fight back to reduce the influence of corporations, and I don't think we can solve all the problems that we face unless we really have a people's movement that reduces the influence that corporations have in America. Citizens, when we come together, can shut coal plants. We can change policy. I think that long term we need a populist movement of people that say, It's just not okay for corporations to run the government. Government needs to represent all the people, not just the people with pocketbooks.

HC: Let's get on to the nuclear power perspective of the Kerry-Lieberman-Graham Senate bill. Outline for us what the bill allowed the nuclear industry to do.

PR: It did two things. One, it subsidized nuclear plants. It's a shame, because we convinced the Vermont Senate to shut a nuclear plant because it was leaking radioactive tritium. And the same day the bill came out, we found out that another plant was leaking tritium into the drinking water in the state of New Jersey.

HC: There's another one that's going to be shut down.

PR: It's not even that it might be shut down, but the same day the bill came out these plants are leaking tritium into the drinking water, which is a radioactive waste. It's just too much of a risk to take, especially when you have studies like the one you commissioned, "Carbon-Free and Nuclear-Free," that prove that the United States does not need nuclear power or carbon generated electricity. Also, the Federal Energy Regulatory Commission says we don't need coal or any nuclear energy to meet our new energy needs. It's an unfortunate joke that in America we continue to insure the nuclear industry and if they have an accident, the industry doesn't actually have to pay for it. If they had to pay for it, like the oil companies had to pay for all the massive oil spills, no one on Wall Street would invest in them, and we'd switch to a clean-energy future.

HC: Couldn't the Price-Anderson Act, which provides for the cost of a nuclear accident to be covered, result in a 100 billion U.S. tax dollars being used to subsidize these nuclear power plants? Did the bill say that?

PR: It's about 60 billion. And it largely subsidized nuclear energy. You can't have nuclear power without essentially having a command-and-control, socialized form of state support for it, because in a competitive marketplace, nuclear power always loses. If you actually took away the subsidies for nuclear, coal, and for other dirty fossil fuels, and made them take the risk of paying for these disasters, clean energy would win almost every time.

HC: The government pays for building the reactors for enriching the uranium, for decommissioning the reactors, and for storing the waste. It's a totally socialized industry in a so-called free market capitalist country. It takes my breath away that the American people would go along with this and yet they would say that free medical care, which most civilized countries now have, that's a form of socialism. I can't understand how the people can be so manipulated. The American people are intelligent, but they're kind of brainwashed.

PR: I think the American people are intelligent, and I think there's an overwhelming amount of information, a huge amount of money spent by each industry, coal or nuclear, every year, just to fool people. People believe what they read in the newspaper, and there are people making tens of millions of dollars to convince people of things that aren't true.

HC: Propaganda. And when you think that the American public in fact owns the airwaves hijacked by Murdoch and the corporations that advertise to their detriment . . .

PR: I think Rupert Murdoch is actually personally starting to think that global warming is a real problem and is struggling to get Fox News to change its editorial policy.

HC: I think his children are pretty disgusted with the way he's going in terms of global warming. But I tell you, if Rupert Murdoch wanted to rein in Roger Ailes, who really runs Fox television, he could. He's much more powerful than Ailes. So it doesn't sound as if he's really serious. Now tell us what you've done with Kimberly-Clark, and how and why.

PR: Kimberly-Clark years ago bragged on their website that the Kleenex brand of tissues all came from virgin forest. They were one of the major drivers of forest destruction in places like the boreal forest, which is a huge temperate rain forest in North America. Greenpeace approached them and asked them, Would you change? Would you stop using forests that are from ecosystems that have been evolving since the last Ice Age ten thousand years ago? Trees in those forests that are over a hundred years old, Would you stop using these gems of diversity of life to make a throwaway product? Would you shift to recycled products? And if you have to log, would you do it in a completely sustainable way? They said no. So for about five years students convinced their universities to cancel contracts, major corporations threatened to cancel contracts, wherever Kimberly-Clark was filming ads, we were there. Activists around the world, from Switzerland to India to Canada to the United States, were protesting Kimberly-Clark. Then, almost out of nowhere, they made one of the strongest commitments of any company to getting out of all ancient forests, to using really significant amounts of recycled content, and to helping to drive the market for sustainably harvested wood. One of their big concerns was that they didn't think there was enough sustainably harvested timber in the world for their products. We said, Exactly. We want you to drive the market for these products, so we can have a more sustainable future. Ultimately, they came around to it. They've been a tremendous leader in helping to reshape how forest products are made.

HC: I don't understand what a sustainable wood product is. I don't understand, as a biologist. Sustainable—what does it mean?

PR: There are ways of logging in which you selectively cut and replant. You ensure that species can still live in that land. You leave the forest largely intact, and you don't touch the forests with the most important biodiversity. Kimberly-Clark is committed to doing that. There are several different ways that people certify that that's done well. But it's a huge step from clear-cutting. Especially from cutting our ancient forests.

HC: When you come back to global warming, the one issue that 189 countries agreed on in Copenhagen was that we must leave the trees intact in the forest. It takes a tree fifty years to get to the stage where it stores the carbon, the same amount of carbon that a tree that's been chopped down has already stored and removed from the environment. So actually, in terms of global warming, we've got to stop chopping down trees. I don't understand, as a mother, a grandmother, a pediatrician, why people use tissues. I use handkerchiefs, and they're so comforting. One day I tried to no avail to get Bloomingdale's to sell handkerchiefs, because they're out of fashion.

PR: That's a great idea.

HC: I thought, the motto will be, "Blow your nose on handkerchiefs, not on trees." Why do we use paper towels in the kitchen instead of tea towels? Why do we use paper serviettes to wipe our mouths? In Australia we wipe our mouths on our sleeves, but Americans are more cultured than we are; you can use cloth napkins. How else? I suppose we have to use paper for toilet paper, but in India they don't. They wash themselves and dry off with a towel. At first when I visited India I thought, "I won't like this much," but it's very fresh and refreshing. Newspapers. How many forests are used to produce one Sunday's edition of the *New York Times*? And most of it's advertising. I think we've really got to start examining why and how we use all this paper.

PR: I think the first is, as you say, reduce, and second is recycle. We ran that campaign a few years ago, when our forest campaign was narrowly focused on biodiversity. Since then we've really focused on the tropical forests that are the cause of 17 percent of carbon dioxide getting into the atmosphere every year. One of the best ways to stop global warming is to stop deforestation. A few years ago we were saying, Let's protect the most important places to store biodiversity. And if logging must happen, let it happen somewhere else, in a sustainable way ecologically, from a biodiversity standpoint. We've really evolved. A lot of conservationists have to say, Now the priority is the Congo, Indonesia, the Amazon. We just can't cut trees there at all, because those areas are so important for storing carbon dioxide.

HC: There's one other thing, and that's baby's diapers. We call them napkins here. When I was a young mother I had three babies under three, all in diapers. They were all made of cloth. I would soak them in a bucket, and every couple of days I'd wash all of them and hang them out in the sun to dry. They smelled so fresh. I went to visit America when my youngest baby was three months old, and some kind woman said, "Oh! You should get disposable diapers." She took me to a shop, and I was amazed. What on earth are we swaddling our baby's bottoms with paper for when (a) there's dioxin in them, because they're bleached by chlorine; dioxin is absorbed through the baby's skin and is a carcinogen; (b) The rubbish dumps spread fecal bacteria into the water supply. They also have plastic on them, which is not biodegradable and lasts thousands of years. People, without thinking what's it's all about, use them because they're convenient, and so they spend money on them. When you have a baby you can buy a set of napkins, and they can last for the baby's life.

PR: The ultimate issues are: how many people are on the planet; how much energy each person uses; how much people are consuming; and how much economic growth there is, because growth is so tied to consumption. It's distorted and ignored, the fact that we're all dependent on the planet and the resources. And the beauty of it, for our spiritual needs.

HC: Growth, economic growth, is antithetical to the salvation of the planet. If we keep using resource after resource, buying this and that to make ourselves happy, it's only got one end, hasn't it?

PR: I'd be willing to bet that the U.S. economy in the Gulf states right now is about to grow, because of all of the money spent on cleaning up the oil spill. So actually that will drive growth. Growth is an optimistic thing. You don't think, This is really good, billions of dollars spent on divorce lawyers. Or that people spend on cancers that could have been prevented, but that's actually a good thing economically.

HC: I know! Is war part of increasing the GDP? We've got it so backward.

I want to get to Exxon Mobil. What are they up to?

PR: Exxon is up to no good. Exxon is like the Darth Vader of the story of global warming. They're the big company out there funding a lot of the skeptics—you know, the small handful of scientists in the public debate who are given an unfair microphone called cash from oil companies. Exxon and a big company called Koch Industries are probably the two biggest companies spreading lies and misinformation and confusing people about what's happening with global warming.

HC: I've read that they've set up separate think tanks in Washington staffed by many of the same people, and they use the same PR firms, like Hill and Knowlton, that the tobacco companies did. The most effective way to affect a debate is to inject doubt into it.

PR: That's exactly right. Exxon and Koch Industries have dozens and dozens of front groups. David Koch, who runs Koch Industries, is the seventh-richest man in America. They are one of the largest privately held companies in the world and are a massive oil company. Koch Industries has actually spent about three times more than Exxon to fund right-wing think tanks like the Cato Institute, American Enterprise Institute, and the Heritage Foundation. All these different foundations create a network or echo chamber of people repeating what the others said to create the appearance that a number of people disagree with scientists. It's probably been even more effective than the tobacco industry. A really good source of information is exxonsecrets.org that Greenpeace created, where we actually track every dollar that Exxon gives to front groups. There's another report that targets Koch Industries. If you go to Greenpeace .org and type in k-o-c-h you'll find our report that shows everything that they fund and the web of people and money that helped to create the conspiracy theory that climate change isn't real.

HC: What influence have you had, apart from putting that data up on your Web pages?

PR: We worked with one of the Rockefeller children, who publicly said, as a member of the original family that created Standard Oil, which Exxon Mobil and all the other companies came from, "You need to stop spreading this misinformation about global warming." These words were stinging, and it really hurt the brand. It got to the point where President Obama in a speech pointed out Exxon as an example of how evil oil is. Their brand was so hurt by the work that Greenpeace and other groups did, they dramatically reduced their funding to skeptics. Recently, unfortunately, they started to get back in the game of funding skeptics again, so we may need to bring the fight back to them.

HC: Is it because you left off the pressure?

PR: My guess is that everybody, coal companies, oil companies, car companies, they're petrified now and are therefore increasing their spending. Because they know that regulations on global warming are inevitable. They're struggling as hard as they can to create a little more uncertainty, to drag out the inevitable a little bit longer, to make sure that when there are regulations, they're weak. I think we're seeing some of the fruits of that strategy in how weak Senator Kerry's global warming bill was. Make a buck for now; it will hurt their kids, their grandkids, and ours.

HC: It reminds me of when I was campaigning very actively against nuclear weapons and for abolition in the eighties. I met a man who made cruise missiles armed with hydrogen bombs. And I said,

"What about your children? Aren't you worried about their future?" He looks at me with eyes like dead stones, and he said, "I'm making money." I said, "Yeah, but what about your children? They won't have a future, they won't grow up," and he repeated, "I'm making money." They don't have to deal with themselves or the emotional ramifications of what they're up to. If only we could open them up to their fundamental moral compulsions and wisdom and knowledge.

PR: In the eighties Sting sang in a song called "Russians": "What might save us, me and you / Is if the Russians love their children too." It was a very U.S. perspective, but we need to touch the hearts of the people like Gandhi touched the hearts of the British. We need to touch the hearts of the people who ultimately are good people, but they're misguided by making money. If they connect it to the fact that they love their children, we might be able to get somewhere.

HC: You've recruited all these young people. I wonder if there's a way to mobilize millions more people through Greenpeace, like kids who stopped their parents' smoking.

PR: Yeah, and got their parents to recycle.

HC: I'd like to discuss the Chernobyl report recently brought up by the New York Academy of Sciences. But also, Greenpeace produced a report on Chernobyl several years ago. Would you summarize what Chernobyl means, how it affected the heath of people, and how many people have died as a result of that ghastly accident?

PR: The national cancer statistics from Belarus say there are about 270,000 cancers and about 93,000 fatal cancers caused by Chernobyl. The death toll is unbelievable, and the legacy of the cancer from Chernobyl is just unacceptable.

HC: The report by the New York Academy of Sciences says that up to a quarter million people have already died in the northern hemisphere. That's genocide. But it's not just people dying now in this generation; they will continue to die for many generations hence, because radiation causes cancer not just by swallowing and eating radioactive food, but it damages the genes in the eggs and sperm, creating genetic disease that is passed on from generation to generation through the reproductive organs. Also, the radiation, like plutonium, lasts for half a million years. Europe is covered with plutonium. The thing that really gets me is that one accident by one stupid man, if you read the history of Chernobyl, has polluted an entire continent, which is Europe, as well as Russia and some of North America. Yet the nuclear industry is forging ahead, like Exxon Mobil. In the process, even if there's not another meltdown, the nuclear waste leaking over eons of time could induce millions more deaths.

PR: The argument you get from the oil industry, even President Obama right before the BP Deepwater oil spill, was saying, "Oil rigs don't spill, or it's very rare." Even if it's every twenty years, risk is the probability it will happen multiplied by the impact. The impacts of these things are so huge that even if it only happens once in a while by a "fluke accident," like that one person at Chernobyl or the massive mess ups and irresponsibility at BP, even if that only happens once every twenty years, we're talking about irreparable damage. We don't need these energy sources. We can use plug-in cars; we can use public transportation; we can use solar and wind and geothermal.

HC: And plug-in solar cars. We don't need to generate electricity with nuclear or with coal; we just cover all the parking lots, as Arjun Makhijani says, with solar panels. You plug in your electric car in the morning, go to work, come back, undo your car, and drive it home, and then plug your car into your house and power up your house from the battery.

PR: You can do the opposite at night. If wind blows a lot at night in your area of the country, plug your car in at night and charge it; you drive to work, you plug it in, you actually sell electricity to your office. You make money during the day, you drive home, recharge it, and have 100 percent clean energy, and you make money.

HC: China is really beginning to make electric cars. Knowing China, there'll be millions of them soon. All we have to do is set up the infrastructure, the grid, the solar panels, the windmills. How much wind power is available potentially in the United States?

PR: You could power almost all of the United States with wind, especially offshore wind, which provides very consistent, reliable electricity. Greenpeace and other groups just worked on a campaign to win the first-ever wind farm in the United States off of Cape Cod. We had companies like Koch Industries putting up money to fight us. We had wealthy liberals saying that they didn't want it in their backyard, so there's a whole range of people against it, but ultimately, we won. Offshore wind is coming to the United States.

Wind energy is very reliable, and if it's offshore, it's flowing non-stop, so it can replace coal plants or nuclear plants. There are some parts of the country where wind blows at night, so you can charge your car; some parts where it flows during the day, and you can charge your offices and homes. In some parts of Western Europe wind energy comprises up to 40 percent of the electricity, and they don't have any problems with keeping the lights on at any point. So wind energy can be a really significant part of the mix anywhere in the world.

HC: We just need to update the grid, because most of the wind is in the western states, and the grid is very minimal out there. But as you pointed out in your Greenpeace report, renewable energy replacing the grid, along with conservation, can produce many more jobs than coal or nuclear and raise the GDP enormously. Then everyone's feeling good about themselves, because they're living from clean energy, not from death-producing industries like nuclear and coal.

PR: That's good GDP. Clean jobs, clean electricity, things that fight global warming. GDP from wars, from oil spills, that's the wrong direction for the world. ∾